# Unveiling Kate Chopin

# Unveiling
# Kate Chopin

## Emily Toth

UNIVERSITY PRESS OF MISSISSIPPI • *Jackson*

http://www.upress.state.ms.us

**Print-On-Demand Edition**

The paper in this book meets the guidelines for permanence and
durability of the Committee on Production Guidelines for Book
Longevity of the Council on Library Resources.

Library of Congress Cataloging-in-Publication Data

Toth, Emily.
Unveiling Kate Chopin / Emily Toth.
p.    cm.
Includes bibliographical references and index.
ISBN 1-57806-101-6 (alk. paper). — ISBN 1-57806-102-4 (pbk. : alk. paper)
1. Chopin, Kate, 1850–1904.    2. Women and literature — Louisiana —
History — 19th century.    3. Women authors, American — 19th century —
Biography.    4. Women authors, American — Louisiana — Biography.
5. Louisiana—In literature.    I. Title.
PS1294.C63T684    1999
813'.4 — dc21                                                   98-31237
[B]                                                                CIP

British Library Cataloging-in-Publication Data available

PHOTOGRAPH CREDITS:
Cammie G. Henry Research Center, Watson Library, Northwestern State University
of Louisiana: Kate O'Flaherty as baby; Eliza and George O'Flaherty;
Kate Chopin and her first four sons; Kate Chopin in riding habit;
Chopin home in Cloutierville; Father Beaulieu.
Missouri Historical Society, St. Louis: Thomas and Eliza O'Flaherty; Kate
O'Flaherty, 1869; Oscar Chopin, 1870; Kate Chopin, 1893.
Elizabeth Shown Mills and Gary Mills: Madame Victoire Charleville.
Dorothy Garesche Holland: Kitty Garesche.
Rosan Augusta Jordan: Chopin home in New Orleans.
Leona Sampite: Albert Sampite.
Mary DeLouche: Maria Normand DeLouche.
Ivy DeLouche: Kate Chopin at the opera.
Lewis Schucart: Kate Chopin's last St. Louis house.
Sister M. Dionysia Brockland, Dr. William Swekosky Collection,
Cardinal Ritter Library, School Sisters of Notre Dame, St. Louis:
Kate Chopin's Morgan Street home.

# CONTENTS

# ACKNOWLEDGMENTS

Virtually everyone who's known me in the last twenty-five years, including thousands of students, has somehow touched my research on Kate Chopin — which makes it impossible to acknowledge them all. More recently, countless e-mail correspondents about Kate Chopin have enriched, or sometimes bedeviled, my days. These acknowledgments, then, are only partial, and I hope those not mentioned by name will feel covered in this general acknowledgment of thanks to everyone. (I also hope that my biographers, if I ever have any, will pull together all my book acknowledgments and create the mega-acknowledgment that really will cover everyone.)

My first personal debt, of course, is to my parents, who instilled in me a love of writing, literature, and learning, as well as an insatiable curiosity about people's lives, and an activist insistence on making the world a better place for women. My mother, Dorothy Ginsberg Fitzgibbons, lived long enough to see the dedication to her in my Kate Chopin book nearly a decade ago; my father, John Fitzgibbons, was already in a nursing home with Alzheimer's disease. Both have since passed away, but I draw on their wit, intelligence, and strength of character every day — or try to.

My family network of supporters continues to encourage writing, literature, and learning: Sara Ruffner, Theresa Toth, Dennis Fitzgibbons, Ellen Boyle, Beauregard, Foxy, and the late Bunkie.

Per Seyersted deserves thanks from everyone who has ever opened *The Awakening.* He opened our eyes to Kate Chopin, and more than two decades ago, he gave me — then a lowly graduate student — a chance to work on his first collection of Chopin's private writings. None of this would exist without him. I am also, as always, grateful to Barbara Ewell for her own Chopin research and for the research tasks she did for me in New Orleans while I lived in exile in Pennsylvania: her energy and organizational abilities remain unsurpassed. Over more than two decades, Bernard Koloski's ideas about teaching Chopin, and about her bicultural roots, have enriched and sparked my thinking. I have also benefited from the dedication, generosity, and good humor of many other Chopinists, in particular Jean Bardot, Thomas Bonner Jr., and Helen Taylor. Heather Kirk Thomas's documentary collections are invaluable, and Cheyenne Bonnell's transcriptions of Chopin's unpublished writings (reprinted in *Kate Chopin's Private Papers*) are also endlessly useful resources.

At Louisiana State University, my generous and talented graduate assistant, Beth Younger, helped this book to happen with her excellent teaching, grading, and advising while I was in the mad throes of finishing it to meet the centennial deadline. Her calm good humor enriches this volume.

Many LSU colleagues have been very helpful as sounding boards, idea mavens, and sharers of wisdom and needed gossip. I owe particular thanks to Pamela Dean, Dominique Homberger, Dorothy Jenkins, Rosan Jordan, Carol Mattingly, Margaret Parker, Robin Roberts, and Gerilyn Tandberg. Robin Roberts nudged me to do this book, and she is right: how often will Kate Chopin have a centennial?

Many LSU students have helped with my Chopin research. On previous projects, Judith Stafford and Janet Wondra were research assistants; Bonnie Noonan and Catherine Williamson also assisted with details. These graduate students transcribed the Rankin-Marhefka Fragments: Brian Arundel, Phyllis Catsikis, Kevin Dwyer, Chris LaJaunie, Cynthia Maxwell, Anna Priddy, Leonard Vraniak, and Steve Weddle. My undergraduate student Michelle Bergeron, in a course on "Tough Cookies in Literature," was the first to notice the Morisot-Chopin link.

Other friends, colleagues, and mentors who deserve particular acknowledgment (in no order except alphabetical) include:

In Louisiana: Patricia Brady, Barbara Davidson, Carmen del Rio, Carol Gelderman, Sarah Sue Goldsmith, Suzanne Green, Susan Larson, Tika Laudun, Lucille McDowell, Susan Tucker, Martha Ward, and Beth Willinger.

Outside Louisiana: Phyllis Bridges, Margaret Cook, Cathy N. Davidson, Janice Delaney, Linda Gardiner, Deborah Martin Gonzales, Annette Kolodny, Amy Levin, Mary Jane Lupton, Veronica Makowsky, Pamela Matthews, Pamela Glenn Menke, Janet Montelaro, Sara Ruddick, Nina Schulman, Elizabeth Snapp, Dale Spender, and Linda Wagner-Martin.

Others whose knowledge and generosity have especially enhanced my Chopin work include, in St. Louis, the author's grandson David Chopin and his family; Martha Baker and John Clifford; Frederick Medler; and Sister M. Dionysia Brockland. In Cloutierville, Louisiana, Lucille Tinker Carnahan was for years my greatest source and greatest friend. Everything I've written about Cloutierville stems from her wisdom. I have also benefited greatly, in Cloutierville, from Leona Sampite, and the late Emma Richter Masson and Mildred McCoy. Elizabeth Shown Mills has been a superb aid in genealogical research.

Kate Chopin conferences in Louisiana have benefited from the excellent work and support of Grady Ballenger, Karen Cole, Tom Fick, Eva Gold, David Hanson, Donald Hatley, Ada Jarred, Katherine Kearns, Carol Wells, Mary Linn Wernet, and their colleagues.

I thank all the libraries and librarians who've aided my research: the Historic New Orleans Collection; Johns Hopkins University; Lakewood (Ohio) Public Library; Library of Congress; Louisiana State University; University of Missouri-St. Louis; University of New Orleans; University of North Dakota; Northwestern State University of Louisiana (especially Carol Wells and Mary Linn Wernet); Pennsylvania State University; St. Louis Mercantile Library; St. Louis Public Library; St. Louis University; National Archives of the Society of the Sacred Heart, Villa Duchesne, St. Louis (especially Sisters Marie Louise Martinez and Mary Cecelia Wheeler); Tulane University; and Washington University (especially Jon Grennan). And most of all, the Missouri Historical Society (especially Martha Clevenger, Peter Michel, Emily Miller, Frances Hurd Stadler, and Carol Verble).

Grants that have suppported this book include a Research and Publication Grant from the Louisiana Endowment for the Humanities, a state affiliate of the National Endowment for the Humanities; and a Council on Research Summer Stipend from Louisiana State University. In the past, other funds supporting my Chopin research have included two Manship Summer Research grants, Louisiana State University; two Louisiana Endowment for the Humanities Research and Publication Grants; a National Endowment for the Humanities Travel to Collections Grant; faculty research funds from the University of North Dakota and Pennsylvania State University; and a residency at the SKMSI Foundation in St. Louis.

For this book, I served as my own literary agent, with assistance from the Authors Guild, especially Tania Zamorsky, and advice from Pamela Ahearn.

At the University Press of Mississippi, I have been blessed with a gifted, innovative, and hard-working editor in Seetha Srinivasan. Hunter Cole, Ginger Tucker, and Steve Yates have provided fine support with marketing and publicity. For production, I want to thank and acknowledge Anne Stascavage, Shane Gong, and Evan Young.

The dedication to this book honors the two people who have done the most to make it possible, and delightful, for me to be the writer I've always wanted to be. Some day Susan Koppelman and I may write about each other's wit, satirical edges, and many perfections and magnificences, and how they have enhanced the twenty books we've written (ten each) during the course of our friendship, which began in the fall of 1972. Bruce Toth, who has been in my life since 1965, has always provided comfort, food, laughter, a willingness to listen to endless kvetching, and an unerring ability to ask the right questions.

Everyone should have a Susan and a Bruce.

*1850–mid-1870 — St. Louis*

February 8, 1850 — birth of Catherine O'Flaherty. First home: Eighth Street between Chouteau and Gratiot

Fall 1855 — Kate O'Flaherty enrolls in Academy of the Sacred Heart (which she attends sporadically for the next thirteen years), becomes friends with Kitty Garesché

November 1, 1855 — death of Thomas O'Flaherty (father) in railroad accident

January 16, 1863 — death of Victoire Verdon Charleville (great-grandmother and teacher)

February 17, 1863 — death of George O'Flaherty (half-brother), a Confederate soldier

1863 — banishment of Kitty Garesché and her family

1865–1866 — family moves to 1118 St. Ange Avenue

1865 — Kate enrolls at the Academy of the Visitation

1867–1870 — keeps Commonplace Book: diary, extracts from authors, poems, comments

1868 — graduation from Sacred Heart Academy

April 1869 — visits New Orleans

April 1870 — Julia Benoist Chopin, Oscar Chopin's mother, dies

June 9, 1870 — marriage to Oscar Chopin of Louisiana, Holy Angels Church, St. Louis

June–September 1870 — European honeymoon, keeps honeymoon diary in Commonplace Book

*Mid-1870–mid-1879 — New Orleans*

New Orleans homes: 443 Magazine Street; northeast corner Pitt & Constantinople; 209 (now 1413) Louisiana Avenue

November 1870 — Victor Jean Baptiste Chopin, Oscar's father, dies

May 22, 1871 — son Jean Baptiste born in New Orleans, baptized in
St. Louis in August

September 24, 1873 — son Oscar Charles born in St. Louis, baptized
in St. Louis

December 27, 1873 — Thomas O'Flaherty (brother) killed in buggy
accident, St. Louis

September 14, 1874 — Oscar in Battle of Liberty Place, with White
League and associated companies, New Orleans

October 28, 1874 — son George Francis born in St. Louis, baptized in
St. Louis

January 26, 1876 — son Frederick born in New Orleans (no baptismal
record found)

January 8, 1878 — son Felix Andrew born in New Orleans (no baptismal record found)

### Late 1879–mid-1884 — Cloutierville ("Cloochyville"), in Natchitoches ("Nak-i-tush") Parish, Louisiana

December 31, 1879 — daughter Lélia born in Cloutierville, baptized
Marie Laïza there

December 10, 1882 — death of Oscar Chopin

1882?–1884? — romance with Albert Sampite

mid-1884 — Chopin and children return to St. Louis

### Mid-1884–1904 — St. Louis

1884–1885 — lives at 1125 St. Ange Avenue, then 1122 St. Ange

June 28, 1885 — death of Eliza O'Flaherty

1886 — moves to 3317 Morgan Street (now Delmar)

June 1887 — first Cloutierville visit since Oscar's death

1888 — "Lilia. Polka for Piano" published

1888 — writes first draft of what becomes "A No-Account Creole"

January 10, 1889 — first literary publication: "If It Might Be" (poem)

April 24, 1889 — brings Oscar's body back to St. Louis from Cloutierville

June 1889 — writes "Wiser than a God"

July 5, 1889 — begins writing *At Fault*

August 1889 — writes "A Point at Issue!"

October 27, 1889 — first short story publication: "A Point at Issue!" in *St. Louis Post-Dispatch*

September 1890 — *At Fault* published at Chopin's expense

December 1890 — becomes charter member of Wednesday Club

August 20, 1891 — "For Marse Chouchoute" (first Louisiana story) published in *Youth's Companion*

March 7, 1892 — writes "Miss McEnders"

April 4, 1892 — resigns from Wednesday Club

April 9–10, 1892 — writes "Loka"

July 15–17, 1892 — writes "At the 'Cadian Ball"

January 14, 1893 — *Vogue* publishes "Désirée's Baby"

May 1893 — trip to New York and Boston

August 11, 1893 — Houghton, Mifflin accepts *Bayou Folk*

October 1, 1893 — hurricane of Chênière Caminada destroys much of the Grand Isle area that Chopin knew

October 21–23, 1893 — writes "At Chênière Caminada"

March 24, 1894 — Houghton, Mifflin publishes *Bayou Folk*

April 19, 1894 — writes "Story of an Hour"

May 4, 1894–October 26, 1896 — writes "Impressions" (Diary)

Late June 1894 — attends Indiana conference of Western Association of Writers

June 30, 1894 — writes "The Western Association of Writers"

July 7, 1894 — "Western Association of Writers" published in *Critic*

July 21–28 — hostile responses to Chopin's "Western Association of Writers" in Midwestern newspapers

August 1894 — first national profile: William Schuyler's article in *The Writer*

December 6, 1894 — "Story of an Hour" published in *Vogue*

March 1895 — sends Guy de Maupassant translation collection to Houghton, Mifflin (rejected)

April 10–28, 1895 — writes "Athénaïse"

January 27, 1897 — grandmother Athénaïse Charleville Faris dies

February 3, 1897 — meets Ruth McEnery Stuart

March 6, 1897 — "Miss McEnders" by "La Tour" published in *St. Louis Criterion*

March 11, 1897 — Reedy's *Mirror* reveals satirical truth about "Miss McEnders"

June 1897 (?) — begins writing *The Awakening*

November 1897 — Way & Williams (Chicago) publishes *A Night in Acadie*

January 16, 1898 — "Is Love Divine?" (*St. Louis Post-Dispatch*) quotes from novel-in-progress

January 21, 1898 — finishes *The Awakening*

January 1898 — Way & Williams accepts *The Awakening*

March 1898 — goes to Chicago, seeking literary agent

Spring–Summer 1898 — son Frederick in Spanish-American War

July 19, 1898 — writes "The Storm"

November 1898 — books transferred from Way & Williams to Herbert S. Stone & Company

December 1898 — visits Natchitoches Parish, sells Cloutierville house, visits New Orleans

March 1899 — Lucy Monroe's review of *The Awakening* in *Book News*

April 22, 1899 — *The Awakening* published (no evidence that it was ever banned)

July 1899 — Chopin's statement on *The Awakening* published in *Book News*

October 1899 — travels to Wisconsin lake country, where she receives English letters praising *The Awakening*

November 26, 1899 — article in *St. Louis Post-Dispatch*: "On Certain Brisk, Bright Days," with "A St. Louis Woman Who Has Won Fame in Literature"

November 29, 1899 — gives reading at Wednesday Club

February 1900 — Herbert S. Stone cancels publication plans for *A Vocation and a Voice*

December 9, 1900 — publishes "Development of the Literary West: A Review" in St. Louis *Republic*'s Special Book Number

1900 — appears in first edition of *Who's Who in America*

1901 — is subject of sonnet "To the Author of 'Bayou Folk,'" by R. E. Lee Gibson

June 4, 1902 — son Jean marries Emelie Hughes

July 3, 1902 — "Polly" published in *Youth's Companion* (last publication)

December 1902 — makes her will

1903 — moves to 4232 McPherson Avenue

July 7, 1903 — death of Emelie Chopin, Jean's wife, and child

August 20, 1904 — has cerebral hemorrhage after day at the St. Louis World's Fair

August 22, 1904 — dies

August 24, 1904 — is buried in Calvary Cemetery, St. Louis

# Introduction

April 22, 1999 is the one hundredth anniversary of *The Awakening*, a novel with an oddly scarlet reputation.

Now recognized as an American classic, Kate Chopin's story was welcomed by most women, but despised by most men. The two women who reviewed it publicly, Willa Cather and Frances Porcher, praised the author's writing talents, but felt they had to deplore her uniquely sensational plot. A century later, though, *The Awakening*'s plot seems very familiar—the tale of a wife and mother who begins to realize that her life is unfulfilling and meaningless. She turns to art and adultery, but neither one fully satisfies her hunger. Ultimately she figures out how to elude everyone's demands, and she does.

Kate Chopin anticipated so much: daytime dramas, women's pictures, *The Feminine Mystique*, open marriages, women's liberation, talk shows, Mars vs. Venus, self-help and consciousness raising. But in 1899, she was a lonely pioneer.

Overwhelmingly, reviewers called Chopin's heroine colossally selfish, stupid and mean. Some even left out *The Awakening* in articles about her career. Inevitably, with men as the powerful reviewers, publishers, editors, and gatekeepers, this view prevailed. Kate Chopin died in 1904, and *The Awakening* was soon out of print. It was reprinted only once, half a century later, through the efforts of an editor at Putnam Publishing whose name is lost to history.

And then, in 1969, a Norwegian scholar named Per Seyersted published Chopin's complete works and the first modern biography, as the women's liberation movement was sweeping the United States. Sixty-five years after her death, Kate Chopin became a star. Although some

Chopin stories — "The Story of an Hour," "The Storm," and "Désirée's Baby" — are now solidly in the American literary canon, *The Awakening* was the book that introduced most readers to Kate Chopin in the 1960s and 1970s. When it was bruited about (wrongly) that Chopin's novel had been banned for immorality in 1899, young rebels raced to read it.

*The Awakening* was also far more of a grabber than *Moby-Dick*, which in the 1970s was being taught as the required great American novel. Chopin's main character — a thoughtful, sensual woman — was much more interesting than an angry white whale. It was possible to identify with Edna Pontellier, and millions of women, and some men, did so immediately.

But what were they identifying with?

The early student rediscoverers in the 1970s saw Edna as a precursor of their own Sexual Revolution, for she says in the novel, in a statement of astonishing bravery for her day: "I give myself where I choose" (XXXVI).* American readers in the 1980s, though, saw Edna as a Baby Boom heroine, an independent woman who moves out of her husband's house, lives on her own, and makes a living from her art. But to readers in Poland, where *The Awakening*'s translation was an instant best seller in 1980, Edna was a heroine of fantasy as much as rebellion: when she moves out, she easily rents a little home of her own. To readers in housing-poor Poland, that was a true American dream.

By the 1990s, literary critics of all stripes had taken on *The Awakening*. Some called Edna (or Kate Chopin) insufficiently aware of her own race and class privileges, while others called her brilliantly attuned to women's silences and inexpressible longings. Critical debates will no doubt continue in the next millennium. Yet ordinary readers

---

*Quotations from Kate Chopin's novels (*At Fault* and *The Awakening*) will be identified in this book by chapter number. Because her short stories and poems are available in so many editions, specific page numbers will not be given for quotations from them.

are most curious about something else: How did Kate Chopin know so much, in 1899?

I asked that question myself in 1972, when I began researching my dissertation on Chopin's writings about white women and people of color. The field of women's history was in its infancy, and we all had to teach ourselves about the First Wave, about those other pioneering writers and thinkers whose work had been buried.

By the 1980s, when I researched and wrote a full-fledged Chopin biography (1990, now out of print), it was easy to see that although she was not an activist, Kate Chopin had been part of a movement, or at least a *zeitgeist*. But her inclusion of sexuality as part of women's liberation still made her unusual for her day, and I discovered that she herself had some passionate secrets.

In the 1990s, a cache of newly rediscovered manuscripts, together with her diaries and letters (all now in *Kate Chopin's Private Papers*), told us many intriguing things about Chopin as a writer and social critic. I began to suspect that ambition, not adultery, may have been her biggest secret — for her manuscripts show that she worked much harder at her craft than she ever admitted in print. She wrote and rewrote, thought and rethought — while creating a network in St. Louis to promote her work. What impelled her to be so passionate about her art, about her presentation of women? I wondered. Where did her knowledge and her drive come from?

As most biographers admit today, writing another person's life story is also writing one's own. And so, in the 1970s, students like me wondered about romance: had Kate Chopin, like so many of her characters, looked outside marriage for fulfillment? In the 1980s, we worried more about finance: had Kate Chopin earned a living from her writing? In my 1990 biography, I answered both questions. Yes, there was another man; No, she did not live on the earnings from her novels and short stories. I also proved that *The Awakening* had never actually been banned.

But I did not yet know what was most important to the mature Kate Chopin. She wrote *The Awakening*, after all, in her late forties, after raising six children and outliving her husband, her parents, and all her siblings. As an adolescent, she survived some kind of assault; in her thirties, she braved scandal and hatred in a small Louisiana town. But she said goodbye to that, and became a worldly and independent author of her own destiny. She had learned at an impressionable age to rely on women, and she listened to women's voices throughout her life.

Now, in my fifties, I understand much more about Kate Chopin. I know, now, the profound effect the death of a mother has on a daughter's life. (Mine died the day my 1990 Chopin book was printed.) I also know how much fathers, absent or present, can shape a daughter's possibilities. I know much more about domestic violence, and why women leave or stay. I know how much deeper and more meaningful women's friendships become in middle age.

This life story celebrates the centennial of *The Awakening* with new materials and a different set of inquiries. This book asks *why* Kate Chopin did what she did, and often finds the answers in the French women whose voices dominated her formative years. If my earlier research was about the content of her life, this book is equally about the content of her character, and how she worked, as Edna does, toward "becoming herself and daily casting aside that fictitious self which we assume like a garment with which to appear before the world" (XIX).

This book is the true story of a St. Louis society belle who — with talent and ambition and a long history of smart, independent female mentors and ancestors — became the author of the most radical American novel of the 1890s.

*Unveiling Kate Chopin* uncovers the inner life of a courageous woman who, a century ago, was a solitary soul, a tough and resilient character who had opinions and who dared and defied. In a new millennium, we need to know about that kind of woman, and how she cast off the veils of Victorian convention. We need to create — as she did — new and distinctive ways of awakening, living, thinking, and growing.

And rebelling.

# Unveiling Kate Chopin

## Chapter 1

# Girls and Women

WHEN KATE O'FLAHERTY was five years and seven months old, her parents packed her off to boarding school.

In 1855 the Sacred Heart nuns did admit tots as young as five to their academy on Fifth Street, a clean, bright building tucked behind brick walls, with its own garden and quiet ways, in the heart of St. Louis. Sacred Heart nuns were famous for their brisk efficiency and keen intellect, and theirs was by far the best education available for girls. But girls who were comfortably supported, and whose parents were alive, were not normally sent away when they were barely beyond the toddler stage. Loneliness is a positive thing in Kate Chopin's *The Awakening*—but little children rarely enjoy it.

There are no obvious explanations. Kate O'Flaherty was born, according to her baptismal certificate, on February 8, 1850, and her first portrait shows a round little girl clutching a bouquet of posies and smiling vaguely. Her gauzy, off-the-shoulder evening gown seems incongruous and coy for a three-year-old, but the picture was made by a traveling artist who carted around prepainted bodies as a sales gimmick. Customers got to choose the body they most preferred for their child.

Already, young Katie was being pushed into a preconceived female role.

Her other surviving childhood picture tells us more about Kate O'Flaherty as an individual—a dark-eyed young rebel sporting disheveled ringlets and glowering at the camera. Fidgety youngsters were often put into neck clamps for photographs, and Miss Katie O'Flaherty looks like one very put-upon little girl.

She had her own agenda, and she wanted to know everything. Where, for instance, did her father go every day? Evidently she whined and nagged so much that one day her papa agreed to take his daughter to work. First they went to early mass (dull on weekdays), but then they rode down to the levee — a thrilling place for a little girl, with monstrous steamships, real Indians, ribald sailors, and disreputable women. Young Katie got to gawk at a raffish world that respectable young girls were not supposed to know anything about.

According to family tradition, the outing created a special bond between father and daughter — but for Kate, it also sparked a lifelong revolt against keeping young ladies ignorant about the rest of the world. For a writer, that was a fine and angry beginning, but it may have made her into a difficult daughter.

The levee adventure is also the only humanizing story that survives about Thomas O'Flaherty. Everything else suggests a humorless, driven, rather sad man who became a stern master, a patriarch who might very well ship an impertinent five-year-old off to boarding school. Especially if she kept asking rude questions and disturbing the peace of the household.

Thomas O'Flaherty was already fifty when his daughter was five, and in the mid-nineteenth century, fifty was elderly: half of Americans died before they reached that age. Thomas was a bootstrap success, having been born in Galway (in 1805) when the British occupiers worked ruthlessly to keep the native Catholics poor, hungry, and illiterate. Still, Thomas contrived to get himself an education, including mathematics and French — and that may have spurred him to leave home, a full two decades before the potato famine unleashed a mass exodus from the Emerald Isle. In 1823 Thomas O'Flaherty set out on his own, because he wanted to. He, and his brother Edmund, wanted wings, not roots.

First they settled in New York, where there were jobs for Irishmen building roads and canals, but two years later, they were restless again. Joined by another Irishman, Roger McAllister, the O'Flahertys headed West — Edmund to Kansas City, and Thomas and Roger to St. Louis, where the gateway to the West was an enterprising businessman's paradise. With a boat and supply store, Thomas soon made a fortune equipping westward trekkers. He invested wisely, and the land he bought in 1842, on Seventh Street between Franklin Avenue and Washington, would be supporting his daughter into the next century.

St. Louis was new enough that even the French-speaking clique that amounted to "old money" did not look down on an immigrant Irishman—especially if he conveniently spoke French. Rather later than most men, Thomas O'Flaherty went courting, and when he was thirty-four, he married nineteen-year-old Catherine de Reilhe, distantly related to a former American governor. Soon the first Madame O'Flaherty was expecting a child.

Meanwhile, eleven-year-old Eliza Faris was growing up in the Charleville family homestead, in the country outside St. Louis. She was a genuine "Creole," as St. Louisans used the word, for her New World heritage went back two centuries, to an intrepid Frenchwoman who had been a frontier bride in Montreal. Her Charleville descendants had lived in the large Louisiana colony since the 1700s, and had earned some money and social standing. But then Marie Athénaïse Charleville, the girl with the fanciful name who would grow up to be Eliza's mother, made a romantic and disastrous marriage to a Kentuckian named Wilson Faris.

Young Faris was both foolish and fertile: while their finances withered, he and Athénaïse kept producing children, every other year. At one point her disgusted father even took over all of Wilson's property. And then in 1843, when their eldest child Eliza was only fifteen, Wilson Faris ran out on the family, leaving them destitute. Like Depression-era children, Eliza saw her secure family's future unravel, suddenly and hopelessly. She learned about fear.

Elsewhere in St. Louis, Catherine O'Flaherty, the wife of the Irish businessman Thomas O'Flaherty, had given birth to a lively, healthy son, George, in 1840. But four years later, she and another infant died in childbirth. Thomas O'Flaherty suddenly needed a wife, preferably one with a social position at least as strong as his. Eliza Faris, with her mother and six younger sisters and brothers, desperately needed money—

and marriage was the only respectable way for a young woman to acquire it.

Somehow they met, and an arrangement was made, with French practicality. In July 1844, just six months after the death of his first wife, Thomas O'Flaherty and Eliza Faris were married in St. Francis Xavier Catholic Church. Thomas was thirty-nine; Eliza was barely sixteen.

Marriages between middle-aged men and teenagers were not common in Eliza's immediate family, and Eliza was a sheltered adolescent, not very well educated, whose English always had a French tinge. In later years she was considered charming and serene; as a bride, her portrait shows, she was lovely. But her early marriage cut short any individual development she might have had. Or, as Kate Chopin wrote in *The Awakening* about Edna's marriage to an older, very settled man with whom she has little in common: she gave up on youthful infatuations, finding a "certain dignity in the world of reality, closing the portals forever behind her upon the realm of romance and dreams" (VII).

If Eliza Faris wanted more from her marriage — if she hoped for a close, romantic relationship, or a companionable union with friendship as well as love — she almost certainly found none of that with Thomas O'Flaherty. In their one surviving portrait he looks prosperous, grumpy, and rigid, while she looks warm, lively, and bright-eyed. He was, after all, older than her father, and he was in control.

Possibly he also insisted that their first daughter be named Catherine — the name of his dead first wife.

The mature Kate O'Flaherty Chopin left behind no writings about her parents' marriage; she hardly remembered it. Nor did she explain why she was sent to boarding school when she was only five. It wasn't just that she had a little sister, for Eliza had grown up in a houseful of children. More likely, a dark family drama triggered sending Kate away.

By the early 1850s, Thomas and Eliza Faris O'Flaherty were living in a comfortable three-story brick mansion in the heart of St. Louis, on Eighth Street between Chouteau and Gratiot (now the site of the Ralston Purina pet food plant). By 1855, the family included four children, three of them Eliza and Thomas's: Tom, seven; Kate, five; and Jane ("Jennie"), two. George, the fifteen-year-old son from Thomas's first marriage, was off at boarding school at St. Louis University, where he wrote adoring letters to his little sister Katie. Another daughter, Marie Thérèse, born between Kate and Jane, had died young.

But the O'Flahertys were not the only ones in the large Southern-style house. Two of Eliza's sisters had married, but Thomas O'Flaherty was still supporting her mother and four of her younger sisters and brothers: three teenagers (Charles, Zuma, and Wilson, who died in an accident), and little Josephine, a twelve-year-old Sacred Heart schoolgirl.

And there were slaves in the O'Flaherty mansion. Although many St. Louisans had qualms about owning other human beings, Thomas O'Flaherty evidently did not. At the time of his daughter Kate's birth, he owned four slaves, about whom we know almost nothing: as property, they were recorded in the Census Book by age and gender, but not by name. The fifty-year-old woman listed in 1850 was almost certainly Kate's mammy.

Five years later, though, a slave family appears in the records for the O'Flaherty household: a twenty-three-year-old slave woman with two little girls, aged four (a year younger than Kate) and one (a year younger than Jane). Both girls are listed in the Census Book as "mulattoes," or light-skinned—and we do not know who their father was. He may have been a white neighbor, or another light-skinned slave. But even in the waning days of slavery in the 1850s, and in the freer atmosphere of the cities, breeding was still something masters liked to control, if they could.

The two little slave girls may very well have been Thomas O'Flaherty's children, living under the same roof with his wife and his white children. (Such living arrangements were not unknown, even without slavery: across the ocean, Karl Marx had a son by the family maid, who lived and worked in the Marx household before, during, and after the birth.)

But for the O'Flahertys in St. Louis, the slave girls would have been a daily reminder to Eliza about male power and female vulnerability. Her church and her French training would both counsel wives to bear up and accept the double standard. Perhaps Eliza's mother, abandoned by her own husband and terrified of poverty, urged Eliza to close her eyes to what could not be changed. After all, Eliza's great-great-uncles had also fathered mixed-race children: one by an Osage woman, another by a black woman. Her mother might have reminded Eliza that no matter how humiliated or betrayed she might feel, Thomas O'Flaherty was an excellent provider. Women had very few respectable ways to earn a living, and wives had few legal rights at all. (The Seneca Falls women's rights conference had taken place just seven years earlier, and it would be another sixty-five years before U.S. women won the right to vote.)

If Thomas O'Flaherty fathered the slave children in his household, he was legally within his rights. But five-year-old Kate, the outspoken child who demanded to know where her father went, would certainly also wonder where the slave children came from. The four-year-old girl may even have resembled Kate. Maybe Kate asked insistent, rude questions that infuriated her father (or horrified her mother). Maybe there were scenes of anger, or terrifying silences.

And all that may be the best explanation as to why, on September 3, 1855, Katie O'Flaherty was sent to boarding school with the Sacred Heart nuns.

There she learned about quiet times, curtseying, and making the sign of the cross. The quiet may have been a comfort after the stress and noise of her crowded childhood home. And yet — there was loneliness. Years later, when Kate Chopin wrote sympathetically about a mixed-race girl who is shunned by both whites and blacks, she may have been thinking about the slave girls in her household ("A Little Free-Mulatto"). When she wrote about a sulky white girl who puts a curse on the circus, she may have been remembering her own impudence ("A Little Country Girl"). But both girls are lonely and sad. Exile, Kate O'Flaherty Chopin knew, is not good for children, and her sentence would be at least four months long. Her tuition was fully paid for the fall semester.

But her first Sacred Heart term ended early, with a sudden crash that echoed through the rest of her life.

All Saints' Day, November 1, is a holy day of obligation in the Catholic calendar, but Thomas O'Flaherty was dedicating the day in 1855 to another kind of obligation. Because of his wealth and carefully chosen civic activities (Irish charities, Catholic lodges, the fire department, and the Mercantile Library), he was among the dignitaries riding the first train across the new Gasconade Bridge to Jefferson City, heralding a new opening to the West. It was a gala, flag-fluttering occasion when the men boarded the trains, cheered by a huge crowd and serenaded by brass bands. For the immigrant Thomas O'Flaherty, who had come to the New World with nothing but his own drive, it was the culmination of his American dream.

But as the first car chugged over the Gasconade in a driving rainstorm, the new bridge, the symbol of Missouri's pride and progress, shuddered, wavered — and collapsed. Cars tumbled helplessly over each other, with shattering glass, grinding metal, and shouts of pain and horror. Mangled tracks and bloody remains rained down below, followed by a deadly silence. Thirty men were killed, and one of them was Thomas O'Flaherty.

At the funeral, he was eulogized by his friend, the slave-owning Archbishop Peter Richard Kenrick. The Catholic Institute praised Thomas O'Flaherty's leaving behind, to his family, "the priceless heritage of an unsullied name." But he also left behind no will and no provision for his wife, his children, his other relatives, and the slaves. It was nine agonizing days before Eliza could get herself and her children named, through an affidavit, as Thomas's official heirs.

And then, at twenty-seven, she suddenly found herself a wealthy widow, in charge of a very large estate (valued at $24,160 in 1861). Widows controlled their property, as wives did not; widows also had legal control of their own children, as wives did not. And so Eliza's first act as a young widow was to bring her daughter Katie home. From then on, Eliza would be the one making decisions about her daughter—

and for the rest of her life, Kate would brood about her father's sudden death, and what it meant for her mother.

Her most obvious musing takes place in "The Story of an Hour," written nearly forty years after the Gasconade. In Chopin's story, a Mrs. Louise Mallard, who has a heart condition, is told her husband has died in a train accident. At first she is consumed with grief, but soon other thoughts creep and slink into her mind. She will not have to live her life for anyone else; she will not have to submit to anyone's wishes but her own. She begins to feel a "monstrous joy" at the thought of her own freedom... whereupon the door opens and her husband walks in, having been nowhere near the crash. The wife's weak heart fails, and the doctors conclude that Louise Mallard died of "heart disease — of joy that kills."

Kate Chopin often used the original names of people who inspired her stories, and she does so in "The Story of an Hour." "Louise" sounds like "Eleeza," the French pronunciation of Eliza's name; Louise, like Eliza, has a sister named Josephine. Even Louise's last name, Mallard, resembles Bullard, the name of a man who died at the Gasconade. "The Story of an Hour" can be read as the story of Eliza O'Flaherty's marriage, the submission of a young woman to someone else's will. It can also be read as a criticism of marriage itself, as an institution that traps women.

And yet, to make her story publishable, Kate Chopin had to disguise reality. She had to have her heroine die. A story in which an unhappy wife is suddenly widowed, becomes rich, and lives happily ever after — Eliza O'Flaherty's story — would have been much too radical, far too threatening, in the 1890s. There were limits to what editors would publish, and what audiences would accept.

But if young Kate's father, irritated by her chatter or her defiant curiosity, was the one who sent her to boarding school at age five — then "The Story of an Hour" is also the tale of her own liberation. Louise Mallard's freedom is an illusion — but in real life, the crash that killed Thomas O'Flaherty liberated his daughter to come home, to be raised among the powerful women of her family. Her father's death kept Kate O'Flaherty from growing up in the typical nineteenth-century patriarchal household, in which a powerful husband ruled the roost — as Léonce Pontellier tries to do, strutting and fuming, in *The Awakening*.

Katie O'Flaherty's roost was ruled entirely by women.

These strong women also had an unusual talent for outliving their husbands. At a time when women often died in childbirth, Kate's female ancestors enjoyed exceptional longevity. Her great-grandmother died at eighty-three, and her grandmother at eighty-eight. By middle age, or sometimes even before, they had left or lost or buried the fathers of their children, and then gotten on with their lives. They were a demographic oddity, and they raised a young girl with a notably independent and quirky vision.

As a girl, Kate was surrounded by the voices of women — from her mammy to her mother and grandmother and great-grandmother, to the Sacred Heart nuns, to her best friend Kitty Garesché. Many of the voices spoke French, some of them exclusively. The deep, blustering voices that dominated most nineteenth-century households were absent from the O'Flaherty/Faris/Charleville home. It was a world of women.

Eliza was not Katie's only mother, for middle-class white babies were routinely nursed by black women. Kate O'Flaherty was also born into a special historical moment, for hers was the last generation of white babies raised by slaves. As a child, Kate knew "the faithful love of her negro 'mammy'" and grew up in a house "full of negro servants, and the soft creole French patois and the quaint darkey dialect were more familiar to the growing child than any other form of speech," her friend William Schuyler wrote in the 1890s. The first soothing motherly voice Katie O'Flaherty heard was her mammy, who may have been Louise, the slave woman named in Eliza O'Flaherty's harried letter to her uncle during the Civil War: "My negroes are leaving me old Louise ran off a few days ago, I suppose the rest will follow soon. God's will be done."

But long before that, Kate and her mammy were separated. Once young Kate survived the first year, the most dangerous time for infants, greater care would have been needed for the delicate new babies, Marie Thérèse and then Jane. Being separated from her mammy was Kate's first loss — one that was universal for white children, but rarely spoken about. "Old Louise" may have been Eliza O'Flaherty's mammy as well: she may be the unrecorded woman who nurtured them all, and had the earliest role in shaping their characters.

Years later, Kate Chopin did write, as many white authors did, about black women's devotion to the white children they raised ("Beyond the Bayou"; "Tante Cat'rinette"). But Chopin also tried to see a black woman's point of view in such stories as "La Belle Zoraïde," in which a slave woman deprived of her own child goes mad. And in the story "Odalie Misses Mass," Chopin created a unique picture of an old black woman and a young white girl who are best friends, separated only by death.

Still, the mature Kate Chopin knew that white people could not truly "know" black people: too much suffering and oppression had separated them. And so her most honest portrayal of a mammy may be the quadroon nurse who cares for the children in *The Awakening*. The nurse is silent — perhaps brooding, perhaps sullen — and seems not to react at all when Edna, moodily, scolds her for negligence. The nurse has no voice at all, and that may be Chopin's clearest admission that white people could not know what a black woman might be thinking.

After her father's death, five-year-old Katie went home again with her mammy and her mother. But during the year of mourning for Thomas O'Flaherty, the baby Jane also died. That made Kate the youngest child, and also the only daughter.

Meanwhile, just four years earlier, Kate's great-grandmother, Victoria (or Victoire) Charleville, had decided she was dying. Having reached age seventy with nothing in particular to live for, she was staying with her daughter Henriette Hunt and Henriette's wily husband, Daniel, a lawyer who urged the older woman to make financial decisions while she could. And so Madame Charleville divided her estate among her heirs, the five of her fifteen children who were still alive. But before she got around to actually dying, she suddenly found a new reason for living: her bright little great-granddaughter.

Katie O'Flaherty's last name always struck Madame Charleville as an unpronounceable Irish barbarism — but the child did need to be educated properly as a young Frenchwoman. Eliza O'Flaherty was not competent to do so: she did not spell very well, and at twenty-seven, she had none of the life experience of her strong, colorful grandmother. Madame Charleville moved to the Eighth Street house, and began.

Over the next two years, Victoire Charleville made sure that Katie learned perfect French. (It was New World French, more Missourian than Parisian, but grammatically correct.) Kate learned French well enough that she was at ease with it all her life, in France and in Louisiana, and she wrote it with no more misspellings and slips of the pen than she did English. In many a short story she uses French expressions easily for local color, and in *The Awakening* even the parrot speaks French.

As a youngster, Katie O'Flaherty seemed naturally gifted in music, another subject in Madame Charleville's homemade curriculum. Kate had daily piano lessons, and by the time she was an adolescent, she could repeat "by ear" any piece of music she heard. In high school she took extra music lessons, and as a mature writer she described the trembling emotional impact of music on such sensitive souls as Edna in *The Awakening*.

But Madame Charleville's best subject for tutoring was one Kate's father could never have taught her. No man could have. Madame Charleville gave her young charge a subject for intense, lifelong fascination, contemplation, and delight: the lives of women. Madame Charleville loved gossip.

She was a colorful, picturesque storyteller whose idea of history was the classic conflict of French drama (and later daytime drama): women torn between duty and desire. In pioneer St. Louis, for instance, the founder's mother, Madame Chouteau, had left her brutal husband to live with her son's partner. They had four children together, but she never married him, not even after her husband's death. Not only did

Madame Chouteau make herself one of the wealthiest fur traders in St. Louis history, but—and this would surely be pointed out—she also outlived her lover by thirty-six years.

Madame Charleville had plenty of other stories from her own family. There was, for instance, the uncle whose mixed-blood descendants grew up to be part of "The Colored Aristocracy of St. Louis." But the best stories were about women. Victoire, Madame Charleville's own mother, had emigrated to the Louisiana colony from an island off the coast of France, married a carpenter named Verdon, and given birth to four children—but husband and wife "kept matters pretty lively at home with continual bickering and quarrels," according to one historian. Eventually, in 1785, "for the salvation of their souls," they got a legal separation—the first one ever granted in St. Louis.

Then, nearly five years later, Victoire Verdon gave birth to another son, whose father's name is lost to history. (Out of mischief, she listed her estranged husband as the father.) Although she could neither read nor write, the canny Victoire created her own market niche, with products appealing to women: she traded buttons, pins, and utensils in short trips downriver. She learned to sign her name with a flourish: "*La* Verdon" (*the* Verdon), and eventually ran a very profitable line of trading vessels between St. Louis and New Orleans. By listening to women's voices and needs, the formerly battered wife had become a tycoon.

The women in Katie O'Flaherty's family loved their mothers and mourned their passing. Just a year after the death of "La Verdon," her daughter—evidently looking for love, and already four months pregnant—married Joseph Charleville. Half a century later, that same Madame Charleville was encouraging young Katie not to judge people rashly, but to face truths fearlessly. Madame Charleville, in short, was very French. Like the French in Louisiana, where she had many relatives and where prenuptial agreements were the norm in bourgeois marriages, Madame Charleville understood that marriage was a practical arrangement, undertaken for social standing and security. Romantic love might come later.

Madame Charleville knew all about the strongest motives of human existence: greed, power, lust, and maternal love. But the greatest lesson, one her great-granddaughter repeated so tellingly in her later stories, was that a woman had to be independent.

In the fall of 1857, when she was seven, Katie O'Flaherty was registered again at the Sacred Heart Academy on Fifth Street, this time as a "day scholar." Through the late 1850s and early 1860s, she was enrolled erratically, either as a boarder or a day scholar, and usually she left school by the end of February. (The school year ended in June, but there were no school attendance requirements.) Until she was ten, Kate never spent an entire year in school—even though her mother paid extra each term for her piano lessons and music books.

As a boarder, she shared one large dormitory room with twenty or thirty girls, and learned routines for privacy, hygiene, modesty, and religious devotion. Since nonessential speech was forbidden, the girls created their own systems of communication with gestures and facial expressions. They also made friendships that lasted for the rest of their lives.

Formally, the Sacred Heart academic program suited what Kate had learned from Madame Charleville at home. It mixed women's wisdom, rigorous intellectual challenges, homely chores, and the celebration of women. The Sacred Heart order, founded in France after the Revolution, stressed high academic standards, while the nuns dedicated themselves to teaching young Catholic girls "of good family" to be pious wives and mothers. But the students were also to be knowledgeable, clear, and independent thinkers, to "meet with adequacy the demands of time and eternity."

The girls were usually taught in English, but the values they learned were in the tradition of French intellectual women. Kate O'Flaherty and her best friend Kitty Garesché were taught fine needlework, plain sewing, and embroidery, but also spelling, penmanship, literature, history, oral reading, "formation of the reasoning power and judgment," "fieldwork in botany as well as gardening," and knowledge of current events and scientific discoveries, "that they may take part intelligently in conversation when at home or in social gatherings." The girls wrote two themes a week — one a letter, and one an essay or literary analysis.

But throughout their schooling, while they might be rebelling or twitching or passing notes during mass, the Sacred Heart girls were hearing over and over, "Hail Mary, full of grace, Blessed art thou among women." They were learning to revere women. Guardian angels were like imaginary friends, and saints aided girls in distress. Our Lady of Good Success helped exam-takers; Saint Cecilia, the patron saint of music, got young girls into the choir. Above all, of course, there was the Virgin Mary, who might intercede to help troubled girls. Her serene presence was also a comfort to lonely children. Sometimes girls who were close friends exchanged pious pictures of the Virgin, small French prints ornamented with lace paper. (One of Kate O'Flaherty's is now in the Missouri Historical Society in St. Louis.)

Meanwhile, at home, Madame Charleville's teachings had given young Katie O'Flaherty a lifelong respect and affection for old women. Kate Chopin's later stories show very little generational conflict: she does not write, for instance, about daughters who defy their mothers or grandmothers to run off and marry unwisely. Her mother characters do not repress or police their daughters; her daughter characters do not break their mothers' hearts. Chopin also shows genuine love and friendship between women across the generations and races. In stories like "Odalie Misses Mass" and "Old Aunt Peggy," for instance, white youngsters revere old African American women as storytellers and vessels of information about the past.

The unwritten story in most women's lives is the story of friendship. Kate O'Flaherty and Kitty Garesché were friends for nearly half a century — but all we have are a few scattered reminiscences, many of them filtered through Kate Chopin's shifty and unreliable first biographer, Daniel Rankin.

"Kate and I first knew each other when, as wee tots, we went as Day Scholars to our old Convent on 5th Street, founded by our Venerable Mother Duchesne," Kitty Garesché wrote to Rankin in 1930. Kitty lived on Ninth Street and Chouteau Avenue, and "As our homes were very near one another, we were constantly together, sharing all our pleasures." But their pleasures were not the traditional ones American mothers encouraged their daughters to pursue, at least in the popular novels the two girls read together, such as Susan Warner's *The Wide Wide World*. In 1850s popular fiction, young girls immerse themselves in housewifely service arts. They learn to pour tea and serve small refreshments; to sew; to care for the sick; to pray; and, if they are wealthy and somewhat worldly, to dance and sing and play the piano as womanly accomplishments. Young girls avoid vanity and stifle any ambitions that are not pious, pure, submissive, and domestic.

But Kate O'Flaherty and Kitty Garesché were not being raised as "American" girls. They were French, from a family background with rules that were more literary and less sanctimonious. And so Kitty's list of their "pleasures" contains nary a word about any domestic arts. In fact, neither girl was being trained to be a wife.

Long before sports were considered appropriate for women, the two girls' pursuits were tomboyish and competitive. They liked climbing the large trees in the O'Flaherty garden, "going recklessly high perhaps— each trying to out-top the other." They enjoyed ice skating and riding Kate's pony, "but principally, and certainly first in our affection, music and reading—veritable passions." The two girls shared what friends give one another: food, activity, intellectual pleasure, tears—and warm and wicked gossip. As Kate recalled, they "divided our 'picayune's' worth of candy—climbed together the highest cherry trees; wept in company over the 'Days of Bruce,' and later, exchanged our heart secrets."

As best friends often do, Katie and Kitty, six months younger, mirrored each other. They had both been christened Catherine; both were from well-respected, wealthy families. Both had some Huguenots in the family tree, and each girl had one parent who was an outsider in St.

Louis: Kitty's mother was the Protestant daughter of a former American ambassador to London. There was a worldliness about both households that was unusual among the inbred older families of the city.

But the two girls also had deep differences. Kate was the baby of her family, while Kitty was the oldest: her portrait shows a neat, earnest, dark-haired and dark-eyed young girl. Kitty never had a wild or rebellious streak — perhaps because her family life, with two parents, was more traditional and staid. Her father, like Thomas O'Flaherty, belonged to various lodges and civic groups; her uncle was a judge; and her family was enmeshed in male St. Louis in ways the Charlevilles and Farises never had been.

Yet the crowded Garesché household had more youngsters, and Kate liked going there to play charades and games. She could also watch, and study, a traditional nuclear family. Kate was one of very few fatherless girls at the Sacred Heart school, and Kitty's family may have made her feel as if she "fit in" somewhat better. Kate was also the only friend allowed to stay overnight at Kitty's, where she would sometimes "help bury and write an epitaph for a pet bird." Their families took both Catherines to museums, lectures, and circuses, and indulged their curiosities — while the two girls shared opinions only with each other.

Kate also shared family secrets with Kitty — about her father's death, her mother's life, and the slaves. Yet another part of growing up for young girls is thinking about their own possibilities, about what they will be allowed to do or be, and their mothers were one guide, although their pasts were very different. Juliette Garesché had had a glamorous London girlhood, while Eliza O'Flaherty had been sheltered on the family farm outside St. Louis — but neither one could ever expect to have a profession. St. Louis had few women's clubs or opportunities; there were no abolitionist or suffrage activities like those that occupied women in the East; and women were not allowed to attend law or medical school or St. Louis University. Kate and Kitty knew intellectual and well-educated and capable teachers and administrators among the Sacred Heart nuns — but those women were cloistered. They had taken the veil, and given up the world.

As far as the two girls could see, they would grow up to be house-wives, and probably restless ones. Kitty's aunt Mariquitta, for instance, spent most of her time shopping, which her devoted husband Julius preferred her to do. Otherwise, he said, she'd fill her head with impos-sible ideas from romantic novels and expect him to spend all his time loving her.

Kate and Kitty were still schoolgirls when the tall, handsome Julius Garesché became one of the first West Point graduates killed in the Civil War, his horse shot out from under him at the battle of Murfreesboro. His widow, Mariquitta, outlived him by only a few years, but Kate Chopin immortalized them both in *The Awakening*. In Chopin's novel, Edna's first schoolgirl crush is on a handsome, nameless cavalry officer, much like Julius Garesché — while the earthy "shrimp girl," a saucy real-ist who talks calmly about extramarital romances, is named Mariequita.

As schoolgirls, though, Kate and Kitty were interested in informa-tion as well as romance. Kate liked to snoop in bureau drawers for for-bidden books, which the two friends would read together, "often 'mid laughter and tears," Kitty recalled. When they read Cecilia Mary Cad-dell's *Blind Agnese; or The Little Spouse of the Blessed Sacrament*, a novel about a pious beggar girl, the girls were inspired to learn Italian. "*Ollendorf's Method* was bought unknown to anyone," Kitty recalled, "and we began the study all by ourselves, as a great secret. I must con-fess that we soon reached a point which seemed to say to our puzzled brains, 'Thus far shall you go and no farther.'"

Before the summer of 1863, when they were thirteen, the two girls had read, according to Kitty: "Grimm's *Fairy Tales, Blind Agnes, Paul and Virginia, Orphans of Moscow, Dickens for Little Folks*, a series: *Little Nell, Little Dorrit*, etc., *Queechy, The Wide Wide World, Scottish Chiefs, Days of Bruce, Pilgrims Progress*. We particularly loved *Zaidee*, a beau-tiful old-fashioned romance; and *John Halifax, Gentleman*. Of poetry we read the metrical romances of Scott, with his *Talisman* and *Ivan-hoe*, with some of the chosen poems of Pope, Collins, and Gray."

Some books had special meanings in their families. *Paul and Virginia*, the romantic French story of two children of nature by Bernardin de

Saint-Pierre, had been a sensational novel in frontier St. Louis in 1797, the year Madame Charleville was married. She eventually named one of her daughters Virginia; that daughter also named her daughter Virginia; and even Kitty Garesché, born half a century later, had a sister named Virginia. A century after its original publication, Kate Chopin used a sensual tropical atmosphere like *Paul and Virginia*'s in her portrayal of Grand Isle in *The Awakening*.

Most of the other books on Kate and Kitty's reading list, though, were popular novels by English and American women: Christian, dainty, obedient—not much like Kate's world. But traces of those books— bits of language, character names and descriptions, even some words about passion and dreams—turn up years later in Kate Chopin's stories. Her Zaïda in "A Night in Acadie," for instance, resembles the bold title character in Margaret Oliphant's *Zaidee*. In Sir Walter Scott's *Ivanhoe* and Grace Aguilar's *Days of Bruce*, young Katie and Kitty encountered heroines who were pure and golden-haired, or dark-haired and passionate—and both types appear in Chopin's fiction. In *Days of Bruce*, the heroine Isabella is, like Edna in *The Awakening*, an unhappily married woman tempted by another man—whose name is Robert.

Christmas 1860 was the last peaceful one Kate O'Flaherty and Kitty Garesché would have together. They were ten years old, and looking forward to their first communions the following spring in their massive, beautiful new parish church, with its Corinthian columns, Italian marble altars, rich frescoes, and costly paintings. That Christmas, Kate's great-aunt Pélagie Charleville Boyer gave her one of her most cherished gifts: a copybook with LEAVES OF AFFECTION stamped in gold on the cover. It was inscribed "To Katie, from her affectionate aunt Boyer, December the 25th, 1860."

At first Kate pasted in magazine pictures, including two sweethearts like the lovers in *The Awakening*, who lean toward each other, with hardly any space in between, as if treading "upon blue ether" (VIII). She copied one favorite poem into her notebook (and much later, wrote underneath it in pencil, "very pretty, but where's the point?")

Before the end of December, Kitty also copied a poem into Kate's notebook: "We Have Been Friends Together," by the English poet Caroline Elizabeth Sarah Norton. Kitty dedicated it "To Katie," and Kate wrote above it, "My sweet friend Kitty."

That was Kitty's last appearance in Kate's notebook, for there were ominous things going on in the outside world. In late December, just four days after the new Church of the Annunciation was dedicated, South Carolina voted to secede from the Union.

With the women at home, and the Sacred Heart nuns, and her best friend Kitty, Kate O'Flaherty was coming of age in a mostly female world — one that nurtured her creative spirit, and encouraged her generosity and her dreams. But it would all change, the year she turned thirteen.

# Chapter 2

## The Spoils of War

THE CONTRAST between the women's quiet world of domesticity and care, and the men's blustery world of power and simmering violence, could not have been clearer in late 1860 and early 1861. Before the war was over, Kate O'Flaherty would, in many ways, be robbed of her innocence.

Kate and Kitty Garesché were enrolled as Sacred Heart day students throughout that tumultuous school year, from September 1860 through May 1861. They were concentrating on the catechism for their first communion, and theirs was supposed to be a time of peace and joy, under the loving image of the Virgin Mary. But already their world was changing, and old ways were crumbling.

"I never went to slave sales, nor do I think Kate ever did," Kitty recalled seventy years later, but slavery was all around them. Ads for runaway slaves filled the newspapers; Dred Scott had started his famous antislavery case at the old St. Louis Court House. Just a short walk from the Sacred Heart Academy, there was a "slave pen," advertising "Negroes available at all times." By the early 1860s, though, many St. Louis households had quietly replaced their slaves with Irish servants. Even Ulysses S. Grant, a West Pointer toiling as a hardscrabble farmer outside St. Louis, freed his one slave in 1859.

But in the 1860 census, Eliza O'Flaherty still owned six slaves. There were three "black" adults (a man, 64, and two women, 28 and 17) and three "mulatto" children (two girls, aged 9 and 6 — the ones born while Thomas O'Flaherty was alive — and a six-month-old baby boy). The father of the baby is unknown, but Kate's half-brother George, twenty, and his uncle Charley Faris, nineteen, were both old enough. By keeping her slaves, Eliza was not retaining a valuable property, for at least two were too young to do useful work. Possibly she felt some kind of responsibility toward the eldest and the youngest. Maybe she felt guilty. But she almost certainly did consider them "part of the family" — which, by blood, they probably were.

On New Year's Day 1861, a crowd disrupted and destroyed the last slave auction in downtown St. Louis. Though some of "Old St. Louis" supported slavery, secession, or both, they were outnumbered by fiercely antislavery German immigrants, who had left the old country to escape inequality and injustice.

By February, half a dozen Southern states had seceded from the Union — including Louisiana, the home of Eliza O'Flaherty's Charleville cousins. In St. Louis, the Sacred Heart convent had already been menaced by "Black Republicans" (fervent abolitionists), and when one Sacred Heart family ran up a Confederate flag over their house, antislavery protesters gathered to boo, hiss, and shout. On February 8, Kate's eleventh birthday, a fire alarm sounded on Market Street, and three or four armed-to-the-teeth "German horsemen" were seen dashing down the street — until they realized the sound was not a call to arms. They retreated, leaving terror in their wake.

In April, Confederate General P.G.T. Beauregard ordered the firing on Fort Sumter, South Carolina. Within weeks, war was officially declared. All over St. Louis, men were dragging out old muskets, demonstrating in the streets, stomping about, and blaspheming and hurrahing and frightening women and children and old people.

And nuns. "The First Communion ceremony was advanced," the Sacred Heart nuns recorded in their journal, "as the parents of many of the children are leaving the city which, they say, will be burnt or pillaged by the soldiers." The sisters' friends begged them to evacuate, and the nuns hid all their valuable objects, important papers, and sacred vessels. But Reverend Mother Tucker vowed to remain in St. Louis as long as possible. "We are not exposed," she said, "and we have no money to pay the expenses of a flight, as the tuitions are most inexactly paid."

(One of the unpaid tuitions was Kate's: Eliza O'Flaherty still owed $30.60 on Kate's tuition for the term.)

Just two weeks after Fort Sumter, on May 1, Kate and Kitty had their communion ceremony in the convent chapel. "We had been prepared most carefully and fervently and I remember how we talked over together the secret emotions of that Day," Kitty recalled decades later. In her "Leaves of Affection" book, Kate put a picture of a young girl wearing a garland and gazing at the Virgin Mary, with a female angel hovering over the girl. Underneath that image of womanly solicitude, Kate wrote: "May 1st, 1861, My First Communion Picture."

But they had little time to feel protected, for they were caught up in "the Civil War with all its thrilling and very sad events for Missouri," Kitty remembered. The most hotheaded youths immediately joined one side or the other, but "Old St. Louis" mostly favored the Southern cause. Kate's half-brother George enlisted for the Confederacy as a private in Company A, Boone's Regiment of Missouri Mounted Infantry. Two days after Kate and Kitty's first communion, self-appointed Confederate troops began drilling at an impromptu outpost they called "Camp Jackson." Young women flocked to flirt with the fledgling soldiers, and for many young people, war still seemed like a lark and an adventure.

By mid-May, the Sacred Heart girls were still in class, learning history and literature, reciting French lessons, and making garlands for Mary Month. The nuns, though, were consumed with dread: Union supporters had threatened to take over their house for barracks and parade grounds. And then, on May 10, a skirmish at Camp Jackson escalated to deadly gunfire, leaving twenty-eight people dead.

That was the day the Civil War came to St. Louis.

The terrified nuns shut down the Sacred Heart school. City girls like Kate and Kitty were bundled home; orphans spent the weekend crouching under convent windows, barricaded by mattresses. All over the city, families were fleeing "the damned Dutch" (German-born Union supporters), the hot-tempered "Seceshes," or both. Every boat that could cross the Mississippi River to Illinois was full; carriages and wagons were commandeered. The next day, four German-American soldiers were found dead in various parts of the city — including one at Seventh Street and Franklin, where Eliza O'Flaherty owned land.

The mayor declared martial law. All drinking places were closed; no one could go out after nightfall; and no minors would be allowed outdoors at all for the next three days. Just ten days after their First Communion, Kate O'Flaherty and Kitty Garesché were separate prisoners in their own homes.

The charming Sacred Heart graduation ceremonies did not take place that year, because school was closed. Over the summer, Union General John C. Fremont opened his headquarters in an elegant mansion just three doors from the O'Flahertys'. Fremont affected the style of a grand monarch, with a 300-man entourage of heel-clicking dandies — while his energetic wife, Jessie Benton Fremont, bustled about recruiting women for hospital work, the first time that had ever been done in St. Louis. But Fremont's incompetence and lavish style enraged President Abraham Lincoln, who fired him after only 100 days. In Kate and Kitty's households, that was considered a Confederate victory.

That fall, 1861, the Sacred Heart nuns bravely reopened their school, with a very large enrollment. St. Louis families wanted their daughters to be safe, and the city was already being overrun by starving women and children, refugees from rural Missouri raids. But searches, seizures, and random violence took place everywhere. Anyone could suddenly be arrested and whisked off to the Gratiot Street Prison, a gray stone fortress at one end of the O'Flahertys' street — while at the other end were the Union headquarters, in a commandeered mansion. Possibly to remove him from the constant surveillance, fourteen-year-old Tom O'Flaherty was enrolled in the commercial course at St. Louis University in 1862, and he stayed through 1864.

Meanwhile, everyone worried about George, Kate and Tom's half-brother, a likable and popular lad. In August 1862, the month Kitty

Garesché turned twelve, George and an unnamed Arkansas army buddy were among forty-nine prisoners captured at a guerrilla camp. After only a few days in the Gratiot Street Prison — where, at least, his step-mother and sister could visit him — George was transferred out of state. His friend, though, had become critically ill, and Eliza offered to care for him in her home. A week later, he died.

George languished in jail for months, until he was freed during a prisoner exchange in Vicksburg. On his way home, he stopped in Little Rock, to console the family of his army friend. George missed the Christmas holidays in St. Louis, and the lively New Year's Day visits, and the sudden early January thaw, followed by severe cold and six inches of snow. That weather proved too much for eighty-three-year-old Madame Charleville. On January 16, 1863, she died, "universally be-loved" and "a lady of estimable character," according to her obituary. She was buried in Calvary Cemetery, in the section next to Thomas O'Fla-herty's grave — and so Kate O'Flaherty lost her first teacher, the old woman who taught her to appreciate the wisdom of women of all ages.

Barely two months later, a shocking notice appeared in the *Missouri Republican*:

D I E D :
At Little Rock, Arkansas, February 17th, 1863,
G E O R G E   O ' F L A H E R T Y ,
of typhoid fever, in the 23rd year of his age.

Kate's half-brother had been a "brave, kind, and gentle young man" and "a bright specimen of humanity in the very early dawn of man-hood." George was also buried in Calvary Cemetery, under the large stone pillar that marked his father's grave.

Years later, Kate Chopin named one of her sons George, and she used the name for the rich, selfish young man in one of her earliest stories, "Wiser than a God." She had known George only in the early bloom of life, and he had been more impetuous than wise. She does not mention George in her surviving diaries, but in a school composi-tion called "The Early Dead," three years after George's death, she asked, "How then express the grief with which we follow the young, the gifted, the beautiful to the silent tomb."

She never found the words.

War brought out the bully in men, and a household run by women was a particular target. One day a Union flag suddenly appeared on the O'Flahertys' porch, because "the Yanks" had tied it there. Kate tore it down.

Within minutes, "the Yanks" were at the door, demanding their flag, and then demanding to search the house. Katie O'Flaherty taunted them: as one old St. Louisan remembered, "the children of '61–'65 were veritable little warriors with their tongues, if not with more deadly weapons." Kate had hidden the flag where the Yanks couldn't find it, in a bundle of scraps—but they could tell that such a defiant girl had something to do with the crime.

They decided to arrest her.

It was not an idle threat. By 1863, soldiers routinely occupied the O'Flahertys' neighborhood, marching to and from the prison, eying the houses of "the disloyal." A German-American soldier had denounced his landlord as a secessionist and then shot him; a merchant who declared that Confederate President Jefferson Davis was "a great man" was sentenced to sixty-three days in prison. It could be deadly to express an unpopular political thought, even by one's choice of clothing: young ladies were frequently seized for wearing secessionist colors, red and white. Some were imprisoned.

When the Yankee flag disappeared, Eliza O'Flaherty may have tried to reason with a stubborn Kate, and warn her about the horrors of prison. But finally Eliza turned to a powerful and persuasive neighbor. Dr. Charles W. Stevens, a Union supporter, agreed to testify that Kate was not a dangerous person who needed to be locked up for the safety of the Union.

Kate O'Flaherty, the young flag thief, was released, and became famous among Southern sympathizers as one who'd stood up to the Yankees. The O'Flahertys' neighbor Anne Ewing Lane even mentioned the escapade in a letter to her sister in Europe, and Kate became known as St. Louis's "Littlest Rebel." But the flag incident was probably more despair than bravado. It was a cry of pain and rage from a young girl in mourning.

Despite the deaths of Madame Charleville in January and George in February, Kate O'Flaherty remained in school during the spring and summer of 1863. There was a steadiness and comfort in the Sacred Heart world, with the students' girlish crushes and intrigues. Kate's "Leaves of Affection" book, which she passed around for autographs in July, is full of loving statements and poems, including this anonymous verse:

> Yes Loving is a painful thrill,
> And not to love more painful still,
> But oh! it is the worst of pain,
> To love, & not be loved again!

Although Kate wrote after the poem her opinion of it ("foolishness"), that snide comment appears to be in a later handwriting.

But there was one great void in Katie O'Flaherty's autograph book. There was nothing from "my sweet friend Kitty" — for Kitty Garesché had been thrown out of St. Louis.

During the Civil War, children were blamed for the sins of their fathers, and wives were punished for the doings of their husbands. And so it was in the Garesché family. Kitty's father, Bauduy Garesché, not only sympathized with the South, but also knew how to make gunpowder. Early on, when he refused to take the Union oath of allegiance, Bauduy Garesché was expelled from St. Louis. Leaving behind his wife and children, he enlisted in the Confederate Army and went to run the powder works in Columbia, South Carolina.

That was in 1861. Two years later, Juliette Garesché made up her mind to join her husband. But among the whisperers of St. Louis, few secrets could be kept, and the Union authorities discovered her plans.

Her home and household goods were confiscated, and she and her home-
less, poverty-stricken children were then banished from St. Louis. Juliette managed to send Kitty and the three younger children to live with
her sister in New York, while she embarked on her own perilous journey to South Carolina.

And so Kate O'Flaherty lost yet another friend, the girlhood chum
with whom she had exchanged her "heart secrets." Much of her heart
went with Kitty. When they were torn from each other, Kate and Kitty
were just thirteen, barely on the brink of womanhood. They did not
see each other again until they were eighteen, finished with school,
and poised to enter St. Louis society. They considered each other lifelong friends — but they could never make up for those lost five years.

In *The Awakening,* Kate honors Kitty in the description of Edna's
closest school friend: one of "rather exceptional intellectual gifts, who
wrote fine-sounding essays, which Edna admired and strove to imi-
tate; and with her she talked and glowed over the English classics, and
sometimes held religious and political controversies" (VII).

The connections Kate Chopin describes are intellectual, not personal.
Perhaps because of her many losses, Chopin herself was also a loner,
one who did not share emotional matters easily.

By July 1863, many Confederate sympathizers in St. Louis had died,
fled, or been banished. After the bloodiest battles, the streets were filled
with the wounded, and an O'Flaherty neighbor called them "creatures
looking as if they had been stolen out of a graveyard." Eliza O'Flaherty, still in mourning for her grandmother and stepson, had heard
that her Charleville cousins died in the horrific siege at Vicksburg,
where the Union soldiers hunkered down and waited for the Rebels to
starve. When they surrendered, the Confederate soldiers were ragged,
even naked; some had eaten their own horses. Vicksburg's civilians,
living in holes in the ground, had subsisted on wallpaper.

But it turned out that the "Charleville boys" were alive, and Eliza
believed they had fought like heroes. Captured with them, and then

paroled, was their nineteen-year-old neighbor, Albert Sampite, who two decades later would play a startling role in Kate Chopin's life. But at the time of Vicksburg, she was just a thirteen-year-old girl, frightened and in mourning.

And then there was another devastating event, whose exact details we can only imagine.

When word of the Rebel surrender at Vicksburg reached St. Louis, Yankee supporters threw on cockades and rosettes, hung up flags, fired guns, whistled and bellowed, and lit off wildly popping firecrackers everywhere. Their houses were especially "resplendent" on Union Row, the O'Flahertys' neighbor Anne Ewing Lane wrote to her sister, but one "outrage" was committed. What Lane reported sounds at first like some small acts of vandalism: "the soldiers going in to Mrs. O'Flaherty's on 8 Street near Chouteau Ave. breaking the vases in her yard and the shrubbery & hoisting a flag over her house."

But there was much more. Like most citizens, Eliza O'Flaherty had lived in fear of the gruff, powerful, German-American soldiers everyone called "the Dutch devils." They seemed foreign, criminal, and menacing, and Eliza had gotten into the habit of wearing her apron backwards, to hide her silverware. Her slaves had run off, or were going to.

After Vicksburg, Eliza O'Flaherty had to be capable, and she had to be brave: she was defending a household of women. At thirty-five, she was responsible for herself, her mother (54), her two sisters (Zuma, 27, and Josephine, 20), and thirteen-year-old Kate. They were four seemingly defenseless women and a blossoming girl, on the innocent edge of adolescence, when a gang of German-American soldiers invaded Eliza's house. Once inside, they menaced her with bayonets—a potent symbol of their power to destroy more than property. For rape has always been the weapon of warriors.

During the Civil War, sexual violence and intimidation were rarely reported (it has been called a "low rape war"). But we also do not know, a century and a half later, what was being described by such words as "abuse" or "outrage." We do not know what Eliza's neighbor meant when she called the invasion at Mrs. O'Flaherty's an "outrage."

With her house full of German soldiers, Eliza knew that patriotism went out the window. She had known all her life that family came first: as a girl of sixteen, just three years older than Kate, she had sacrificed herself in marriage, to save her family. Twenty years later, when she confronted the German soldiers with bayonets, we do not know who said what, and what threats may have been exchanged.

But Eliza hoisted the Union flag, because they demanded it, and did whatever she had to do, and evidently it was enough.

Eight months later, Eliza wrote to her uncle that "I was forced by a compy of dutch devils at the point of the bayonet to illuminate my house & to hoist a flag, it was to celebrat the taking of Vicksburg, they threatened to burn the house over our heads —." Eliza was discreet ("Pleas burn this letter," she wrote), and said nothing about her fears for her vulnerable daughter, just growing into womanhood. Perhaps she assumed her relatives would read between the lines and know whether Kate had, or had not, been molested. Or maybe Eliza could not bring herself to say any more. Shame is a powerful silencer.

The effect on her young daughter cannot be known. In wartime, most civilians feel powerless — but Kate O'Flaherty also saw her mother powerless before the bayonets of soldiers. It would have been an indelible picture: a woman pitting her values — love and care of others — against the mighty and indomitable power of men. But whatever "outrage" was committed by the soldiers, Eliza O'Flaherty showed her daughter how to survive.

Although her school remained open, Kate O'Flaherty stayed home during the fall of 1863 — evidently writing, reading, and thinking. She behaved as adolescent victims of abuse do: she withdrew and hid. A stepladder in the attic at home became her refuge, summer and winter. With a big shawl on cold days or "in airy dishabille in the dog days," she pored over stacks of fiction and poetry (the formal library had "solid and pretentious cyclopaedias" and Roman Catholic religious works). She much preferred reading Sir Walter Scott "to doing any sums or parsing stupid sentences." But she had started intense reading, especially Scott, as a social activity, sharing laughter and tears with her best friend Kitty. Reading had always been a comfort and an escape. She knew and loved the power of words.

But now Kate was reading Scott's tales of knighthood by herself, without Kitty, and with a firsthand knowledge of war. The chivalry of Scott's knights seemed a kind of mockery to one who knew what war really involved. Without Kitty, *Ivanhoe* could only remind her of her many losses.

A year later, Kate O'Flaherty was in school again when Confederate General Sterling Price's armies moved toward a massive attack on St. Louis. Schools and businesses closed; hordes of citizens fled. Others barricaded themselves in their homes until the threat passed. But that spring, the ragged Confederate armies finally surrendered in Virginia, on Palm Sunday. On Good Friday, five days later, President Abraham Lincoln was shot, and he died on Easter Sunday.

There was no joy in the end of the war, and no romance in what Kate O'Flaherty Chopin remembered and wrote about those years. The Lost Cause had little bright sheen for those who lived through it. Young men died, or lost their will to live. Women, she seemed to think, knew better how to survive — but we will never know what "outrage" she survived in her own home.

In her short stories, a quarter century later, Chopin wrote about old men who lost their memories, or waited vainly for their dead sons to return ("A Wizard from Gettysburg"; "The Return of Alcibiade"). She also described the grim loneliness of the battlefield itself ("The Locket"), but no one wanted to publish that story. By then Americans were boosting the Spanish-American war, and no one wanted to think about a young woman like the one in Chopin's story, who hears that her soldier lover is dead and feels a "spasm of resistance and rebellion. . . . Why was the spring here with its flowers and its seductive breath if he was dead! . . . The soul of her youth clamored for its rights; for a share in the world's glory and exultation."

Kate Chopin's finest stories of the Civil War are those with women's souls, the voices she knew best from her childhood. She describes women who spend their lives dwelling in the pre-War past, including a child-like widow dedicated to her dead husband's memory and a tortured lady remembering the burned plantation and the lover who dashed off to glory and never returned ("A Lady of Bayou St. John"; "Ma'ame Pélagie"). Chopin also wrote poignantly about black women forever scarred by war: in "Beyond the Bayou," a former slave known as "La Folle" (the foolish one) cannot cross the bayou near her cabin because during the war she had been frightened literally "out of her senses."

In her Civil War stories, Kate O'Flaherty Chopin describes what she remembered from the war: dreams of bravery and romance; terror, loss, ashes, and a lifetime of mourning. For the crucial years between eleven and fifteen, Kate O'Flaherty became a woman in the midst of street violence, sudden death, and constant clamoring fear. She lost her first teacher, a woman of great knowledge and compassion; she lost her cheerful, loving brother; and she was yanked away from her dearest friend and closest confidante. With Kitty she could have laughed, and cried, and shared her heart's secrets—but Kitty was gone. And there was the "outrage," and the knowledge that her mother could not protect her from everything. The women's world was not enough of a shield and a wall.

For Kate O'Flaherty, the war years were a bitter coming of age.

## Chapter 3

# The Voice of
# a Young Woman

MODERN PSYCHOLOGISTS talk about young women's "loss of voice" in their teens. While growing up, young women too often grow down, learning to silence themselves and stifle their opinions. Faced with puberty and pressure to conform, they retreat from being individuals.

Kate O'Flaherty's coming of age was also bound up with the woes of war. She had lived in a cozy and secure world of women, with spirited widows and nuns, and her beloved friend Kitty. She was being raised under the "Victorian umbrella" of women who cherished and protected young girls.

All that was shattered when she lost her brilliant great-grandmother; her school was closed; her brother died; her best friend was wrenched away — and Union soldiers abused her and her mother. She had reason to hide in the attic, reading — and studying — novels like *Ivanhoe*. Some three decades later, in *The Awakening,* the beautiful Madame Ratignolle resembles Scott's golden Rowena. But Adèle Ratignolle is also a mother-woman: she recognizes that Edna is a troubled soul, in need of friends.

After the war, though, Katie O'Flaherty was lucky. In two all-female schools, she had the cure most recommended for young women's loss of voice. Her teachers and role models and student leaders were all women and girls. She saw women doing everything, and not shying away from expressing their opinions. Kate was also, in her last years, something of a school celebrity, both as a scholar and a creative writer. Like most authors — but without recognizing it — she found her vocation very early.

She also found herself a new mentor, a teacher who could fill the place in her life and her heart first opened by Madame Charleville. Her new mentor encouraged Katie O'Flaherty to write judiciously, but also gracefully — with thought, and with humor.

Outwardly, the teenaged Kate O'Flaherty became more sedate. In her first young-adult portrait, made when she was sixteen, a year after the end of the war, she stands against a classical backdrop. She carries a fan, and wears a fashionably flounced hoop skirt. Physically, she was becoming a woman, and that year her family moved to 1118 St. Ange Avenue, half a dozen blocks southwest of their original home.

The new house was even more full of people. Besides Kate, her mother, grandmother, and brother Tom, Eliza's brother Charley and sister Josephine remained. The three live-in servants were now Irish: two women in their twenties and a thirteen-year-old girl. Kate's mammy, who may have been the first tender voice of her life, was gone, and what became of the other former slaves is unknown. If Kate befriended the youngest Irish servant, who was about her age, no one recorded anything about that.

Two other families also shared the household. There were the settled McAllisters: Eliza's sister Amanda, her husband Roger (originally Thomas O'Flaherty's business partner), and their children Nina, Andrew, and Marie (all younger than Kate). Then there were the newly-wed Tatums: Eliza's sister Zuma (known as "Puss") and her husband John, whom she'd married during the war, when he sneaked into St. Louis under the noses of the Union troops. Zuma had become pregnant almost immediately, but the infant did not survive. Two years after the wedding, she and John had already buried two children.

Suddenly it was no longer a women's household. John Tatum, a steamboatman, was often away — but Roger McAllister was a solid, middle-aged merchant, powerful in the community. He was the kind of man who came home at night, and commanded family meals. And so, just as she reached puberty, in the O'Flaherty/Faris/McAllister/Tatum household, Katie O'Flaherty got to observe married couples for the first time. Aunt Amanda had married sensibly, Aunt Zuma had married romantically, and both were in their late twenties or early thirties — the ages of disenchanted wives in Kate Chopin's fiction.

If, as has been said, a writer's whole capital is her childhood, Kate O'Flaherty's youth was a rich one for learning about women, marriage, and independent widows.

The move to a new home may have been one of the ways Eliza O'Flaherty tried to comfort her daughter after the war. They moved away from the site of the "outrage" and from sad, bitter, and terrifying memories. Eliza may have decided that Kate, as an adolescent, needed to be in a house where she would be protected from violence — and the only way to do that was to have men about.

Kate also had a change of scene for school. She spent the 1865–1866 school year as a special student at the Academy of the Visitation, a pretty campus inside a stone wall that separated it from "Kerry Patch," the squalid Irish ghetto (later portrayed in Chopin's "A Vocation and a Voice"). Since the Visitandines had long been noted for their musical programs, the year was Kate's chance to concentrate on her music, to spread her wings in a different direction. The "Viz" year was also Eliza O'Flaherty's healing present to her daughter, a valuable and effective therapy. Kate loved the piano, and a girl who played the piano would often sing along. And so, literally, Kate O'Flaherty began reclaiming her voice.

For the academic year that began in 1866, Kate returned to the Sacred Heart Academy, where the education was more academically challenging and also more innovative about women's roles. The older girls' curriculum aimed to create "intelligent, active, unselfish women, with minds and hands trained for the sphere in which God has placed them, whether it be home-life or some wider social field" — an unusually progressive statement. The students were to "take part intelligently in conversation," write interesting and correct letters, and discuss scientific discoveries and current events. They were also required to think, and to judge: of Isabella II of Spain, Kate O'Flaherty wrote in her notebook that the queen "is beloved by her subjects, but her character is not stainless."

Except for conversation, the Sacred Heart students were really not being trained to be wives, at least in the traditional American sense.

The Sacred Heart nuns also worked on ways to encourage their girls, but not through cutthroat competition in which one wins and the others are losers. Rather, they stressed excellence, and those who were not first still shared the glory. (In modern terms, they made the school into a web, a community rather than — as men might — a hierarchy in which only one could be top dog.) In music as well as traditional academic subjects, Sacred Heart students competed vigorously for honors and prizes, including colored ribbons, medals, and crowns. At their assemblies, some girls would win so many crowns that they could not fit them all on their heads. And so they would drape the crowns over their arms, creating a charming, jolly, and colorful picture.

The greatest honor of all was to be a Child of Mary. Most honors were given by the nuns, but Children of Mary were chosen by their schoolmates as well as their teachers. They represented the best that Sacred Heart life had to offer: leadership and hard work, piety and popularity, and scrupulous kindness to younger girls. Children of Mary were supposed to be studious, capable, and well rounded, and they were everyone's favorites.

Katie O'Flaherty had barely returned to the Sacred Heart school when the election took place on October 14, 1866. The election was dramatic, and the suspense intense until the new members were chosen. Kate's cousin Aurore "Lovy" Charleville and her friend Lizzie Thornton were chosen as Under Sacristans; Lizzie Bulte was Librarian; and the "Other Members" were Francis ("Frank") Blakely — and Katie O'Flaherty.

A month later, on November 21, Kate, Frank, and another girl named Mary Farrell were officially inducted into the Children of Mary. They received special medals which many Children of Mary wore on their belts, and they had the right to sign their names with a special flourish:

Katherine O'Flaherty, E. de M. ("Enfant de Marie," or Child of Mary)

As an "Other Member," Kate had no special duties in school, and that suited her: all her life she tried to evade organizational responsibilities, and relished being an insider-outsider. The religious "Rules of the Congregation of the Blessed Virgin Mary" were the same as those for any Catholic: celebrating holy days, taking communion, and saying daily prayers. But the Children of Mary had other duties that were traditionally female: they were supposed to join adult sodalities and do charity work, which might also include running lending libraries. As an adult, Kate Chopin paid dues to the St. Louis Children of Mary Sodality, and to the St. Louis Mercantile Library—but she rarely volunteered to do anything for long.

Another section of the Rules was less difficult, since it fit with the values she'd learned in the world of widows at home. The Children of Mary were warned against bad practices and "occasions of sin," such as "evil companions, quarrels, contentions, murmurings." The Children of Mary were specifically, and explicitly, supposed to be kind to women. The adult Children of Mary took that very seriously—including one very compassionate nun who saw Kate O'Flaherty, still sorrowing, as a soul in need.

Madam Mary Philomena O'Meara was only six years older than Katie O'Flaherty. (The Sacred Heart sisters were called Madams, not Madames or Mesdames.) Born in Ireland, Mary O'Meara had grown up as a curious, strong-willed, but lonely child, who used to take a statue of the Virgin Mary to bed with her for comfort. As a schoolgirl, she also climbed trees and loved books, but after her prayers saved her sister's life, Mary O'Meara dedicated herself to "love and service" in religion. At the end of 1863, the year of Katie O'Flaherty's sorrows and losses, nineteen-year-old Mary O'Meara took her vows as a Sacred Heart nun.

Kate O'Flaherty called her "our much loved teacher, Madam O'Meara"; Kitty Garesché remembered her as "one of our nuns most gifted for composition in both verse and prose." From the beginning, her pupils adored her, and she dedicated herself to making the Children of Mary into "valiant women." Her classes were exciting and exacting. She loved history, which she considered the stories of people and their foibles. She liked to tell vivid and colorful tales of monks and queens and heroes — just like the stories Madame Charleville had used to entertain and instruct little Katie. Although she was in a school that celebrated its French origins, Madam O'Meara considered the writing of good English "the best all around test of culture."

Madam O'Meara was an excellent conversationalist with a long memory and exquisite tact. She also appreciated "the interior life," the growth that might take place within a child long before it appeared on the surface. In Katie O'Flaherty, she found a gifted girl who needed to recover from the sharp pain of many losses all at once. She needed to express herself, not simply drown herself in others' stories. Writing, Mary O'Meara suspected, would be Kate O'Flaherty's cure. It would let her hear and find and use her own voice.

In 1867, at seventeen, Katie O'Flaherty began her commonplace book, a plain notebook with lined pages and a green and black mottled cover, on which was printed "Katie O'Flaherty. St. Louis." It had no lock; it was not private; and much of it consists of passages copied from well-known writers, along with character sketches of famous rulers and political figures, almost all men. She recorded famous last words of famous people, and noted odd historical events, such as the Venetian "Espousals of the Adriatic." Sometimes she even corrected long-winded authors: when Longfellow went on and on in his novel *Hyperion* about spring as "the rising of the broad grene curtain," St. Louis schoolgirl Kate O'Flaherty changed his line to a brisker "the opening of the scene."

Kate did begin her notebook with a solemn, pompous passage from the English novelist Edward George Bulwer: "To many minds at the commencement of one grave and earnest pilgrimage, I am vandal enough to think that the indulgence of poetic taste and reverie does great harm and lasting injury." But after the second such passage, from T. B. Macaulay's *Ranke's History of the Popes,* young Kate wrote her first surviving opinion: "It is to me a subject of wonder that a mind such as Macaulay's, so enlightened and free from bigotry, should have considered the Catholic Church a mere work of 'human policy.'"

She soon grew more blunt. In her view, *The Life and Letters of Madame Swetchine* by the Count de Falloux was "a queer book — which did not interest me much." (The book was often assigned to Sacred Heart students as punishment for misdeeds, so Kate O'Flaherty may have also done something to deserve it.) Neverthless, she did appreciate a good character sketch, in the portrait of Monsieur de Fontenelle, a great misanthrope: "I like it because I can glance over it as an occasional reminder that a monster once lived upon earth."

The portrait of Fontenelle inspired her to do what budding writers do: apply the knowledge to her own life. She was reminded, she wrote, of "a joke told at my expense." Her mother sent her into the parlor one afternoon, she wrote, "to entertain a gentleman, who, though deemed bashful has never yet succeeded in making that ingredient in his composition known to myself." She chose the piano to fulfill "my mission of entertainer," and she tried everything, from operas to sonatas to waltzes and jigs — after which he told her "there was nothing on earth he disliked more than music — at any time — in any place — and of any kind from a brass band to a jew's harp."

A less talented writer might have recorded the anecdote and then explained it, but Kate O'Flaherty let it stand. Already she was developing her comic timing — which depends on knowing when to stop.

Adolescents of every era go through wide mood swings, alternating between romantic earnestness and hilarious cynicism. In her original compositions, Kate O'Flaherty often rebelled against pious platitudes. In an essay about a classmate's death, for instance, she wrote seriously about death and sorrow, but then grew enthusiastically morbid: "Lift one of those marble hands, which clasps so confidingly the jeweled cross; how cold it is — its chill sends a shiver through the frame; drop it, — hear how heavily it falls against the alabaster bosom." In a supposedly serious poem about an old man's regrets and losses, Kate O'Flaherty was even more subversive, piling on sentimental clichés, such as "memories of yore" and "his mother's knee," and ending with bright-sounding utter nonsense:

> His cottage home in his jasmine frame,
> Still smiled beneath the linden shade,
> When the south-wind an early pilgrim came,
> And the wild flowers a rich mosaic made.

We cannot know whether Madam O'Meara was amused or horrified by Kate O'Flaherty's parodies of mawkish poetry. Years later, a biographer reported that young Kate's "essays and poetic exercises were thought to be quite remarkable, not only by the scholars, but even by the sisters." If Madam O'Meara tried to discipline Kate's imagination or stop her flow of words, there is no evidence in the notebook. Kate kept on with it — committing ridiculous misspellings, and mangling pompous passages.

But she never mocked her best teacher, or the lively female community at the Sacred Heart Academy. Kate O'Flaherty's earliest original poem that survives, "The Congé," celebrates a Sacred Heart tradition, the last day "at which the day scholars are permitted to mingle with the boarders." Above the poem, Kate O'Flaherty explained that "The 'Madam' alluded to was our much loved teacher Madam O'Meara."

Besides showing the youthful poet's wit and ear for meter, and her wry portrayal of her own clumsiness, "The Congé" pokes fun at her little cousin Nina McAllister's hefty appetite, while praising the dexterity of Kate's own friend and age mate Frank (Blakely, another Child of Mary). But the heroines are the nuns, Madam O'Meara and Madam Hamilton, who trust the girls with responsibilities, feed them dinner, contrive unusual intellectual treats and entertainments, and make them feel respected, safe, and loved. "The Congé" recognizes the devotion of women to the education of girls and shows Kate O'Flaherty's gifts as a "teller of marvellous stories."

*The Congé* — 1867

The Congé is past and the frolic and fun
Was over, before it seemed scarcely begun;
For with playing and romping and teasing away,
The quick fleeting hours soon filled up the day.
But the morning was not to amusement devoted
For Madam to all of her "Brights" had allotted
The task (this displayed a heart ever trusting)
Of arranging and breaking and mending and dusting,
Her chemical tools, which of delicate make
We could easily handle and — easily break.
There was Lizzie who thought with importance of air
That we could do nothing if she was not there,
And Frank — thinking much, and speaking but little
Who handled with safety tools e'en the most brittle
While Katie O'F, poor unfortunate lass
Broke impliments stoutest as though they were glass.
But this war of destruction, thanks, soon was to cease
And the room and its contents left happily in peace.
For kind Madam Hamilton, with due form and state,
Announced the dinner no longer could wait,
And arranging the girls with artistical taste,
Led the way to the hall without trouble or haste.
But ye Fates! On arriving I found 'twas my doom
For want I presume of more benches or room,
To sit between Lizzie and Nina my cousin
Who seemed to have appetites due to a dozen,
And gave me scarce time to breathe or to think
With asking for butter — the bread — or a drink.
But between these demands which indeed were not few,
I found time to admire an arrangement or two
Of the garlands of flowers and pigs à la fry

Which in every direction were greeting the eye.
But all these howe'er beautiful sink into nought,
In considering the fun which the afternoon brought;
For through cellar and basement and garret so high,
We tumbled and tossed in the game of "I spy."
Now into the barn yard — the loft or the stable,
Hiding in every place — any place that we were able;
And thrown into ecstasies of foolish delight
At not being found or at seeking aright.
But at length Madam M. with mysterious air,
Comes whispering that the girls must prepare
To enter a room, shut out from all light,
To see a strange thing — a most wonderful sight;
Which sight we soon found was a new source of pleasure
Got up by "our Madam" whose mind is a treasure,
Ever teeming with jewels of science and fun,
And in whom we all think sets and rises the sun.
'Twas a strange magic lantern which displayed a queer sight
Of devils in every conceivable plight.
Of hills and volcanoes; St. Peter's at Rome;
Of Pantheons at Paris — or a neat cottage home.
Of monkies and tigers and elephants rare —
All displayed with precision and mentioned with care.
But my keen disappointment one cannot conceive.
When, at the best part we are told we must leave;
For fear that the already fast fading light
Would leave us in fear at the coming of night.
And as I reluctantly arose to obey,
Though my reason said "homeward" my heart bade me stay.
So greatly put out — nearly ready to cry,
I kissed my companions — bade Madam good bye —
And secretly knowing I'd no time to waste
Turned my steps towards home with all possible haste.

For most Sacred Heart girls, the end of school meant the end of their protected female community. It was their last chance to consider what kinds of women they would be. Madam O'Meara believed that Sacred Heart graduates should become "companions intellectually of their husbands, mothers fit for their sublime trust, women able to bear life's responsibilities and courageous to meet them." Through literature they would learn about "the nobility and beauty of the life before them."

Probably at Madam O'Meara's urging, Kate O'Flaherty began collecting passages about women. She copied descriptions of art works emphasizing women's power, and passages comparing the "natural" qualities of German women with the snobberies of Englishwomen. From Lady Blessington's *Conversations with Byron*, Kate O'Flaherty may have been comparing herself with the Lady at the same age: "a just matured woman, full of loveliness and love, the kind of creature with whose divine sweetness the gazer's heart aches."

At her Sacred Heart graduation on June 29, 1868, Kate O'Flaherty was, for the last time, the center of attention for her many intellectual and musical achievements. At the ceremonies she played an instrumental duet ("duo de Norma") with a classmate, and read her original essay on "National Peculiarities." She won a first blue ribbon, the highest honor for day scholars, and shared the very highest honor, the gold medal award of "excellence of conduct and proficiency in studies" with three other students, including her friend Frank.

But graduation was both a pinnacle and the beginning of yet another loss. She would leave behind the brick convent building with its brick walk and tall lilac bushes, whose sweet fragrance scented the air after late spring rains. She would abandon the quiet halls, the rustling curtseys, the cakes and teas and smiling rituals of kindness, and the nuns whose life work was to nurture "our children."

She would enter St. Louis society, a world in which young women were viewed as lovely prizes. Men, though, would be making the rules.

# Chapter 4

## Belle and Bride

THE TWO FRIENDS were going to make their debuts together. Kitty Garesché turned eighteen in the summer of 1868, six months after Kate O'Flaherty, and that fall Kitty and her family were back in St. Louis. The two Katherines had been apart for five years, ever since the Gareschés were banished, in that grief-filled year when both girls turned thirteen. Sent to her aunt's in New York, Kitty had continued her Sacred Heart education at Manhattanville, and she and Kate still mirrored each other: both had been elected Children of Mary.

Once the war ended, the two friends could write letters, and the bond they shared in childhood had been stretched — but not broken. With their debuts, they expected to recapture the warmth, excitement, and "secret emotions" they shared with their first communions — until Kitty's life took a sudden tragic turn. Just as workmen were completing a new home, from which she would make her debut, her father — the munitions expert Bauduy Garesché, whose work for the Confederacy had sent the whole family into exile — died suddenly. Instead of dancing at parties and balls, Kitty was in mourning.

On her own, Kate O'Flaherty was "already fast acquiring that knowledge of human nature which her stories show," her friend William Schuyler wrote years later. She was a bit too smart, or too forthright, for high society. Although she was "one of the acknowledged belles," known for beauty and "amiability of character," she was also noted for "cleverness" — which, for women, is not always praise. Often it means that a young woman is unwilling to hide her intelligence. She has a voice, and she wants it to be known that she has brains.

Kate O'Flaherty at eighteen was an "Irish Beauty," Kitty recalled. Not tall, she had "very abundant dark hair" that "drooped in a wave, lower on one side than on the other, which gave her a very arch, sprightly expression." A portrait showing her in profile reveals the masses of long wavy hair that were considered a woman's glory in the mid-nineteenth century. For everyday, a belle would wear her hair pinned up; for evening, it would cascade in waves and curls about her shoulders. But Kate also had direct brown eyes, that "looked right at you" — anticipating Edna in *The Awakening*: "Mrs. Pontellier's eyes were quick and bright. . . . She had a way of turning them swiftly upon an object and holding them there as if lost in some inward maze of contemplation. . . . Her face was captivating by reason of a certain frankness of expression and a contradictory subtle play of features. Her manner was engaging" (II).

Kate O'Flaherty also had "a droll gift of mimicry" and quite a bit of realism:

> Though she was the object of great admiration, she accepted it in a matter-of-fact way and did not seem a bit vain. She had remarkable self-possession, a certain poise of manner, though very sweet and simple. Her laugh was quiet; her voice gentle and low. It seems to me that in her, intellect predominated and kept the passions cool.

By the time Kitty shared those memories with an inquiring priest, she had been educating girls for over half a century. She knew what was worth cherishing in American girls growing up, and that it was rare for a young woman on the brink of society to be introspective. Kate may have looked Irish, but she was thoughtfully French in her attitude. She did not lose her head over men, nor over being the belle of the ball.

Instead, her passion was for music. With its old French heritage and its newer German immigrants, St. Louis was one of the country's most musical cities. Some kind of performance went on every night of the week: philharmonic societies, German bands, touring Italian opera companies, and concerts of every description. When Kate wrote about the Norwegian violinist Ole Bull, she was anticipating Edna's love of music in *The Awakening*:

> To describe the effect his music had upon me would be impossible. It seemed the very perfection of the art, and while listening to him, I for the first time longed to be blind, that I might drink it all in undisturbed and undistracted by surrounding objects.

Madam O'Meara had taught the Sacred Heart girls to concentrate, undisturbed and undistracted, and their daily prayers and quiet times encouraged meditation and a thoughtful, clear-eyed contemplation of life. That was not part of a belle's schedule, and Kate O'Flaherty resented her loss of privacy. She says nothing in her diary about the real purpose of a débutante season, as a marriage market, but with the canny women of her family, she may have hashed over exactly how to recognize the right man — the one who would not restrict her.

In the late 1860s, contemporary fashions required endless fittings, which also added to a belle's feeling of confinement. In one 1869 portrait, Kate O'Flaherty is dressed in a lady's walking costume, including a high feathered headdress (pinned to her hair with lethal-looking hatpins); a gown with elaborate flouncings and ruchings over a corset that pinches in her waist; and an overskirt with trailing bustle. Overall, she looks brittle and miserable, and she hated the artificial social rituals that stole her energies from her real love. On December 31, 1868, for instance, she told her diary about endless rain, and added:

> What a nuisance all this is — I wish it were over. I write in my book to day the first time for months; parties; operas, concerts, skating and amusements ad infinitum have so taken up all my time that my dear reading and writing that I love so well have suffered much neglect.

Likewise on March 25, 1869: "In three more days Lent will be over — and then commence again with renewed vigor — parties — theatres, and general spreeing. I feel as though I should like to run away and hide myself; but there is no escaping."

She did devise escape games, including "the art of making oneself agreeable in conversation," which she described to her trusted confidante, her diary. One didn't even need to be able to speak, she wrote, for

> All required of you is to have control over the muscles of your face — to look pleased and chagrined, surprised indignant and under every circumstance — interested and entertained. Lead your antagonist to talk about himself — he will not enter reluctantly upon the subject I assure you — and twenty to one — he will report you as one of the most entertaining and intelligent persons, — although the whole extent of your conversation was but an occasional "What did you say?" "What did you do?" — "What do you think?"

She was, in fact, rather pleased with her ability to play the social game:

> A friend who knows me as well as anyone is capable of knowing me — a gentleman of course — told me that I had a way in conversation of discovering a person's characteristics — opinions and private feelings — while they knew no more about me at the end than they knew at the beginning of the conversation.

She did try to keep up with pursuits of the mind. She joined a German Reading Club, and copied favorite passages, especially about women, in French, English, and German script. The spring of 1869 was a season of activism for St. Louis women, who were breaking out of traditional molds. Kate Field became a New York journalist; Phoebe Couzins, once a famous belle, became the first woman ever admitted to Washington University's law school. That February, a delegation of ten "women's rights women" traveled to the state capital at Jefferson City to lobby the legislators — who were outraged, and declared that the women had "unsexed themselves by coming here with their demands."

Turning nineteen that month, Kate O'Flaherty was obviously wondering whether intellectual and political women had to be misfits. She copied a definition of "Blue Stockings" ("a title for pedantic or ridiculous literary ladies"), and a passage from the British novelist Dinah Mulock's *The Woman's Kingdom,* telling what "makes a house bright."

Almost invariably, the women of the family. The men make or mar its outside fortunes, but its internal comfort lies in the women's hands alone. And until women feel that — recognize at once their power and their duties — *it is idle for them to chatter about their rights.*

Kate O'Flaherty underlined the sentence about rights, and underlined *rights* twice — but did not say whether she agreed or disagreed. Like so many bright young women, she fancied herself the only nonconforming, uncomfortable individual, the only one who did not fit in:

> I am invited to a ball and I go. — I dance with people I despise; amuse myself with men whose only talent lies in their feet; gain the disapprobation of people I honor and respect; return home at day break with my brain in a state which was never intended for it; and arise in the middle of the next day feeling infinitely more, in spirit and flesh like a Liliputian, than a woman with body and soul.

Young Miss O'Flaherty also expressed her thoughts in rational, well-constructed sentences — which put her even further out of step with her contemporaries:

> I am diametrically opposed to parties and balls; and yet when I broach the subject — they either laugh at me — imagining that I wish to perpetrate a joke; or look very serious, shake their heads and tell me not to encourage such silly notions.
>
> I am a creature who loves amusements; I love brightness and gaiety and life and sunshine. But is it a rational amusement, I ask myself, to destroy one's health, and turn night into day? I look about me, though, and see persons so much better than myself, and so much more pious engaging in the self same pleasures — however I fancy it cannot have the same effect upon them as it does upon me.

Possibly Kate's critical temper inspired Eliza O'Flaherty to arrange a pleasure trip — an all-female cruise — to New Orleans in the spring of 1869. Besides Kate and Eliza, the group included Mrs. Sloan, the wife of a socially prominent businessman, and her daughter Mamie, Kate's schoolmate; a woman named Rosie, otherwise unidentified; and

Nina McAllister, Kate's little cousin. Kate had strong, sometimes rude opinions about her companions: "Not remarkably gay for me when one reflects that Mother is a few years older than myself — Rosie an invalid — Mrs. Sloan a walking breathing nonentity — Mamie a jovial giggler and Nina a child."

Nevertheless: "N. Orleans I liked immensely; it is so clean — so white and green. Although in April, we had profusions of flowers — strawberries and even black berries." There was one "delightful" evening when Kate and Mamie slipped away from their elders to dine in "a dear little house near Esplanade St., a house with an immensity of garden" — like the house Edna occupies in *The Awakening*. Mamie flirted with the hostess's brother, while Kate devoted herself to treats and gossip:

> I quaffed all sorts of ales and ices — talked French and German — listened enchanted to Mrs. Bader's exquisite singing and for two or three hours was as gay and happy as I ever had been in my life. Mrs. Bader had been but a year married, she was the famous Miss Ferringer — Singer and Schauspielerin, who in order to support indigent parents went upon the stage, thereby not only retaining respect, but gaining it from every quarter. Her talents and womanly attractions won her a kind and loving husband — Mr. Bader — one of the first merchants of New Orleans a man worth $600,000.

Although she probably did not know it, Kate O'Flaherty in this passage captured almost everything notable about New Orleans: music, food, the many languages, and the union of love and money and pleasure. From Miss Ferringer's story, she also got the germ for what became, years later, her first story accepted for publication: "Wiser than a God." But she left out of her diary the daring thing that young women always did in New Orleans: they learned to smoke cigarettes. And so did Kate O'Flaherty.

Back in St. Louis, she gave only two more weeks to her diary, in May 1869. Mostly she copied long quotations, some from Alphonse de Lamartine's *Graziella* (a partial inspiration for her later "At Chênière

Caminada"). She copied some Byron ("The Siege of Corinth"), and "Short Extracts from different authors," under such headings as Adversity, Affection, Books, Conduct, and Death. But after her quotations on "Life," she stopped writing in her diary for a year.

She also wrote "Emancipation. A Life Fable," her first surviving short story, about a caged animal who has air, light, food, and drink—but the moment the cage door is open, he races out in "mad flight," eagerly "seeing, smelling, touching of all things." Inspired by Victor Hugo's similar tale (*The Man Who Laughs*), the story is about a male animal—instead of the bird in a gilded cage who symbolizes confined women in nineteenth-century women's writing. Kate O'Flaherty may have resisted identifying with restrictions on women—but at the same time, she was playing the most traditional of female roles.

She was being courted, by a dashing Frenchman.

Exactly when Kate O'Flaherty and Oscar Chopin met is unknown; nor do we know whether they flirted in French, English, or both. Although he was American-born, Oscar's English almost certainly had a French quality, and compared with the other eligible young men in St. Louis, he was far more suave, with a mustache, a continental European background, and cosmopolitan experiences.

Aurelian Roselius Oscar Chopin had been born on September 30, 1844 and raised on the family plantations in Natchitoches ("Nak-i-tush") Parish in northwest Louisiana. The last name was pronounced "Show-pan," and most of their neighbors in and around the village of Cloutierville ("Cloochy-ville") were from France or descended from French immigrants. Grandiose first names, like Oscar's, were very fashionable.

We cannot know how much Oscar Chopin told Kate O'Flaherty about his family, especially at first. His mother, a Louisiana native, was kind, gentle, and fragile; his father, a French-born physician who hated everything American, was cruel and brutal. Oscar had grown up watching his mother beaten, and had once helped her to escape.

But when war broke out, Dr. Chopin packed the whole family off to France, where, at Château-Thierry, Oscar was an undistinguished student at the Collège de la Madeleine. He ended his school days by failing his baccalauréat, the examination for the French General Certificate of Education—whereupon he and his friends (who also failed) drowned their sorrows in Paris at a brothel called the Boum Magenta. There the women were "kind enough" to "give our little rods a bashing," Oscar wrote to his cousin. "Mine is no longer in good condition, poor thing."

Oscar claimed to dislike aristocratic women ("prudes") and to prefer "working girls" with their "noisy and natural laughter and their bold looks." He adored the ladies of the evening, with their "big fascinating eyes, charming sighs, smiles, which get you, right there in the heart, little feet you can't forget, heady perfumes . . . and then . . . well, you know the rest."

Oscar also had at least two mentionable love affairs: "the lovely blue-eyed blonde of the railway" and "the brunette from the Faubourg Montmartre in Paris"—and he affected a world-weary tone: "These love affairs, however, have long since been replaced in my heart by many other more and more pleasant ones," but "I can't help sympathizing with these two tender creatures and, as I remember them, my heart (which is not very tender) melts."

His heart had quite recovered, though, once he arrived in St. Louis, to learn the banking business in the firm of his late great-uncle, Louis A. Benoist. The plan was that Oscar would become a cotton factor, the gentlemanly middleman between cotton growers and buyers. However, twenty-two-year-old Oscar immediately appreciated more than business, he told his cousin:

> St. Louis is really a charming place. . . . its delights are as great as those of the Rivoli in Paris . . . the women here are more beautiful than our lovely ladies in Paris. It is charming. It is interesting. There is indeed a vast opportunity for love and I can assure you that the god Eros is not forgotten here.

Oscar was ready for love, and Kate had impressed at least one other visitor during the winter of 1869. A New Yorker named J. H. Tighe wrote to a St. Louis friend that he wanted to be remembered to "Miss Katie O'F—" who was "a charming specimen of female loveliness."

Meanwhile Kitty Garesché, still in mourning, had steppped onto a different path: in January 1870, she joined the Sacred Heart nuns. While her contemporaries danced through the winter social season, Kitty devoted her time to silence and prayer, wide reading, and "the training in manners at an age when youth most desires to shake off control."

Kitty had grown up in a household of many little ones, with a strong father, while Kate had lived among women of independence, spirit, and dignity. Still mirroring each other, each one chose the world in which the other was raised. Kate became the mother of many little ones, the center of a nuclear family; Kitty spent her adult life in the middle of a society of women.

But in 1870, just before her twentieth birthday, Kate O'Flaherty mostly knew that she had lost her best friend once again — and that her own life was about to be irrevocably changed. That winter, there were many parties at Oakland, the lavish Benoist estate outside St. Louis, with its romantic stone watch tower, four stories high, for gazing at the stars. One of the frequent guests was Oscar Chopin.

Only a few years removed from Paris, Oscar knew the latest dance steps and fashions. He may have found the midnight suppers at Oakland, with their hearty roasts of venison and pig and duck, a bit unsophisticated after the flavors of France. But Oscar evidently had truly French values — for he appreciated not only the beauty of young women, but also their intellectual agility.

"She always treasured the memory of the time at Oakland when love came to her heart," their son remembered half a century after his mother's death. But Kate O'Flaherty's diary entry on May 24, 1870 shows only that she had given up writing in favor of living:

> Exactly one year has elapsed since my book and I held intercourse, and what changes have occurred! not so much outwardly as within. My book has been shut up in a great immense chest buried under huge folios through

which I could never penetrate, and I — have not missed it. Pardon me my friend, but I never flatter you.

She did not even mention Oscar Chopin's name, and her entry also suggests that she alone made the decision to marry him.

All that has transpired between then and now vanishes before this one consideration — in two weeks I am going to be married; married to the right man. It does not seem strange as I thought it would — I feel perfectly calm, perfectly collected. And how surprised every one was, for I had kept it so secret!

Two weeks later, she wrote again: "*June 8th Wednesday* Tomorrow I will be married. It seems to me so strange that I am not excited — I feel as quiet and calm as if I had one or two years of maiden meditation still before me. I am contented — a . . . ." Evidently she was interrupted. Her next entry, under the heading "Three Months Abroad," begins with "*June 9th* My wedding day!"

Kate Chopin never idolized the man she married, although she knew women who did. They were the ones who, as in *The Awakening,* "worshiped their husbands, and esteemed it a holy privilege to efface themselves as individuals and grow wings as ministering angels" (IV). But she was never one of them. Even on the day she married Oscar Chopin, she expressed the opinion that his behavior was not perfect.

"My Wedding Day! How simple it is to say and how hard to realize that I am married, no longer a young lady with nothing to think of but myself and nothing to do," Kate O'Flaherty wrote in her diary on June 9, 1870.

Like Edna in *The Awakening,* a Kentucky Presbyterian who marries a Louisiana Catholic, Kate O'Flaherty was marrying an outsider, a foreigner in St. Louis eyes. That — and dreams and fears about sex — may have kept her from sleeping much the night before her wedding. She awoke on her last maiden morning "before the household was stirring," and "The whole day seems now like a dream to me," she wrote.

Looking for omens, she glanced out the window "to see whether the sun would shine or not."

And then "We went to holy communion this morning, my mother with us," but "I went to mass and could not read the prayers in my book" and "I dressed for my marriage — went to church and found myself married before I could think what I was doing." Still, "it gave me a double happiness to see so many of my friends at mass for I knew they prayed for me on this happiest day of my life."

The wedding took place in Holy Angels Church, a neat brick Gothic building, just three years old, on St. Ange Avenue. Her parish priest, Father Francis M. Kielty, was a roaring Irishman, known for the "trenchant pen" with which he wrote vigorous, opinionated articles in St. Louis periodicals. He also had (and this was considered praise) a "most keen sense of the ridiculous."

And then, at the reception: "What kissing of old and young!" Kate wrote. "I never expect to receive as many embraces during the remainder of my life" — whereupon Oscar committed his first *faux pas* as a husband: "Oscar has since confessed that he did not know it was customary to kiss and that he conferred that favor on only a very few — I will have to make a most sacred apology for him when I get home."

Oscar was evidently a reserved cultural outsider, like Edna in *The Awakening* — confused by the enthusiastic caresses of the natives, and unsure what to do. Natural-born writers like Kate O'Flaherty Chopin do find their material everywhere, sometimes at the most unlikely moments. And so one of the first inspirations for Edna Pontellier may have been a certain ill-at-ease bridegroom named Oscar Chopin.

Then Kate and Oscar were off on their European honeymoon, while Kate looked back to the women of her family: "It was very painful to leave my mother and all at home; and it was only at starting that I discovered how much I would miss them and how I would be missed."

Like many diary writers, especially a century ago, Kate O'Flaherty Chopin retreated from expressing her deepest thoughts, especially the

sad ones. Although she was starting out on the adventure that was supposed to be "this happiest day of my life," it was also the end of something. Not only the end of her "maiden years" and the start of adult responsibilities — but also the end of her life in a circle of women and girls,
whose motives were known, whose warmth could be relied upon, and
whose knowledge of the world was sophisticated, crisp, and independent.

She would now be, forever, defined as a wife, and take her assigned,
and much more narrowly defined, place in a patriarchal world. She
was now, as she wrote, "Mrs. Chopin and not Miss Katy."

On their honeymoon train from St. Louis to Cincinnati, the newlyweds Kate and Oscar Chopin met "several acquaintances" who joined
them in "consuming a few champagne bottles that had escaped the dire
destruction of their companions to meet with a more honorable con-
summation by the bride and groom."

Kate was certainly thinking about another kind of "consumma-
tion," but her first sexual experience with Oscar Chopin may not have
taken place on the overnight train, which pulled into Cincinnati at six
o'clock the next morning. Sex would have been uncomfortable and
strained: Pullman cars were equipped with double-decker bunk beds
only. Possibly there was an acrobatic, comical sexual encounter with
groping and poking about the Pullman beds — or perhaps they just
waited for a real bed, two days later.

Kate Chopin's diary hints that they waited — or at least, that whatever they did beforehand was unsatisfactory.

Cincinnati, she recorded quickly, was the "Queen City" where "the
sole life sustaining article of the inhabitants is *Beer*, simply Beer; without it they would cease to live." She admitted she knew that from personal observation. The next day, Sunday, June 12, they were in Philadelphia, "a gloomy puritanical looking city," but they stayed in the
elegant Continental Hotel, known for its green velvet and marble.

The next morning, Kate Chopin wrote the most romantic passage
in her entire honeymoon diary, in a discreet code that suggests sexual
enlightenment and pleasure: "It was a *lovely* night! and I thought of

how the moonlight looked at Oakland. The moon knew better how to honor the sunday than did the people — for it filled us with — happiness and love." Philadelphia looked "a little less gloomy."

Then, on the train to New York, they met a celebrity: "Miss Clafflin, the notorious 'female broker' of New York." This would have been a thrilling encounter, for "Miss Clafflin" was a very scandalous figure — either Victoria Woodhull or Tennessee Clafflin, the adventurous sisters who started out as small-town Ohio fortunetellers, then went east and made their fortunes through Cornelius Vanderbilt, the Great Commodore. While they were publishing a women's rights newspaper advocating votes for women (as well as free love and magnetic healing), Vanderbilt set them up as the first women stockbrokers in the United States. Woodhull, who brashly ran for the U.S. presidency two years later (the first woman to do so), was soon known as "Mrs. Satan."

Both Clafflin sisters fit Kate Chopin's description: "a fussy, pretty, talkative little woman." Miss Clafflin "discussed business extensively with Oscar" at first, but then turned to Kate and "entreated me not to fall into the useless degrading life of most married ladies — but to elevate my mind and turn my attention to politics, commerce, questions of state, etc. etc."

Kate "assured her I would do so — which assurance satisfied her quite."

The new Mrs. Chopin liked to record colorful events, and especially things that were pompous, ridiculous, or venal. She was intrigued by "the 'Bulls and Bears of Wall St.' bellowing and grunting in the Stock and Gold Boards," but it took two weeks of waiting in New York ("a great den of swindlers") to get a ship to Europe. On July 4, the Americans on board made a "faint effort" to celebrate their national holiday, whereupon the "Dutch" band "scraped out 'Hail Columbia' and a few other martial strains, whilst we were occupied in dining, and some, more patriotic than their companions, laid aside knife and fork to give vent to a feeble 'bravo' — after which 'order was restored.' "

Oscar, raised in French-speaking Louisiana and spending his early manhood in France, would have found raucous demonstrations of American patriotism odd, and possibly humorous. But one wonders what memories a "Dutch" (German) band might have triggered for Kate on July 4. Exactly seven years earlier, the "Dutch devils" had invaded her mother's house to celebrate the Vicksburg victory, and had committed their "outrage." Those memories may be why Kate Chopin wrote only one shipboard diary entry after July 4, and it was one mentioning school ("I had studied at school about the atmosphere of these northern regions"). Maybe she was remembering Madam O'Meara, the thoughtful nun whose dedication and intuition saved Kate O'Flaherty from overwhelming adolescent sorrow and silence.

Love was a healer, too, as she watched the beautiful North Sea: "The moon is out again, full and round like in Philadelphia, but how many thousands of miles closer it looks! it seems so immense too, and the stars appear so huge that one can scarcely imagine them so very, very far off."

Honeymoons are intended as an intimate and romantic time, but the newlywed Chopins were rarely alone. The Griesingers, New Orleans friends, accompanied them through most of Germany, and in Cologne they ran into Kate's St. Louis neighbor, Vernon ("Bunnie") Knapp, on a Grand Tour and taking a course of lectures. (Half a century later, after a long career as an attorney, Vernon Knapp would write an article calling Kate Chopin "the most brilliant, distinguished and interesting woman that has ever graced St. Louis.")

Travel could be exhausting. On July 20 in Stuttgart, for instance, Kate wrote despairingly, "Rose late — feeling not well & staggered at the amount of unpacking and washing to be given out; which interesting occupation engaged my time till 5 in the afternoon." She worried, too, about the future, buying a black lace shawl, some brussels and valenciennes lace, and tables and linens "in anticipation of that house keeping which awaits me on the 'other side.'" Despite the endless packing and reshuffling of bags and trunks, and hiring and paying off valets and maids and washerwomen and drivers, the Chopins travelled quickly, by train and railroad, to the major German cities: Bremen, Cologne, Bonn, Mayence, Wiesbaden, Frankfurt, Heidelberg, Stuttgart, and Ulm.

By the end of July they were in Switzerland, where they traveled for almost a month. They had seen the houses of famous men (Beethoven, Goethe), and visited the usual cathedrals and castles and tourist attractions, which Kate recorded, rather dutifully, in her diary.

She found disasters, shocks, and dangers much more interesting. Railroad connections failed; drenching rain destroyed her best outfit. One time a careless child drowned; on another occasion, hotheaded students threatened to have a duel. The young Mrs. Chopin expressed very curmudgeonly opinions, such as her comments on a lead cellar in Bremen, filled with "dried up remains — the mummies they call them — ghastly old things that would have been infinitely more discreet in crumbling away hundreds of years ago." At the Cologne zoo, the Chopins and Griesingers saw "any number of wild beasts that showed their teeth in the most wonderful manner — but we weren't at all frightened, which I set down as an instance of bravery on our part."

Despite her German Reading Club, Kate Chopin never succeeded in speaking German well, nor was Oscar any better: in Heidelberg, for instance, they set off for the castle "like true mountaineers," but could not summon up enough German even to find the right path. With one amiable driver, "we understood one half of his communications and guessed at the other," and they entered French Switzerland with great relief: "Not that we ever succeeded in talking German; but what excrutiating efforts have we not made."

Even when they could, the newlyweds did not spend every waking moment alone together. When Oscar went off once to "witness these Germans' interpretation of a galop — a waltz etc.," Kate wrote in her diary: "Dear me! I feel like smoking a cigarette — think I will satisfy my desire and open that sweet little box which I bought in Bremen." In Zurich, she boldly went outside alone, rowing on the lake and boasting, "I find myself handling the oars quite like an expert." She took walks by herself, and in Switzerland she even drank a beer alone, in public.

The new Mrs. Chopin rarely sounds self-effacing in her diary. The nuns had taught her to write with self-confidence, and she writes about her new husband with more humor than sentiment. When the young couple tasted the water at the famous boiling springs at Wiesbaden, for instance, Kate "thought it shocking," but "Oscar of course found it delicious." Days later, when they set out to scale a Swiss mountain, Kate rode on horseback, but Oscar stubbornly marched on foot with two "perfect Yankees." Later on, Kate praised the view, but concluded slyly that "Oscar is very tired from his walk up and down the mountain."

Kate's own health was excellent except for references to headaches and "feeling badly," and those references come roughly every 28 days, keeping track of her menstrual cycle. As for their spiritual health: when in Europe, the Chopins behaved like relaxed European Catholics, often skipping mass. "Intended to go to church," Kate wrote once, "but what is it they say of the paving stones of the lower realm?" They did, however, make a point of attending mass at the Fribourg cathedral. After all, it did have "what is considered, the finest organ in the world."

All summer, they were dogged by the possibility of war between France and Prussia. Troops were massing and moving, and when war was finally declared, hotels cleared out immediately, in panic and confusion. Oscar, safe in France during the American Civil War, had not lived through wartime; Kate, in St. Louis, had known years of anxiety and fear. But she had also grown up among French women, at home and at school, and had always known that France was the pinnacle of culture. And so she worried that the war might keep her and Oscar from even getting there: "For what is Europe out side of Paris?" she agonized.

Somehow they did get to France, probably aided by Elihu Washburne, the American ambassador, who was married to one of the Gratiots of St. Louis. By the time the Chopins reached Paris, the leisurely and beautiful city was preparing itself for a Prussian invasion. Residents were fleeing; cows were being pushed through the streets; and troops were drilling in the green woods of the Bois de Boulogne. To Kate, it was all too familiar.

On September 4, while she and Oscar stood watching, the imperial government collapsed, and she wrote, "I have seen a French Revolution!" The gendarmes had dispersed, and "the Garde National has taken under its care the public buildings and places of the city." (One member of the National Guard was Edgar Degas, the painter-to-be — but he and Kate Chopin did not meet in Paris.) Kate and Oscar watched the people tearing down the imperial eagles and strutting through the Tuileries, and she concluded, "What a nation."

There was little to do afterwards, and the Chopins barely escaped before the city gates were closed and the Parisians settled in for a long siege and a famine. Among those settling in were Degas and two painter friends, Berthe Morisot and her beloved sister Edma — whose story appeared, nearly three decades later, in *The Awakening*.

Although Kate and Oscar would always have Paris, she would never see it again. She wrote about it later, in a few stories ("A Point at Issue!"; "Lilacs"), but only with a few broad brushstrokes. She never got to know Paris, and all she saw was, again, the fearful face of war.

Back in the United States, the Chopins returned to St. Louis, where Kate "embraced the dear ones left behind." She was now a married woman, sexually experienced, and ready to set out on her life's journey as the mistress of her own household — but without the women whose care, advice, and gossip had surrounded her all her life.

She also had a new project. By the time the young Chopins made their way to New Orleans, in early October, Kate was expecting her first child.

## Chapter 5

# Walking in New Orleans, Swimming at Grand Isle

"BECOMING A WOMAN" is sometimes described — by men — as some kind of vast, mystical change that happens along with the loss of virginity, or the changes of puberty, or both. But women know that "becoming a woman" is not the most radical or difficult transformation in a female lifetime. Especially during the childbearing years, being a woman often means giving up one's self: a good woman is supposed to efface herself while caring for others. Often she has to conceal or defer her own desires. She has to stifle her most assertive inner voices until, after the years of motherhood are over, she comes into her own.

What is far more challenging is to become a "person": an individual who makes her own choices and becomes the center of her own story. After years of self-sacrifice, many a woman discovers, with surprise and delight, that she has the talent to be the chief actor, and the director, in her own play.

But even at twenty, Kate Chopin intended to be an individual. She had never masked her intelligence, nor hidden her courage. With Oscar, she was learning about the men's world that had been mostly invisible while she was growing up, and that knowledge helped her to develop a certain empathy with men, and especially with boys. She was developing what Virginia Woolf calls "the androgynous mind." Still, her greatest loyalties and her deepest knowledge came through her connections with women. As Woolf also says: a woman thinks back through her mothers.

When Kate and Oscar Chopin arrived in New Orleans to set up housekeeping in the fall of 1870, there was an ogre waiting: Oscar's father.

Kate evidently had not met him on her trip to New Orleans in the spring of 1869, nor had he attended her wedding to his son. But she had heard all about him, and much later she would write about his type: the angry, unregenerate Frenchman who loathed everything "American." In New Orleans, that meant virtually everyone who spoke English and lived outside the French Quarter, where the old Creoles had hunkered down, grumbling about bad times and rude upstarts. ("Creole" in the 1870s meant a white person, born in the New World, of pure French or Spanish ancestry.)

Dr. Victor Jean Baptiste Chopin not only shared the Creole prejudices, but he was also a genuine Frenchman, born in Loupiègnes, a small French village seventy miles northeast of Paris. After getting some kind of medical training, he took off for Mexico to make his fortune, but somehow wound up in Natchitoches Parish, a pocket of French-speaking settlers in overwhelmingly "American" north Louisiana. There he sought and found himself an heiress, Julie Benoist, with an impeccable French lineage and a great deal of land. At their wedding, she was only fifteen; he was twenty-four. In his eyes, and under the Napoleonic Code that was the basis for Louisiana law, his young wife was totally his property. Happily giving up on medicine, Dr. Chopin settled down as the master of a plantation, where he made the lives of his wife and slaves a living hell.

Under his rule, his wife could not take her own surrey even to go to mass. When she pleaded to be allowed to visit her mother, Dr. Chopin locked her in her room, and sent her mother's coachman away. Her one pleasure was her piano, but when friends asked her to play it, she would say sadly that it was old and out of order. Her husband would not allow her to get it fixed.

Julie Benoist Chopin gave birth to five children in thirteen years and was in her early thirties when, in a singular display of courage, she left her husband and stayed away for several years. She did not do it alone: her eldest son Oscar, who left home himself when he was fourteen, undoubtedly helped. (In Kate Chopin's story "In Sabine," a hot-tempered young man helps a battered wife to escape her brutal husband.)

But when Dr. Chopin pursued his wife, her own widowed mother—who was buying and selling land with Dr. Chopin—was no support. Her church counseled obedience, and neighbors shrugged, for it was well known that "Frenchmen beat their wives." And so, as dutiful Catholic women did in those days, Julie Benoist Chopin returned to her husband. She gave birth to their last child, Marie, just three days before the firing on Fort Sumter ignited the Civil War.

His wife had not been Dr. Chopin's only victim, for she was not the only living creature he "owned." (Later Kate Chopin portrayed a similarly cruel slaveowner in the character of Armand, the husband in "Désirée's Baby.") With his wife's money, Dr. Chopin had bought a huge Red River plantation with nearly a hundred slaves, and he became famous for his brutality. Local legends even confused him with Simon Legree, the incarnation of evil in *Uncle Tom's Cabin*. When slaves continually ran away, and overseers refused to work for him, Dr. Chopin ordered his eldest son to do the job. But Oscar chose to toil in the fields himself, with the chained slaves, rather than treat them cruelly. Eventually, when he could stand no more, Oscar ran away to live with relatives.

Three years later, when Oscar was seventeen, civil war was declared. Willingly or not, Oscar and the rest of his family sailed to France with Dr. Chopin, who left his plantation properties in the care of a neighbor. In 1864, when the rampaging Union troops raided the Chopin plantation, they ate all the food, killed the animals, and smashed what was left of Julie Chopin's beloved piano, throwing the pieces into the yard. In France, though, Dr. Chopin prospered by investing in French railroad stocks. After the war, he and his family returned to muttering, embittered neighbors. Other families had lost fathers and sons and everything they owned—but Dr. Chopin still had plenty, and he filed suit with the French and American Claims Commission to get restitution for the rest. Local resentment may have pushed Dr. Chopin to move to New Orleans with his wife, while their children seized the opportunity to escape. The younger ones stayed behind with relatives in Natchitoches

Parish, while Oscar's seventeen-year-old sister Eugénie, perhaps to spite her father, married a rich Irishman.

Oscar himself was working in St. Louis when his mother died in April 1870. She was forty-two, a sweet and broken spirit, and her gentle son was engaged to marry a young woman who hated cruelty toward slaves and shared his mother's love of music.

When Kate and Oscar Chopin settled in New Orleans in early October 1870, Dr. Chopin was living alone in the St. Louis Hotel in the French Quarter — but the newlyweds deliberately chose a house outside the Quarter, across the Canal Street dividing line. "The American side," up from the river, had become more prosperous and more suitable for up-and-coming businessmen wanting to regenerate New Orleans. Still, the young Chopins' choice of neighborhood seemed calculated to enrage Oscar's father. Their house (which no longer exists) was at 443 Magazine Street, between Terpsichore and Robin (now Euterpe), in the area called "the Irish Channel."

That way Oscar both tweaked and avoided his father, while protecting his own wife. Raised among independent widows, women of warmth and spirit, Kate had never been confronted with a family monster. The new Madame Chopin was not, however, a vulnerable young woman. She was a self-possessed adult who knew how to run a household, including how to keep accounts and organize domestic help. She had watched capable women all her life. A young bride who liked physical activity, and who made fun of her new husband in her diary, was not apt to be buffaloed by his bitter, vicious father, a man who thought "the Irish voice was distressing to the sick."

Kate Chopin also spoke French, and she had a husband who cherished her. And so, according to one source, "Dr. Chopin was unable to make sarcastic remarks to his son's vivacious young wife. Her brown eyes looked too calmly at him. . . . Her fair young loveliness won his admiration. Always at ease, her quick change from vivacity to quizzical seriousness baffled him." She also chose a most clever way to torment him: "He detested music. She made him listen to her as she played the piano and soothed his irritability with French melodies heard in his youth and now almost forgotten."

He had met his match, yet the young Mrs. Chopin must have dreaded her future. How would such an impossibly grouchy Grandpère treat her and her new baby? Would she be forever tiptoeing about his anger, staying out of reach of his rage? Her worries did not last long. Already suffering from a "long and painful malady," Dr. Chopin made a will in mid-October, and died a month later. After the funeral mass in the St. Louis Cathedral in the French Quarter, he was buried next to his wife, in St. Louis Cemetery Number 3.

Old Creole custom required six months of full mourning. If Kate Chopin followed the custom, she wore black, and no jewelry, for most of her first pregnancy — during which time she was also being judged by Oscar's other relatives. But she was no prisoner, and certainly no victim.

Until his orphaned nine-year-old sister Marie came to live with the young couple, Oscar's only relative in New Orleans had been Dr. Chopin. But droves of aunts and uncles and cousins lived in Natchitoches Parish, mostly centered around the village of Cloutierville. Once the cotton season ended in October or November, prosperous merchants and planters and wealthy ladies, all of whom had servants to pack their trunks and carry them to the landing, would take the packet boat to New Orleans and stay for weeks at a time. For the women, visiting and shopping for clothes and delicacies were the central activities — along with inspecting Oscar's new bride.

Although she had French roots, and was even related to several Cloutierville families on her mother's side, the new Madame Chopin was a thorough outsider in the eyes of Oscar's family. New Orleans was still occupied by uniformed Union soldiers, and Kate Chopin had come from a state that had not seceded, and a nation that had won the war. To Oscar's relatives, Kate's Midwestern origins, her frank and forthright ways, and her insistence on doing strange things — such as taking long walks by herself—made her seem more Yankee than Southern. They regarded her with great suspicion and disapproval.

Some merely shook their heads, whispering quietly among themselves. Others, knowing that Oscar no longer had parents to advise him, warned him sternly about his duty. Allowing Kate to "go on, always in her own way" was "more than unusual, it was horrible." When the scolding was particularly intense, Oscar would tell Kate what had been said, and often they would laugh about it. Sometimes Kate would do wickedly accurate and hilarious imitations of the advice givers.

Oscar was a rare man who preferred an original woman, one who was neither quiet nor stay-at-home. Possibly Kate had no idea how odd it was to take her long, solitary strolls around New Orleans, smoking her Cuban cigarettes. In New Orleans, ladies rarely went about unescorted—and, of course, no lady smoked at all. During her walks, she also jotted down descriptions of what she saw, and was particularly interested in the colorfully painted mule cars that served as rapid transit.

On at least one occasion, Kate Chopin took a "green car" out to City Park and the Metairie cemeteries, which were a favorite cool spot for walks and picnics, and she stopped for refreshments in a private garden on the shell road, midway between the city and Lake Pontchartrain. (In chapter XXXVI of *The Awakening*, Edna meets Robert in such a garden and declares, "I don't mind walking. I always feel so sorry for women who don't like to walk; they miss so much—so many rare little glimpses of life; and we women learn so little of life on the whole.")

But even at twenty, Kate Chopin was learning about life, and writing it down. She had the solitary soul of a writer, and New Orleans was a fascinating place to watch. Its entertainments and pleasures included horse racing, with frenzied betting; superb performances of comedies and serious drama; and some of the best singers in the world at the French Opera House, the first in the United States to stage *Lohengrin* and *Tannhäuser*. Mardi Gras had long been a series of rowdy street celebrations, more like gang wars than parades; but in the 1870s it began evolving into the elaborate, ritualized pageant of floats and krewes, costumes and queens that it is today. Kate Chopin also listened to older New Orleanians' colorful stories, including their memories of the slave dances in Congo Square at Orleans and Rampart Streets, before the war. She would describe those intricate, sexual dances two decades later in "La Belle Zoraïde."

But once her pregnancy began to show, Madame Chopin was confined at home. Maternity clothes had not yet been invented, and an obviously pregnant woman (as she shows in *The Awakening*) was not to be seen in public. Accustomed to a houseful of female relatives, Kate must have been lonely, and the name of only one woman friend (Mrs. L. Tyler) is known.

She did have servants, including a quadroon named Alexandrine: the New Orleans racial designations ("mulatto," "quadroon," "octoroon," designating degrees of blackness) were thoroughly new to a Midwesterner. New, too, was the bandana tignon Alexandrine and other servants wore — but by old New Orleans law, passed generations before, women of color were forbidden to wear extravagant or colorful headdresses. New Orleans provided so much to see, and to ponder.

These were all things that Kate Chopin could discuss in great detail with her mother, her closest friend, who often came and stayed for months. "Companionate marriage," in which a wife's best friend is her husband, was not an American social ideal until the 1920s; in Kate Chopin's day, a woman's best friends were her mother, female relatives, and a few school friends. Eliza O'Flaherty shared Kate's first Mardi Gras in 1871, and then stayed on for the time when a daughter most needs her mother: the birth of her first baby.

Kate Chopin's doctor was Charles Jean Faget, a Frenchman and French Quarter physician who had attended Dr. Chopin in his last illness. Dr. Faget was a tall, thin, odd-looking man with grizzly black hair, who wore a priestly hat and cape and imitated the soft voice and melancholy manner of a priest. He was financially impractical, intensely religious, and internationally renowned for discovering how to distinguish yellow fever from malaria. (Still used today, the test is called "Faget's sign.") For that he was decorated as a Chevalier of the Legion of Honor, and much later Kate Chopin drew on him for her story "Dr. Chevalier's Lie," about a generous doctor who conceals the sordid truth about a country girl in the big city.

Even during the stress and excitement of her first pregnancy, Kate Chopin was gathering material.

She also gave birth in the most modern way. Until Queen Victoria chose to use chloroform for the birth of her eighth child in 1853, American and English physicians (all male) had resisted using the drug, arguing that women should "bring forth children in sorrow," as the Bible ordered. The pain in giving birth was supposed to make women love their babies more. But Dr. Faget, like his twenty-one-year-old patient, was no slave to old customs that were cruel to women. Exactly twenty-three years later, on May 22, 1894, Kate Chopin described her son's birth in her diary:

> I can remember yet that hot southern day on Magazine street in New Orleans. The noises of the street coming through the open windows; that heaviness with which I dragged myself about; my husband's and mother's solicitude; old Alexandrine the quadroon nurse with her high bandana tignon, her hoop-earrings and placid smile; old Dr. Faget; the smell of chloroform, and then waking at 6 in the evening from out of a stupor to see in my mothers arms a little piece of humanity all dressed in white which they told me was my little son! The sensation with which I touched my lips and my fingertips to his soft flesh only comes once to a mother. It must be the pure animal sensation: nothing spiritual could be so real — so poignant.

(Edna in *The Awakening* remembers childbirth much less happily: "an ecstasy of pain, the heavy odor of chloroform, a stupor which had deadened sensation, and an awakening to find a little new life to which she had given being added to the great unnumbered multitude of souls that come and go" — XXXVII.)

As a concession to Oscar's relatives — or as penance — Kate and Oscar named their first child after his late grandfather, Jean Baptiste Chopin. Then in mid-June, three weeks after their baby's birth, Oscar departed for Paris, where he sold stocks, settled his late father's business affairs, and stayed at a grand hotel where he could order oranges and chocolate and cigars from room service. By the time Oscar returned to New Orleans, his baby son was three months old and had been baptized in Kate's old parish church in St. Louis.

Back in New Orleans, little Jean had the quadroon Alexandrine as his nanny, the first woman from whom he heard the soft Creole patois Kate Chopin quotes in "La Belle Zoraïde." A younger woman of color, one who was breast feeding herself, must have been hired as a wet nurse. And so, like most middle-class white children in the South, Jean Chopin grew up associating love and warmth and tenderness, lullabies and soft voices, with darker skin.

But the lifelong responsibility for another living creature was now Kate O'Flaherty Chopin's. She entered a new phase of her life with joy and doubt and fear, emotions she describes over and over in her fiction: a woman's bashful delight in discovering her pregnancy ("Athénaïse"); her terror of hereditary madness ("Mrs. Mobry's Reason"); and her overwhelming love for a child's soft gentle flesh ("hot, plump body pressed close against her, and the little one's warm breath beating her cheek like the fanning of a bird's wing" ["Regret"]).

For Kate Chopin, as for every new mother, having a child meant that she was no longer free to indulge herself in social pleasure or creative solitude. For the rest of her life, she would be expected to do what Edna in *The Awakening* finally refuses to do: "Remember the children."

Within the next seven years, Jean Chopin acquired four younger brothers. The next two Chopin boys were born in St. Louis: Oscar Charles (September 24, 1873) and George Francis (October 28, 1874). Then there were two born in New Orleans: Frederick (January 26, 1876) and Felix Andrew (January 8, 1878). Finally a girl, called Lélia but baptized Marie Laïza, was born December 31, 1879 in Cloutierville.

Nineteenth-century women often had babies close together. Respectable ladies were not supposed to know about birth control, for gentlemen were supposed to use condoms ("French letters") with prostitutes, not with their wives. After 1873, with the passing of the "Comstock Laws," it became illegal in the United States to disseminate any kind of birth control information through the mails — which also meant magazines, newspapers, or letters. Abortion — routinely and often safely performed for centuries by midwives — became illegal for the first time in the United States. The Catholic Church, then as now, opposed birth control.

Because there were no antibiotics, and few cures for childhood infections or waterborne parasites, many babies, especially poor ones, died. But all of Kate Chopin's little ones lived — and all of them pulled on her energies. In 1874, a portrait of Oscar Chopin with their son Jean shows a portly businessman with receding hair, a mustache, and well-trimmed beard. He looks quite robust and cheerful. But a photograph of Kate, two years later, with her first four sons, shows a sad-looking, weary woman without a trace of the slight smile that plays around her lips in earlier and later pictures. At twenty-eight, she looks closer to forty.

Kate Chopin had reason to worry, for Oscar was far better as a father and husband than as a businessman. For the first time since her father's death when she was five, Kate's world depended on a man's ability to make money. Exactly what Oscar did for a living during their first years of marriage is unclear, although he inherited some money and land from his father. In 1872, two years after settling in New Orleans, Oscar finally appears in the city directory as a cotton factor, the middleman who lent money to the planters and procured their supplies. The factor sold the planters' cotton, and then received back interest and commissions at the end of the cotton season. It was a respectable and thriving profession before the war, but everything depended on a good cotton harvest — which, after the war, could not be depended upon.

The Chopins moved twice in New Orleans, each time to a somewhat more prestigious address. By 1874, they and their growing family lived at the northeast corner of Constantinople and Pitt, in uptown New Orleans. (That house no longer exists.) Two years later, they moved again, to a side-by-side duplex at 209 Louisiana Avenue (now 1413–

1415), between Coliseum and Prytania. The Chopins rented their side (1413) from a sugar dealer, and their two live-in servants, a cook and a laundress, lived in a one-story service building in the back.

The downstairs area included front and back parlors with elaborate acanthus-leaf ceiling medallions and two fireplaces (the medallions and fireplaces still exist). Behind the parlor was a dining room, and stairs led to three or four large bedrooms. Kate and Oscar moved in with four sons, and their fifth, Felix, was born in that house — a lovely cottage surrounded by a lush profusion of shrubs, trees, and flowers that perfumed the air on warm evenings.

They enjoyed entertaining friends in that house, according to a Mrs. L. Tyler who frequently visited them: "Oscar, ever jovial and cheerful and fun-loving and really very stout, liked to romp with the children through the house and about the gardens. 'I like disorder when it is clean' was his favorite saying." Kate, meanwhile, was a distinctive personality who "enjoyed smoking cigarettes, but if friends who did not approve of smoking came to visit her, she would never offend them. She was individual in the style of her clothes as in everything else. She loved music and dancing, and the children were always allowed to enjoy themselves."

As for the marriage: "Kate was devoted to Oscar and thought him perfect." Another informant, Mrs. John S. Tritle (the former Nellie Hoblitzelle of St. Louis), agreed: "Kate was very much in love with her Oscar," and although she was a social favorite, she and her husband always preferred each other's company to anyone else's.

Mrs. Tyler and Mrs. Tritle were both interviewed long after Kate and Oscar were gone, and they were reluctant to say anything overtly negative. But we can read between the lines to suspect that Kate Chopin never truly fit in, that Oscar was too kind and fun-loving to be good at business, and that the children were loud, undisciplined creatures.

In short, they had a lively, exciting, spontaneous and creative life. And yet — Kate O'Flaherty had been a young woman who liked being alone with her "dear reading and writing." She must have begrudged time spent always attending to the needs of others. Even with servants, the mother had to administer, to give care, to notice, to budget, to watch.

But all the while she was watching, Kate Chopin was gathering material, and she had help in her thinking from a special, and later very famous, source. Several years before he became known as an Impressionist and a sketcher of lovely ballerinas, the French painter Edgar Degas spent five months in New Orleans, starting in the fall of 1872. He lived with his uncle, Michel Musson, on Esplanade Street, the wide, tree-lined boulevard at the edge of the French Quarter. From that house — like the double cottage of the Pontelliers in *The Awakening* — he strolled about the city observing cotton merchants, people of color, and other interesting subjects.

There are more than a few clues that Degas met Kate Chopin — also a solitary stroller — during that short time. Both his uncle and his brother, René De Gas, belonged to the Cotton Exchange with Oscar, and his uncle's office was next door to Oscar's on Carondelet Street. But certain other facts make it apparent that Edgar Degas gossiped with Oscar's wife with some depth and intensity.

The painter was lonely and away from the people and the world he knew best — and so was Kate Chopin, a St. Louis native and a daughter who missed her mother. The young Madame Chopin was a lover of art and music, and so was Degas. He was also considered rather asexual, and therefore no threat to the husbands of women he might meet.

It takes no effort of the imagination to think that Oscar Chopin might introduce his colleague's nephew, the painter, to his own wife, to pass some time with her. Moody, puppy-like, and androgynous, like Robert in *The Awakening*, Edgar Degas could easily entertain Kate Chopin with French stories, and gossip about people he knew who were safely away in France. He could tell her about the siege of Paris (as part of the National Guard, he had helped overthrow the government, while she and Oscar watched). But more important, Degas could tell her about some of his friends — lively and fascinating information that she used a quarter century later in *The Awakening*.

In France, one of Degas's dearest friends was Berthe Morisot, an ambitious and talented artist who would be one of the first French women to make a professional career in painting. (Mary Cassatt, who had the advantage of being both rich and American, would become the only other well-known female Impressionist.) Dedicated to her art, Morisot would avoid romance and marriage until well into her thirties, and she was truly "a courageous soul," one that "dares and defies" — the words the pianist Mademoiselle Reisz uses in *The Awakening* (XXI). But Chopin's Edna Pontellier cannot dedicate herself solely to her painting — and Degas knew just such a woman.

She was Berthe Morisot's own sister, with whom Berthe studied and painted, side by side, for twelve years. Degas was close friends with both of them, and the two sisters were gifted soulmates who never spent a day apart — until suddenly, in 1869, Berthe's sister decided to marry. She moved to live with her naval officer husband in the provinces far away from Paris — and she gave up her art. She became one of her husband's possessions, and her life was one of sadness and unfulfillment.

Her name was Edma Pontillon — a name so much like *The Awakening*'s Edna Pontellier that it cannot possibly be coincidental.

Degas connects with *The Awakening* in other ways. One of his New Orleans neighbors was Madame América Olivier, a music teacher who gave piano lessons to the children of Estelle and René De Gas, the painter's brother. (Her house is part of the background in Degas's "Children on a Doorstep.") Her husband was a cotton merchant, and a member of the elite Pickwick Club. He was everything a proper husband should be.

His first name was Léonce, and his wife did not love him.

Instead, she came to love her across-the-garden neighbor, René De Gas. During the spring of 1878, a few months after Kate Chopin gave birth to her last son, Léonce's wife and René De Gas eloped together, deserting their spouses and children and fleeing to Paris, never to return. Edgar Degas, who was very fond of René's wife, broke off all contact with his brother for a decade. But the story was known all over New Orleans, and when Kate Chopin created the character of a perfect husband who bores his wife, thus throwing her into the arms of a far livelier lover, it was easy to know what to call him: Léonce.

For the mismated spouses in *The Awakening*, then, Kate Chopin combined the real-life names that she must have heard, first, from Edgar Degas: (Edma) Pontillon and (Léonce) Olivier. And so, years before she was ready to write *The Awakening*, Kate Chopin already had the names — and some of the story — of Edna and Léonce Pontellier.

Many of Kate Chopin's deepest emotional ties remained in her women-centered world in St. Louis, where she and the children sometimes spent whole summers. Eliza O'Flaherty's house was still full of the people Kate had known all her life. Eliza's mother, Athénaïse Faris, was still living there, and so were Eliza's sister and brother-in-law, Amanda and Roger McAllister. The McAllister children, Andrew and Nina, still lived at home, as did Kate's brother Tom, who completed just two years of a four-year commercial course and was working as a clerk.

In St. Louis, as in New Orleans, Kate Chopin had an unconventional physician to attend her in childbirth. Dr. Frederick Kolbenheyer, an Austrian-born physician trained in Vienna, was famous for his radical political views, especially the fierce hatred for the Hapsburg monarchy that led to his getting "a hint to leave the country." Once he arrived in St. Louis in 1871, at the age of twenty-eight, he found kindred spirits in the newspaper circle surrounding Joseph Pulitzer, himself a fiery, wire-haired immigrant. Dr. Kolbenheyer lived in south St. Louis among the poor German immigrants he mostly served, but he also became a trusted friend of Eliza O'Flaherty. He was known for his outspokenness, quick temper, and fascinating conversation.

Three months after Dr. Kolbenheyer attended the birth of her second son, Kate's brother Tom met an untimely end. Kate was evidently not close to him, and little is known about him: years later Kitty Garesché thought that Kate had been an only child. Tom did have a bit of a wild streak, and one Saturday afternoon, he and several buddies decided to have a kind of drag race with their teams of horses. But something went awry, and a friend's horse started running wildly.

Bravely or recklessly, Tom threw the friend out of the buggy and plunged onward with the runaways — only to be thrown from the buggy himself. When he was found, minutes later, his neck had been broken, and he was dead. Thomas O'Flaherty Jr. was buried next to his father and his half-brother George, in early January 1874, beneath the obelisk in Calvary Cemetery.

Before she was twenty-four, then, Kate became Eliza O'Flaherty's only surviving child. That may also be why she spent the summer of 1874 in St. Louis. But Oscar, in New Orleans without his wife to rein him in, got into some serious trouble.

In Louisiana, Reconstruction was a violent time, and New Orleans was especially full of bribery, corruption, bitter memories, and hatred for the current Yankee occupiers. Black men were voting; white former Confederate soldiers were not; and Louisiana's white men were endlessly fearful about conspiracies among black men to "murder the whites and outrage their women." (In that context, "outrage" did mean "rape" — but what it meant in St. Louis in 1863, in the "outrage" at the O'Flahertys', we cannot be sure.)

In Louisiana in 1872, the various factions managed to elect and then inaugurate two governors simultaneously. One was a Southern Democrat and the other a Northern carpetbagger, and both sides steamed for a confrontation. By the summer of 1874, supporters of both parties were drilling in New Orleans, and most of the soldiers were Confederate veterans.

Oscar may have been atoning for not serving in the war when he joined "The First Louisiana Regiment" — part of the Crescent City White League, formed to protect, in some vague way, the rights of white men against "the African race." (Another White League member was Michel Musson, Degas's uncle.) Oscar's commander, of Company B, was a Magazine Street neighbor and lawyer, Frank McGloin, who wrote newspaper poems and articles about white superiority and the gloomy future of all humanity.

Some sixty men were in Company B by September 14. Kate Chopin was still in St. Louis, awaiting the birth of her third child, when the White League and associated members, including Oscar, took their troops into the streets. Oscar's company occupied a pool hall, while other Leaguers — imitating French street fighting — fanned out and made barricades of iron street crossings, sewer covers, wagons, and mattresses. Later that afternoon, the White Leaguers attacked the Metropolitan Police.

The League had few weapons, and once the police opened fire with their cannons, and then fled, the Battle of Canal Street was over in fifteen minutes. But some twenty-seven people were killed, including White Leaguers, police, and bystanders. More than a hundred were wounded. Thinking they had won, Oscar and his companions wore pieces of black ribbon in their buttonholes to honor their dead. But a week later, federal troops and warships with guns trained on the city restored the carpetbagger governor to office. In some eyes, though, the White Leaguers were heroes. By the time Kate returned to New Orleans, the "White League Waltz" and the "People's Rights Quick Step" had been published and acclaimed.

But from the federal point of view, the White League companies were revolutionists and traitors, and there was at least one suggestion that they be tried for murder. That was something to terrify a mother of three small children. Evidently it wasn't done, however, and three years later Oscar's name appeared on another Crescent City White League membership roll, as a member of the Ogden Guards. This time, though, he stayed out of trouble.

Kate Chopin's opinions are not recorded, but as a mother and a past victim of men's violence, she could not have cheered the White League's attacking the police. She must have feared for Oscar's life, and for their children, and for the young women of New Orleans.

Her attitudes toward race and racism, however, cannot be determined from the stories she wrote two decades later. She describes failed efforts at integrating the races in schools and saloons ("In and Out of

Old Natchitoches," *At Fault*), but the stories do not push particular ideas. She is much more sympathetic when she portrays mothers: the slave who goes insane when she thinks her child has died; the old family servant who conquers a thirty-year fear of the outside world to save a white child ("La Belle Zoraïde"; "Beyond the Bayou").

Motherhood, not race or politics, dominated Kate Chopin's years in New Orleans, and it linked women across the color line. Mammies still nursed white children, and babies were more important than battles. And women's voices (as Kate O'Flaherty had learned in early childhood) were both softer and more sensible than men's.

October through May was the New Orleans social season. For the rest of the year, husbands who could afford it sent wives and children away from the crowded, hot, disease-ridden city. When the Chopins were not in St. Louis, they were often at Grand Isle, a Creole resort where Kate Chopin, though she spoke French, was a foreigner, a Northerner, and an outsider.

With her Midwestern upbringing, Kate may have been shocked — as Edna is in *The Awakening* — to read racy books passed around and discussed freely. Whether she blushed during discussions of childbirth or the telling of risqué stories cannot be known. But she was, even more than in New Orleans, someone who is (as Madame Ratignolle says in *The Awakening*) "not one of us" (VIII).

Grand Isle in the 1870s was a charming place populated by middle-class Creoles. It was easily reachable by boat from New Orleans, and from the dock, a mule-drawn tramway carried guests to the *pensions* (boarding houses) and the sandy beaches of the Gulf of Mexico. The Grand Isle that Kate Chopin knew had a *pension* like the Lebruns' in *The Awakening*: a big house surrounded by smaller cottages connected by bridges, an easy stroll to the beach. Each family had its own bath-house, but there were also general dining and dancing parlors, and sleeping quarters for a hundred servants. The best hotel, Krantz's, was the model for Klein's in *The Awakening*.

For young mothers like Kate Chopin, Grand Isle was wholesome: no open canals or cisterns or swarming mosquitos threatened children or adults with deadly diseases. No one locked doors. The island was a tropical paradise, with palm trees and vines, orange and lemon trees, acres of yellow chamomile, and no streets — only grassy green or sandy paths. It was seductive to the imagination, too, with tales of shipwrecks and pirate gold from Barataria Bay, the old haunt of the pirate Jean Lafitte. (Kate O'Flaherty had read about him in school, in Byron's "The Corsair.") Everywhere there were birds and strange, rare odors and perfumes, and above all, as in *The Awakening,* "The voice of the sea" (VI).

During the week, Grand Isle was the domain of women and children, with long, languorous afternoons of croquet and swimming (in heavy woolen or flannel suits). On weekends, husbands came on the steamer for card parties, dancing, gambling, recitations, and whatever amateur musical performances someone might have gotten up. There were also excursions to Grand Terre, the abandoned sugar plantation where visitors could climb the old fort and watch the wriggling gold snakes and sensuous lizards. Grand Isle had an atmosphere of lazy sensuality, few obligations, and a European approach to religion: there was no regular priest to say mass.

Two decades later, when Kate Chopin wrote about Grand Isle, she was recreating a vanished time and place. In October 1893, a hurricane devastated the resort she had known and killed some 2,000 people. Three weeks later, she wrote "At Chênière Caminada," a Grand Isle story with all the remembered local color and sensuous atmosphere: the sky, the sea, the birds, love and music and death, all amid the magical atmosphere of the island.

Five years later, in *The Awakening,* Chopin returned to Grand Isle before the hurricane. On the beach on an August night, Robert tells Edna stories about hidden pirate treasures and strange spirits. While all the husbands are off in New Orleans earning a living, Edna and Robert (who lives with his mother in the big house) take an excursion to Grand Terre, where they see the lizards and snakes wriggling about.

They also listen to insufferable amateur musical performances, watch the children, torment young lovers, and make flirting jokes together. When Edna learns to swim at Grand Isle, she appreciates for the first time the power and beauty of her own body, and her awakenings finally end at Grand Isle.

Kate Chopin gave birth to her fifth son just before the 1878 yellow fever epidemic, which killed 4,000 people and cut off postal service to and from the world outside New Orleans. Because it was believed that yellow fever might come through the mails, Kate could not even write to her mother.

Kate and Oscar, though, were close partners. Having watched women administer their own property and money, Kate had none of the shrinking from business affairs that was considered proper among Southern ladies. (In Louisiana, she was always considered a bit of a Yankee.) Oscar did talk with her about his business, which involved not only cotton, but also market prices on commodities such as sugar, whiskey, cigars, molasses, and corn, and odd lots of other things: hermetically sealed fruit, playing cards, candles, brooms, brushes. Though cotton factors themselves purported to be rather aristocratic (as shown in Degas's painting, "Bureau de Coton"), Oscar's work was very practical, and not luxurious.

As she had with her father, Kate even visited Oscar's business. In the last entry in her New Orleans diary (now lost), she describes a "journey with Oscar through the district of warehouses where cotton is stored and when sold passes under presses of immense power, reducing bales to half their size for better storage aboard ship." They saw the "pickeries where damaged cotton is bleached and otherwise repaired. The whole process of weighing, sampling, storing, compressing, boring to detect fraud, and the treatment of damaged bales is open to public view." But everywhere, during the visit, Kate heard ominous messages: "too much rain for cotton" and "the cotton was shedding."

The cotton crop had been poor for several years, and Oscar — whose business depended on lending money to cotton growers, and then being reimbursed — was sinking hopelessly into debt. Between June 1878 and December 1879, there were three judgments against him for city taxes, and he was losing the mortgage on his grandmother's property in New Orleans. Starting in 1876, he had bought some land in Natchitoches Parish, possibly on the advice of his very practical wife and her mother, who had lived all her life on income from Thomas O'Flaherty's wise real estate investments.

But whatever financial shrewdness Kate Chopin brought to the marriage was not enough. Oscar was either improvident or unlucky, and a woman's fortunes rose and fell with her husband's. His failure meant a wrenching change in her life. By the fall of 1879, with Kate expecting their sixth child, the Chopins had to give up living in New Orleans: they could no longer afford it. The servants packed up everything, and Kate and Oscar and their five sons left the crowded, raffish, but always exciting city to set up rural housekeeping in the small French village of Cloutierville, Louisiana.

For the first time in her life, Kate Chopin, a city-bred woman with a taste for fashionable clothes and urban amusements, would be living in a small town. Also, those country relatives of Oscar's, the ones she had mocked and imitated with such relish early in her marriage — they would now be her neighbors.

# Chapter 6

## Cloutierville: The Talk of the Town

FROM THE TIME Kate Chopin landed in Cloutierville, Louisiana —
with a tired, vexed brood of five youngsters, a sad husband, a servant or
two, and another baby on the way — she was eagerly watched. Towns-
people loved misbehavior, drama, and sensational secrets, and once
Madame Chopin settled in, those seeking amusement were rarely disappointed. She was not a Southern lady, she was not a country woman,
and — wittingly or not — she knew how to discombobulate, fascinate,
and enrage the local populace.

Cloutierville was a little French village, "two long rows of very
old frame houses, facing each other closely across a dusty roadway,"
Kate Chopin wrote in an 1891 story ("For Marse Chouchoute"). Some
700 people lived either along the street or in the cabins and small houses
in the fields beyond. None of the houses had the intricate ironwork or
fancy wooden "gingerbread" that decorated so many ordinary New
Orleans homes. Nor did they have the brick burgher solidity of St. Louis
buildings. To an unappreciative urban eye, the houses in Cloutierville
might seem to have very little character at all.

The land, though, had its appeal. Springtime was gorgeous, when
the cotton plants sent out their green shoots against the red-brown soil,
and the countryside was perfumed with sassafras and chamomile, and
violets, magnolias, and roses made carpets of many colors. In the summer, there were swift and sudden storms, trailed by moist, simmering
sunshine. By August, days were long and hot and dusty, and everything
seemed limp and overripe. In September, there would be warm rains,

followed by the dusty beauty of autumn, with sugar cane glittering like green silver. The grass was thick, deep, and very green, and a violet haze trembled over the forests. By October, the first frost would send pecans falling from the trees. There would be a kind of death in the air, and in the clear Cane River, trees loomed like skeletons.

Every winter, because the climate was colder than it is now, local paths were muddy and icy, and Kate Chopin, who had always valued fitness and exercise — walking, rowing, horseback riding — was confined to her home. Sometimes people would see her gazing out the back door at sundown, over the lonely fields and forests. When the air was clear, she might see all the way to Shallow Lake and Bayou Derbonne. But the nearest larger town, Natchitoches, was half a day's journey away. Like her character Edna in *The Awakening*, Kate Chopin, turning thirty, seemed to be pondering her place in the universe — and finding it not at all to her liking.

Oscar, though, was a native son, born in the Cane River country, from a "good family." His younger brother Lamy now ran Dr. Chopin's old Red River plantation and was also a local favorite — a small, bright-eyed, red-cheeked man, famous for his hospitality. Kate and Oscar arrived around the time Lamy's first child, Eugénie (Nini), was born. Lamy's wife, the former Cora Henry, had also lived in the area all her life.

Although there was still some resentment of young men who had not served in the war, Oscar was considered generous and likable. His father — an outsider — had been a monster, but his mother had been gentle and kind, and Oscar was known to have defended her.

Kate, meanwhile, was related, through her mother, to many local people, including the grocery store owner and notary and dry goods merchant, but she was still an outsider. Anyone not born and raised in Cloutierville would always be a foreigner, an "étranger" (male) or "étrangère" (female). Kate's French, though fluent, was also different, with a St. Louis emphasis, and perhaps a touch of Canada. Cloutierville natives, neither Canadian nor Acadian ("Cajun"), were mostly descended from people who immigrated directly from France to Louisiana.

Kate's "foreign" accent may have made her seem aloof and unfriendly, and her conversation was almost certainly abrupt, by the standards of leisurely rural speech.

She may not have been aware of any of this, especially at first.

Eliza O'Flaherty traveled to Cloutierville to be with Kate for the birth of her sixth child. Kate's new family physician was Samuel Oglesby Scruggs, a Virginia-born doctor who had married into an old French family, the DeLouches. He was a renowned raconteur, a Mason, and virtually the only Protestant in town.

In Cloutierville, where neighbors' eyes were always upon them, Oscar and Kate did conform to Catholic expectations. They owned a bedside *prie dieu,* a prayer stand with velvet knee cushions, and their daughter Lélia was baptized promptly, in St. John the Baptist Church, on February 29, 1880. (Of the five Chopin sons, three were baptized in St. Louis, but no baptismal records have been found for Frederick or Felix in St. Louis or New Orleans.)

By baptizing their daughter "Marie Laïza," Kate and Oscar conformed to the Church's insistence that every child be given a saint's first name. But they always called her Lélia, a popular Cane River country name and a link with George Sand's daring novel *Lélia,* about a passionate, ambitious woman who finds most men inadequate. Baby Lélia's name also honored "Lil" (Lélia) Chouteau, one of Kate's St. Louis friends. Nearly a decade later, Kate Chopin's first publication would be a polka called "Lilia" (a common misspelling).

Lélia herself grew up to be a dramatic storyteller, who claimed that *The Lilia,* the packet boat operating between the mouth of the Cane River and the town of Natchitoches, had been named after none other than herself. Her mother would certainly have approved.

Kate and Oscar, Lélia, and the boys all occupied a large white house toward the end of Cloutierville's one street, on the road heading toward Derry. Their handsome house, with its outside staircase, had been built for the village's founder, Alexis Cloutier, some sixty-five years earlier, with handmade square nails, a lower story made of brick, and an upper one of heart cypress. Its special features included wainscoting, French doors, four fireplaces, and a high pitched roof sheltering the front and rear verandas from sudden thunderstorms.

As was customary, the Chopins lived only on the second floor, avoiding mosquitoes and breathing cooler air. Their quarters were busy and cramped. Kate, Oscar, and the baby occupied one large bedroom, which doubled as a parlor; the five boys squeezed into the other bedroom. The lower story, dirt-floored, was for storage, while the outbuildings included a kitchen, a carriage house, a stable, and quarters for two live-in servants, both widows. Martha Field, 55 and "Black" (according to the census), was a cook; Cora William, 45 and "Mulatto," was a washer-woman. Both helped with child care, and the Chopins also hired a maid and a yard man. An overseer farmed the land behind the house.

Mrs. O'Flaherty, when she visited, stayed in a small back bedroom and no doubt heard about her daughter's unhappiness. When Kate turned thirty, Eliza was just fifty-one, and they were lifelong friends and kindred souls.

Oscar, however, had a job that only added to his popularity. Just beyond the Chopins' house, toward the church, was his general store, bought with money salvaged from bankruptcy. He stocked everything, including foodstuffs (salt meat, flour, cornmeal); apparel (ladies' dresses, men's hats, shiny shoes); and supplies (kerosene, saddles, harnesses, plow points, and bolts of fabric). To his best customers, Oscar gave *lagniappe* ("lan-yap," a little extra). But he was most popular because he gave credit to everybody, and rarely bothered them for payment.

Kate sometimes helped out — possibly to keep an eye on her too-generous husband. On Saturdays, during sales, she spent all day at the store, meeting a rainbow of people, including the blacks, the whites, the light-skinned people of color from Isle Brevelle, the Texans passing through, and even the local Chinese, imported from Cuba as field hands after the war. The store was the place for loafers, lovers, busybodies, and storytellers, and it was where Kate Chopin listened and learned.

One of the first people she met in Cloutierville was Father Jean Marie Beaulieu ("Bole-yay"), the middle-aged, French-born village priest. A short man with a very large head, small mouth, and sad eyes, Father Beaulieu wore a cassock and intoned doleful sermons even at weddings, where he would describe "The little amount of happiness that one enjoys in marriage, the usual dissensions that prevail therein; the terrible scandals which too often burst into the open." Still, he would conclude with a sigh, marriage was valuable. It produced good citizens, gave children to the Church, and was "a cure for concupiscence."

Father Beaulieu did not believe that women should be original thinkers. Rather, he urged each wife to be "submissive to your husband; be for him full of tenderness and love, but remember above all that you belong to God and that nothing in the world can authorize you to do what the law forbids you." If Kate Chopin tried to consult Father Beaulieu about feeling depressed or lonely or overwhelmed in a village where she had few friends and many hostile observers, she found little or no sympathy.

Virtually all the stories passed down about Madame Chopin in Cloutierville describe how she did not belong. She was opinionated, without the tactful roundaboutness people develop when they live closely together for generations. She also lacked the simplest country skills: one day, evidently deserted by servants, she was forced to figure out how to milk a cow herself, aided only by her adolescent neighbor Emma Perrier. Half a century later, "Miss Emma" was still repeating the tale of Kate Chopin's ineptitude and calling her a "dirty lady."

Kate Chopin's impatient urban habits also worked against her. When she was in a hurry (something highly uncommon in Cloutierville), she might head next door to Oscar's store, where—in full view of the neighbors—she would leap onto his horse's back and take off down the road. She rode bareback and astride, her legs on either side of the horse, her hair waving in the breeze. Local people were scandalized.

"Her love of horseback riding they never understood," one observer said years later. Yet her horseback riding, like her walking, was physical exercise as a form of escape. She never wanted to be the conventional angel of the house—nor did she want to look like a plain country woman. Although talking about what to wear is often a bond between women, no one in the Cane River country dressed the way Kate Chopin did.

Her "tight-fitting clothes, her chic hats and a good deal of lavender colors in all her costumes" were a source of wonder. Half a century later, they were still clucking over her favorite costume, "a fantastic affair — a close-fitting riding habit of blue cloth, the train fastened up at the side to disclose an embroidered skirt, and the little feet encased in pretty boots with high heels. A jaunty little jockey hat and feather, and buff gloves rendered her charming." She favored orchid and purple, with a rose at her throat, and all the girls admired "the little hat with the plume." When she rode sidesaddle, the elderly ladies of the town agreed that Madame Chopin was "lovely" — but shocking.

During the day, while most Cloutierville women were home with household chores, or the ones with servants were visiting or napping — Kate Chopin might stroll slowly up and down the street, sporting her fashionable parasol. Crossing the street, she would lift her skirts provocatively, displaying her ankles. Or, in the afternoon, she might don a fashionable riding habit and take her "promenade on horseback" down Cloutierville's one street. Every man working outside would suddenly drop everything — to gawk.

She also smoked Cuban cigarettes, which she rolled herself, with cigarette papers and an adroitly applied clot of saliva.

Kate Chopin loved pretty things, and her source of comfort was the one known to women for centuries: when you're bored, shop. Through Oscar's store, she ordered expensive and modish clothes from New Orleans, and sometimes did not pay the bills. Oscar, her tolerant husband, may have been her only friend.

Decades later, Kate Chopin's daughter claimed that her mother had been a local "Lady Bountiful," dispensing "advice and counsel, medicines, and, when necessary, food to the simple people around her, and in this way learning to know them and to love them too." In reality, though, she was more likely to patronize at least some of the "simple people" — if she paid much attention to them at all.

Kate Chopin was required to attend to her second cousin, Aurore (Lovy) Charleville, who had been another Child of Mary at the Sacred Heart Academy. Lovy had dedicated herself to a teaching career and was twenty-eight when she married a first cousin whose nickname was "Chouchoute" (a name Chopin used in one of her first Louisiana stories). In Cloutierville, in the summer of 1882, barely thirty, Lovy died in childbirth, and the newspaper notice of her death may have been written by Kate Chopin, then thirty-two. Kate's last child was two and a half, and Kate had apparently figured out how to avoid having any more children.

But in the last pages of *The Awakening,* when Madame Ratignolle gives birth in agony, Edna feels a "flaming, outspoken revolt against the ways of Nature" (XXXVII)—a rebellion that must owe something to the last moments of Lovy Charleville.

As Kate Chopin observed, Cane River country people were passionate in their loves and hatreds. After the war, which left many aristocrats penniless, quiet social evenings had replaced balls and duels and grand gestures. But some Cane River people still claimed to fall in love like a pistol shot (Chopin used that in "Désirée's Baby"), while others married in haste and repented for the rest of their lives.

One was the wife of Sylvère DeLouche, the son of Dr. Scruggs' wife from her first marriage. On Kate Chopin's thirty-first birthday, February 8, 1881, the whole village turned out—as it was wont to do— for Sylvère's wedding to the beautiful, Cuban-educated Maria Normand, noted for her superb sewing. Sylvère was already a well-known "sodden drunk" who would drink too much and fall in the river, ruining the fine white linen suit Maria made for him. He was not the kind of groom Madame Normand wanted, and she refused to attend her daughter's wedding. But Maria's father, who doted on her, gamely gave a small reception at home, with cakes and champagne. As expected, the Normand-DeLouche marriage proved to be unhappy, and Maria Normand's marital troubles echoed throughout Cloutierville. Eventually she turned to another man, and both left their mark in some of Kate Chopin's most passionate and intense stories.

By 1881, Madame Chopin certainly knew that motherhood would never be enough to fill her mind and use her energies, although it was certainly easier in Cloutierville than in the cities. Everyone minded everyone else's children, dances included a *parc aux petits* for young children (as in Chopin's "At the 'Cadian Ball"), and babies were rocked away in *branles*, tiny cotton hammocks suspended from hooks in the ceiling. The baby "who has not swung in a *branle*," Chopin wrote later in the story "Loka," "does not know the quintessence of baby luxury."

Children began school at age eight, and by 1882 Kate's sons Jean, Oscar, and George were all old enough to attend the small village school across the street from their house. Kate herself continued to love reading, and later a St. Louis friend wrote that while in Cloutierville, she kept the works of Charles Darwin, Thomas Huxley, and Herbert Spencer as "her daily companions," because "the study of the human species, both general and particular, has always been her constant delight." (But except for Oscar and perhaps Dr. Scruggs, she would have had no one to talk to about the readings that most intrigued her.)

Local entertainments, meanwhile, seemed very strange to an urban matron. For young people, there were Saturday night dances, as in Chopin's stories "At the 'Cadian Ball" and "For Marse Chouchoute," with accordion music, squeaky fiddles, square dance calls in French and English — and many opportunities for flirtation and seduction. There were also showboats and traveling circuses (as in Chopin's "A Little Country Girl"), but those seemed very amateurish to an opinionated young woman used to Norwegian violinists and French opera companies.

Most often people met for parties in each other's homes, with conversation and card playing, a pot of gumbo, and baked meat pies. Kate Chopin did share the local obsession with card games, and years later, in her "A Night in Acadie," a justice of the peace who is supposed to be at a wedding is found playing cards instead. But in Cloutierville in the 1880s, there were also great dinners, sumptuous feasts of game birds put on by Dr. and Mrs. Scruggs — after which the doctor would do his most colorful storytelling. His best-known claim was that Harriet Beecher Stowe had been staying in his house when she got the idea for *Uncle Tom's Cabin* — but the proof, he said, had somehow vanished. (Kate Chopin alluded to that tale in *At Fault,* her first novel.)

The Chopins also held their own *veillées,* informal and spontaneous parties with word-of-mouth invitations: "We are goin' to pass *veillée* at the house." Guests played cards, or put on an "evening of music" (*soirée musicale*), with everyone playing the piano, singing, and dancing. The Chopins could have given formal dinners (Kate owned heavy monogrammed silver forks, engraved KO'F), but she and Oscar preferred informal evenings playing board games on their long green velveteen-topped table.

Still, Kate Chopin was growing restless. She may have begun lying about her age: in the 1880 census, she is listed as twenty-seven instead of thirty. Other men had certainly noticed Madame Chopin, who "was the prettiest thing around." She was not domestic, but socially powerful, and — maybe her Yankee ways again — considered rather aggressive for a woman. She was undoubtedly more popular with men than with women, and by 1881, she had been married for eleven years. Oscar had grown stout and predictable, lovable and comfortable and gentle. He was a good husband, but held no surprises.

Kate was given to long rides, sometimes at night, and her favorite flowers were the "four o'clocks," which opened at four in the afternoon and bloomed all night. Later she wrote, in a rare first-person story: "I could not help thinking that it must be good to prowl sometimes; to get close to the black night and lose oneself in its silence and mystery and sin." (Afterwards, she crossed out the words "and sin.")

Meanwhile, she and Oscar stopped living together for much of the time, although his health may have been part of it. Many Cane River people lived with low-grade malaria, and in late summer 1881 Oscar went to Hot Springs, Arkansas to "recuperate his health," according to the local newspaper, which reported in September that "He is looking well, and is enthusiastic in his praises of the healing qualities of this great resort for the ailing of humanity." But the wholesome food, hot and warm and cold baths, and hours of rest did not cure whatever may have ailed the marriage, or troubled his wife.

Oscar had been home barely a month when Kate left for St. Louis to stay with her mother for several months. It was a form of birth control, but she may also have decided that she preferred her mother's company to that of her husband — or to the carping tongues of his relatives.

In April of the following year, 1882, Oscar had some kind of illness, and so did six-year-old Fred. The Chopins bought "crude petroleum" to put in puddles and stagnant bodies of water, to keep mosquitoes from breeding.

In the fall of 1882, Oscar became really ill, with a violent attack of "swamp fever," the local term for any lingering fever believed to arise from decaying vegetation or foul air or swamp miasma. Although it is fairly dry today, Natchitoches Parish in the 1880s was crisscrossed with bayous, and yellow fever epidemics were not uncommon. Oscar's doctors were very worried. In late October Dr. Scruggs visited him eight times in four days, then left him alone for two and a half weeks.

In New Orleans, Dr. Faget would have been summoned, since he knew how to distinguish yellow fever from malaria — by taking the patient's temperature. A rising temperature meant yellow fever, which might run its course; otherwise, the illness was malaria, the "swamp poison," with its enlarged spleen, false recoveries, and increasingly violent attacks. Although malaria was deadlier, it did have a proven, well-known, inexpensive and easily available treatment: quinine.

But Dr. Scruggs was a country doctor who had taken his medical training forty years earlier. He may not even have owned a thermometer. Evidently he thought Oscar had yellow fever, because his first prescription was calamine, given for "gorged" liver (easily confused with an enlarged spleen). By early December, the doctor was paying daily visits to Oscar; on December 7, he also treated three Chopin children. Finally, on December 8, nearly six weeks after Oscar's first recorded attack, Dr. Scruggs gave him quinine.

It was not a dangerous drug, although an overdose could cause nausea, diarrhea, and vomiting in a severely weakened patient. The standard dose for malaria patients was ten grains, but Dr. Scruggs and his partner Dr. J. F. Griffin, who visited twice on December 8, evidently decided to make up for lost time. And so they gave Oscar forty grains, or four times the usual dosage.

A day later Dr. Scruggs paid another house call and performed a "distention." Dr. Griffin did another on the next day, December 9.

On December 10, Oscar Chopin died.

Oscar's death was not recorded in the church register in Cloutierville — an odd omission, especially since it was reported in the St. Louis newspaper ("On the 10th inst., after a short illness"). The lack of a church record may have been Father Beaulieu's doing: he did have pointed likes and dislikes. One thing he disliked was making house calls, and he would do so only if the summoning party first caught and saddled Father Beaulieu's horse. That meant clambering through the adjoining overgrown pasture, which was also the cemetery. With her husband dying in the house, Kate Chopin could scarcely have managed that — and her stories, written in St. Louis a decade later, do suggest a grudge against the village priest.

Chopin's Cane River country tales include a village priest obviously based on Father Beaulieu. Short, middle-aged, with a long, flapping cassock, Chopin's Père Antoine will make house calls only when a house is not too far away ("For Marse Chouchoute"). In any case, his spiritual ministrations are not powerful. A cabin he blesses is swept away in a flood; a drunken young man he counsels goes off to be killed in a brawl (both in Chopin's novel, *At Fault*).

The fictional Père Antoine also knows nothing about family loyalty. He browbeats a young girl for loving her grandmother, the only one who takes care of her, and when the young girl becomes ill, the priest says lazily that he would make a house call, "if I could." But he's much, much too busy. He is "picking the slugs from his roses" ("Love on the Bon-Dieu").

In short, Kate Chopin wrote about "Père Antoine" — Father Beau-lieu — as a way to get revenge for her miseries in Cloutierville. Maybe she just sensed that the village priest disliked her, but possibly he also failed to come when Oscar needed the last healing hands, the final rites. She could never forgive a man who failed her that way.

The newly widowed Kate Chopin was immersed in sad duties and bit-terly painful obligations. She had to order a coffin from the local car-penter, and find $75 to pay for it. She had to sort through mounds of confused and disorganized papers and records. Hardest of all, she had to explain to her six children, ages not-quite-three to eleven, that Papa was gone, and would never laugh and play with them again.

Because bodies were not embalmed, the wake and funeral had to be held quickly. Oscar was buried in the little cemetery next to St. John the Baptist Church in Cloutierville, and for the first time Kate spent Christmas as a single parent — something she would do for the rest of her life.

Eight years later, she wrote about the grief of widowhood for the first time in her novel *At Fault*: "Of course Thérèse had wanted to die with her Jérôme, feeling that life without him held nothing that could reconcile her to its further endurance" (I). But Chopin had grown up in a houseful of widows who missed their husbands to varying degrees (and sometimes not very much at all). She knew how to be a single mother and how to handle money much better than Oscar had, for his bad management and generosity to all had left her more than $12,000 in debt. Oscar owed seven years' worth of unpaid taxes on property in the French Quarter, and also owed taxes on five pieces of land in Natchi-toches Parish, including his family's own home. He was in debt for rented livestock, vehicles, store expenses, newspaper subscriptions, and expensive hats from New Orleans ($94 — possibly Kate's). There were also medical and funeral bills, property inventories, and inheritance pa-pers to handle.

Most women of Kate Chopin's class would have turned their finan-cial affairs over to the most capable or eager male relative. But the widow

Chopin, always an *étrangère* and rather a Yankee, chose instead to run Oscar's businesses herself. That was not odd for the great-great-granddaughter of the steamboat entrepreneur "La Verdon," but it was very unusual in the Cane River country in the 1880s.

Under Louisiana law, Kate Chopin had to petition to be named legal guardian of her children; otherwise Oscar's brother Lamy inherited custody. Four months after Oscar's death, she was officially named "Tutrix" of her children, by which time she was also running Oscar's store and the plantations very skillfully. She corresponded with New Orleans cotton factors, drew up contracts with local planters, farmers, and sharecroppers, stocked the store, kept careful financial records, and got people to pay their bills—which no doubt caused some resentment.

There was not enough money, though, to pay all the debts. A year and a day after Oscar's death, Kate held a public auction, selling $8,100 worth of land, along with all the real and personal property she could spare—but it was still not enough. She owed money to lawyers, along with many other smaller debts, and it was a full fifteen months after Oscar's death—March 1884—before the final accounting was finished.

Meanwhile, Kate Chopin was doing things that few women did. She was a resourceful mother, and she was supporting herself and her children on her own work and clearheaded accounting. As the widow of a well-liked man, she might even have been admired by villagers in Cloutierville—if she had not been involved with someone else's husband.

While he was alive, Oscar was a buffer for his wife. Whatever criticisms were made of her could not be made of him—except that he did not control her properly, according to local critics. She, meanwhile, could mimic disapproving priests and relatives and neighbors—and know that Oscar would laugh and egg her on, privately. Oscar also shared her interest in words. He was well educated in two languages, and his surviving letters are lively and humorous. He fit in well with the oral culture of Cloutierville, among storytellers like Dr. Scruggs—but a woman storyteller would have been less common, and less welcome.

At home, of course, while Oscar was alive, Kate could have said whatever she liked. She was still a married woman, and therefore protected. But once Oscar was gone, men flocked to aid or console the handsome Widow Chopin. "There were many young ladies and young matrons who were sometimes a little jealous of the lovely Kate," Cloutierville neighbors said much later. "When Oscar died, some of the wives felt that their husbands' sympathy for the young widow prompted them to be a little more solicitous in helping her to solve her problems in the store and on the plantation than was necessary."

Everyone, including his wife, knew who was "sweet on Kate."

Albert Sampite ("Al-BEAR Sam-pi-TAY") had been married for eleven years when the Chopins arrived in Cloutierville. His wife, Lodoiska ("Loca") DeLouche, had lived there all her life except for a short term in boarding school in Bardstown, Kentucky. (Her exotic name came from her father's chance meeting with a Russian duke.) Albert was a restless traveler, but Loca was a homebody, a tiny, plain country woman, loyal and hardworking, who sustained many sadnesses. Of her six children, only two lived past infancy.

The son of French immigrants, Albert Sampite had seemed to be an excellent marriage prospect. He had wealth, good looks, social position, and charm, and Loca's happy mother gave her two parcels of land as a wedding present. Albert also had a strong constitution, having survived the siege of Vicksburg and walked home, barefoot, to Cloutierville, over a hundred miles in the blazing July sun. After the war he owned three cotton plantations (Oscar Chopin was his factor), and he became one of the richest landowners in the area, employing forty-two people and making enough money to invest in Colorado land.

But by the 1880s, Albert Sampite was unhappily married, and hardly a model husband. He preferred gambling and drinking and riding about at night, and he was an inveterate roamer. Thirty-eight the year Oscar Chopin died, Albert was lean, vigorous, with a well-trimmed mustache, pointed eyebrows, dark eyes, and long goatee. He could look devilish, or devilishly handsome, and "Ladies' men run in the Sampite family" was a local saying. "He was what some might call a womanizer," his descendants used to say. "Even when married, he demonstrated an un-flagging interest in women" — especially a certain young, restless, and fashionable widow who shared his love of fine horses and his talent for business.

They all moved in the same social circles. Since Mrs. Scruggs was Loca's mother, the Scruggses' feasts included Chopins and Sampites as guests. After Oscar's death, Kate inherited land that adjoined Albert Sampite's, and so it was not unseemly for them to meet and discuss where hers ended and his began. They had a mutual interest in farming and land and horseflesh, even after Kate sold that parcel of land at auction to pay her debts.

Respectable women were supposed to stay at home, as Loca Sampite did. But Kate Chopin kept up her interest in exploring Cloutierville, on horseback and on foot. Much later she wrote about the muddy banks, the slimy spring turf, the woods, and the night ("Vagabonds"), as well as snakes, owls, uncanny night creatures, and silvery mists ("Ti Frère"). The warm dark country nights, lit only by the stars, could conceal many an escapade.

But there were also everyday chances for Kate Chopin and Albert Sampite to meet: at the landing when her merchandise arrived; at her store, to carry the goods — and to shelve them in the cellar. Possibly he even watched her moving about, scarf on her head, the way Alcée Arobin watches Edna arrange her little house in *The Awakening*. Village flirtations could take place at the general store, as in Chopin's later story "Azélie," or in church ("Love on the Bon-Dieu"), or in the woods ("A No-Account Creole"). Or would-be lovers could just happen to be away from home at the same time, in the same town ("At the 'Cadian Ball"). Dances were improper for a widow, but there were always weddings, wakes, and christenings. And in the summer, afternoon torrential rains might force two people to take refuge in a house, alone, as in Chopin's "The Storm." That story's hero is named Alcée — the name for all her heroes inspired by Albert Sampite.

Yearning is common in Chopin's stories — including women's yearning for men who are not their husbands ("A Respectable Woman," "A Lady of Bayou St. John," and *The Awakening,* among others). At least one of Albert's descendants heard that he and Kate were lovers while her husband was still alive — which could explain Kate's restlessness, and Oscar's stay at Hot Springs without her, and even Kate's trips to St. Louis without Oscar.

But after Oscar's death, in any case, the affair blossomed. Exactly when, where, and what we will never know, and if anyone wrote down dates and places and descriptions, none of those survive. Eleven years after the first spring of her widowhood, Kate Chopin wrote in her diary: "I had loved — lovers who were not divine," and added a little later, "And then, there are so many ways of saying good night!" — but we cannot know if she meant some kind of intimacy with Albert Sampite.

Decades later, a playmate of the Chopin children used to say that Albert and Kate had been "fond" of and "admired each other," but she refused to be more specific. Albert's little great-niece, Ivy DeLouche, heard throughout her childhood that Albert did have an affair with Kate Chopin, but other grandchildren heard it was merely an infatuation on his part, or hers. Yet Marie Sampite, Albert and Loca's daughter, always claimed that "Kate Chopin broke up my parents' marriage."

Whatever happened did mean something to Kate Chopin, for the memory of Albert Sampite lurks everywhere in her fiction. She especially recalled him when she chose the French first name Alcée for her most handsome, rough-edged male characters. The name is pronounced "Al-say," exactly the same as the shortened form of Albert Sampite's name: "Al. S-----é."

In "At the 'Cadian Ball," Alcée Laballière is a successful planter who plays cards and talks crops and politics, unless a "drink or two could put the devil in his head." Handsome and sensual, he works stripped to the waist and pants "a volley of hot, blistering love-words" into the face of his prissy cousin Clarisse. In the sequel, "The Storm," Alcée has an illicit, sexually ecstatic meeting with a woman he did not marry, whose "lips seemed in a manner free to be tasted, as well as her round, white throat and her whiter breasts." That story, with its descriptions of "quivering ecstasy," was not published until 65 years after Chopin's death.

But Chopin did publish *The Awakening*, with the roué Alcée Arobin and his lustful pursuit of Edna, the discontented wife and mother who is an outsider among the New Orleans Creoles. Arobin loves the night and horses; he is good-looking, with an insolent manner; and he pursues Edna in a practiced way, with charm and "animalism." In *The Awakening*, as in "The Storm," the Alcée character awakens a woman to sexual passion she has never known before.

As Kate Chopin's stories show, Albert Sampite had become part of her imagination, indelibly. But by the time she gave him a part in her fiction, he was no longer a part of her life.

If she had wanted to marry Albert, that was not possible. Among Catholics there was no divorce; under Louisiana civil law, if a divorce took place because of adultery, "the offender may not marry his or her accomplice." In any case, the storm of indignation that would have engulfed both Cloutierville and St. Louis would have been intense and unceasing. In Chopin's first novel, *At Fault*, the Catholic heroine renounces the man she loves — because he is divorced.

Chopin no doubt got advice from everyone. Father Beaulieu had opinions about the sanctity of marriage, and about the behavior of widows. Eliza O'Flaherty was urging her daughter to come home to St. Louis. In Cloutierville, Eliza's irascible cousin Landry Charleville took it upon himself to accost Kate in the street, during one of her promenades on horseback. He grabbed the bridle of her horse and shook his finger while scolding her furiously.

Kate listened awhile, then decided she had heard enough. She pulled out her little whip, and whipped him.

But Albert Sampite, even if he had been single, was not her match. Unlike Oscar, who was truly a French gentleman, Albert was neither widely traveled nor well educated, and he was not a reader of books.

His surviving writings show him as fairly inarticulate, at least in English. In a typical letter to his wife, he complains about their son: "Why don't Alphonse write. I haven't hunted any since he was here, he can make war to snails of nothing else."

And then there was Albert Sampite's other side. He was irresistibly charming when sober, but he drank steadily and did not seem to be drunk — until he turned haughty, violent, and cruel. That was when he would beat his wife with a leather strap.

Wife beating was not uncommon in Cloutierville, and some villagers claimed it was a French custom, even a right, for men to beat their wives. But Kate Chopin had not grown up with scenes of domestic discord. In a household of women, she had not seen drunken or angry fights. She did not expect them in marriage, nor did Oscar, who had helped his mother escape. And so, in yet another way, Kate Chopin was an outsider. She did not have to take any abuse from anyone.

Chopin may have had some compassion for Loca Sampite, as a suffering woman. She may have heard that Loca ordered expensive black taffeta dresses from New Orleans, in an effort to compete with Kate's urban sophistication. But when Chopin later wrote a story called "Loka," she made the title character ugly, clumsy, and dull-witted — without a shred of sisterly sympathy.

In Cloutierville, Kate Chopin was the center of a swirl of chatter among people who had never truly liked her, and there was no well-loved husband to be her buffer and protector. Possibly Albert also threatened her, and maybe she knew that batterers do not change. Or Albert may simply have outraged her by meddling with her money. Among his papers, kept in a coffee can and passed down to his descendants, are letters to his children, deeds to land, and five IOUs, all dated 1883, from Cloutierville residents promising to pay a total of $301.08, at 8 percent interest, to Kate Chopin.

Was Albert helping her collect the money owed her — or was he helping himself to her money?

In any case, very suddenly, Kate Chopin decided to give up the store and the plantations and go home to her mother. Indeed, nothing in her early life or readings would have encouraged her to throw everything over for a grand passion. Her mother had not married for love — and if, as a widow, Eliza O'Flaherty had any serious suitors, no information has survived. Her grandmother and great-grandmother had been practical Frenchwomen; her great-great-grandmother, whom she had never known, did have a child out of wedlock, but never reconciled with her estranged husband. And she never, ever gave up any of her property.

Only one of Kate's relatives, her mother's sister Zuma, had had a famous romance — the sudden marriage slipped past the occupying Union troops, during the war. But as a married couple, Zuma and John Tatum were soon burying children who died young. Later, Zuma was famous for being ill-tempered and complaining.

Kate Chopin was, like her mother, a practical Frenchwoman. When her turn came, she chose to escape the hue and cry, the impossible entanglement, and the sad memories of Cloutierville. Whatever Albert Sampite meant to her, it was not enough. Edna, in *The Awakening*, makes a similar choice when she leaves her lover, Robert, to be with a mother-woman, Madame Ratignolle. Both Kate Chopin and Edna Pontellier choose a woman's duty and love for another woman over the uncertain passions of a man.

When Kate Chopin left Cloutierville for St. Louis, she left behind some of her boys, for awhile, with Oscar's brother Lamy. She left a walnut dresser to her neighbor Emma Perrier, and two crystal filigree perfume bottles to Lodoiska Grandchamp, another Cloutierville friend. To Albert Sampite, she left her long, green-topped gaming table, and an oil lamp of clear glass with an amethyst tinge — useful for anyone who rode around at night.

By the middle of 1884, Kate Chopin was back in St. Louis. She had left as a twenty-year-old bride; now her oldest child was thirteen. Weary from being a single parent and sick at heart over her life in Cloutierville, Kate Chopin returned to what she thought would be a haven. She would be a daughter again, in her mother's house.

# Chapter 7

# St. Louis and At Fault

FOR KATE CHOPIN, moving back to St. Louis was not the frantic flight of a scandalous woman or a broken-hearted widow. Nor was it solely the ragged retreat of an exhausted, still-young woman who yearned for the safety and comfort of her mother's love.

Chopin also returned to St. Louis as the mother of young children, as the head of a family, and as a woman who loved reading and writing and was fascinated by the newest scientific thinking. All that made her a misfit in Cloutierville, where storytelling was a great popular art but private reading was rare. Too, the lack of a lending library, such as the Mercantile in St. Louis, made it hard for her even to get books.

She also worried about her children's education. The Cloutierville school, just nine years old, had only the most basic curriculum: geography, grammar, history, spelling, reading, arithmetic, philosophy, and a miscellaneous subject called "Scholars Companion." There was no science, and after the elementary years, there were no schools at all in the little French village. The Chopin youngsters would have had to go to boarding school, which was very expensive. With her children gone, Kate Chopin would have been even more alone, a foreigner and an outsider.

Meanwhile, the best public schools in the United States in the 1880s happened to be in St. Louis. The first kindergartens in the country were started there, and many of the public school teachers belonged to the "St. Louis Movement," a circle of Hegelian philosophers. Central High School's rigorous curriculum included ancient and modern history, English literature, geography, Greek, and Latin, as well as the newest mathematics and natural science. There were even sports teams for the boys (Felix Chopin became a quarterback). Kate Chopin may have doubted what she wanted for herself—but there was no doubt about the best place for her children.

At first the Chopin brood moved in with Eliza O'Flaherty, her sister Amanda McAllister (now widowed), and the McAllister young adults, Andrew and Nina. Like Edna and Adèle in *The Awakening,* Eliza and Amanda shared an intimate friendship and a loyalty to one another. They had also lived in the same household for most of their lives. But Kate's return, with her children, made the home at 1125 St. Ange much too crowded, so the Chopins and Eliza O'Flaherty moved across the street, to 1122.

Eliza, now fifty-six and gray-haired, had been a widow for nearly three decades. She still had her slightly French accent ("half lost r's, and a certain precision in the use of words"), as well as her "indescribable air of caste and good breeding" and "a way of saying gently very positive things to her grandchildren." Kate was proud of her mother's speech, and in her mother's home again, she felt secure and loved in the world of women she knew best.

But it did not last long.

Eliza O'Flaherty had cancer, and on June 28, 1885, she died. After the funeral at Holy Angels Church, she was buried in Calvary Cemetery, near the rest of the family. Kate Chopin was "literally prostrate with grief."

Yet from childhood on, she had learned from her mother about surviving grief and death. In every decade of life, she had lost at least one person close to her, although the death of her mother was the most devastating. Eliza had been her anchor through all the other sorrows, and had been with her, sharing women's wisdom, for the births of the children. Her mother had remained a serene presence through all her daughter's heartaches. But now Kate Chopin, at thirty-five, was a motherless child who took her place at the head of a generational chain.

Her first step was to move to a home of her own, away from memories and old patterns. Within a year, Chopin and her children had moved to a house at 3317 Morgan Street (now Delmar) between Grand and Jefferson, in a newer part of the city. It was a grand, three-story Federal-style home with intricate stonework, called (in St. Louis) the Lafayette Square type. In many cities it would be called a small mansion.

(Exactly when Kate Chopin bought the house, for $8,900 from one Jan Hoffman, is unclear. A handwritten note with a photo of the house, which was new, gives the date as July 3, 1883 — but at that time Chopin, widowed, was still living in Cloutierville and engaging in her perilous flirtation with Albert Sampite. The same note also lists five Chopin children, omitting Lélia, and says — incorrectly — that Chopin lived in the house until her death. She may have bought the house in antici-pation of returning home to live, or the actual purchase date may have been July 3, 1885, just after her mother's death, when Kate would be inheriting from her mother's estate.)

In any case, the move put Kate Chopin and her children half a city away from the old neighborhood and such relatives as Aunt Amanda, who would surely notice that Kate had stopped going to mass. After the Cloutierville years, in which she was the center of scandal and dis-approval, Kate Chopin always preferred privacy. Like her character Edna Pontellier, she was rather a solitary soul who wanted only certain kinds of people around her.

Yet the return to St. Louis threw Kate O'Flaherty Chopin back with the people who had always known her. Mother Kitty Garesché now lived in Michigan, and Kate visited her for comfort, and at home there were countless relatives. Her mother's many cousins and their daughters, for instance, had mostly married "solid men" and were now among the city's social elite. Some belonged to the Daughters of the Confed-eracy; most were seen at the opera, the theater, and other musical and social events. Their job (never stated so blatantly) was to be ornaments to their husbands, and to smooth the way for their husbands to succeed in business — the wifely role that Edna pointedly rejects in *The Awakening*.

Chopin had moved back into a familiar web of kinship and friend-ship, among people who remembered her as a clever, outspoken young belle. She still had strong opinions, and there was no social-climbing husband to restrain her. In St. Louis, she was neither a foreigner nor an outsider: if she broke rules, she knew it. As a widow in St. Louis, Chopin was taking on a role she had been observing all her life. She was home.

Two years after her mother's death, Kate Chopin ventured back to Natchitoches Parish, for good family reasons.

Oscar's sister Marie, the little orphan who had stayed with Kate and Oscar in New Orleans, was now married to a fast-talking would-be lawyer — and Kate wanted to look him over. Phanor Breazeale had started out as a penniless farm boy who, in his teens, had had to flee to Texas after a murky political brawl. Adventurous and rude, he was wildly inappropriate for a well-bred young lady from one of the finest families of the Cane River country. When Marie jilted her respectable fiancé in favor of Phanor, he gave her an engagement ring that he'd won in a poker game — leaving her relatives shaking with rage.

Kate Chopin couldn't wait to meet him.

She arrived in Natchitoches after a long, weary journey with ill-tempered and sickly children; one even had a fresh case of the measles. Nevertheless, she had to meet Phanor, greet the Breazeales' baby daughter, and inspect Marie — who, like Kate, had grown agreeably stout. Both were now matronly-looking mothers who chattered away happily in French, always at ease with each other.

Kate and Phanor also got along famously. They rolled and smoked cigarettes together, told old tales and made up new ones, played cards until all hours, and made fun of hypocrisies and pretensions. Phanor, raised a Catholic, had run away from home three times rather than take communion. Later, out of contrariness, he joined the Masons, but announced to all that he was a militant atheist, and remained one the rest of his life. Kate Chopin, a renegade Catholic, was thoroughly in sympathy with that, and Marie and Phanor were family favorites with her from then on. They egged her on, and they all made each other laugh.

The Breazeales also gave Kate Chopin the germ for the first story she worked on for publication, eventually called "A No-Account Creole."

The story's heroine is torn between two suitors: an ambitious New Orleans businessman and a penniless Creole farmer. There was some of Phanor Breazeale in each one, and a bit of Oscar Chopin, too, in the businessman who dreams of not having to work very hard — and perhaps a bit of Albert Sampite, too, in the raw emotions of the Creole who loves and loses.

In Natchitoches Parish, Kate and her brood stayed with her brother-in-law Lamy, his wife Cora, and their daughter Nini at the plantation in Chopin, Louisiana (Lamy, as postmaster, had named the postal district after himself). Kate also needed to inspect her remaining property, including the Cloutierville house that she was renting out, and Oscar's grave, in the small Cloutierville cemetery, also had to be visited. Whether she saw Albert or Loca Sampite is not recorded.

During and after that return trip in 1887, Kate Chopin was still adrift and bereft. After her mother's death, she had felt that she was alone in a world without meaning. Yet she had always been writing and reading, for pleasure and consolation. Books had been her escape after the wartime "outrage," and at the height of her débutante year she had complained to her diary that "my dear reading and writing have suffered much neglect."

During her married years in Louisiana, Chopin had also been writing — not only diaries, but entertaining and colorful letters that her mother saved. So it was that Dr. Frederick Kolbenheyer came upon the talent that Kate Chopin would use for the rest of her life. He had been her obstetrician in St. Louis, and her son Frederick may have been named after him, but Kolbenheyer was not simply a medical man. Like the best doctors, including Dr. Mandelet in *The Awakening,* he knew about the secrets of the human heart. And unlike the doleful Father Beaulieu in Cloutierville, Kolbenheyer had a wide-ranging knowledge of human possibilities, venalities, and hopes.

He knew much more, for instance, about money and the vulnerability of even the shrewdest of women. Some of Eliza O'Flaherty's estate had reportedly been swindled away by a trusted friend who preyed on widows, and Kolbenheyer recognized that Kate Chopin might not be able to support her family on her inheritance, her Cloutierville house rental, and her Louisiana land holdings. She also needed a consuming interest that would be all her own.

Dr. Kolbenheyer was definitely a radical thinker. Impressionable adolescents, including some of Kate Chopin's children, admired his big black beard and piercing eyes, but were sure he was some kind of an anarchist, "bordering on a bomb thrower." Born an aristocrat (in 1843 in Austrian Poland), Kolbenheyer had studied both philosophy and medicine in Vienna, and he knew Kant, Schopenhauer, and Hegel better than almost anyone else in St. Louis. He was a spellbinding talker who could discourse for hours on the life and career of the great emperor Napoleon, but he believed in serving those who needed it most. He devoted his medical career to caring for the poor on the South Side, where — in Fritz Roeslein's book store — he became vice president of Joseph Pulitzer's *Post-Dispatch.*

Kolbenheyer is probably the one who introduced Kate Chopin to Pulitzer and to his partner John Dillon, and theirs was the first daily newspaper to publish a Chopin story. But his most important contribution was to repeat to Kate Chopin what Madam O'Meara, her beloved Sacred Heart teacher, had told her more than twenty years earlier: You have a talent, and you must write.

Chopin's very first publication turned out to be a piece of music: "Lilia. Polka for Piano," put out by H. Rollman & Sons in 1888. That year, Chopin also played an offstage role — and perhaps an unwitting one — in a very large drama in Cloutierville.

In May 1888, Loca Sampite left her husband Albert after twenty years of marriage. That September, she filed for a legal separation, listing what he had done to her: violence, cruelty, blows with his hand and a leather strap. She had fled to her mother's and then returned to try again (with "patience and forebearance"), but his "ill-treatment, outrages & violent words & conduct" grew worse. She had had to flee their house with nothing except the clothes on her back, and his beatings left her an invalid for a year. She asked for a monthly allowance, custody of their two children, and a division of property.

Albert, as batterers do, evidently made some moves toward a reconciliation: he visited their daughter at boarding school at least once, bringing money.

Meanwhile, the woman Loca perceived as "the other woman," Kate Chopin, was obviously creating a life for herself apart from the Cane River country. In January 1889, Chopin became a published author, in the Chicago magazine *America,* with a somewhat ambiguous poem called "If It Might Be":

> If it might be that thou didst need my life;
> Now on the instant would I end this strife
> 'Twixt hope and fear, and glad the end I'd meet
> With wonder only, to find death so sweet.
>
> If it might be that thou didst need my love;
> To love thee dear, my life's fond work would prove.
> All time, to tender watchfulness I'd give;
> And count it happiness, indeed, to live.

In Cloutierville, the poem was no doubt passed around and chewed over for clues and secrets. Charitable souls would assume that Chopin was writing about her late husband, Oscar, and perhaps she was — although she may also have been musing, in a what-if vein, about Albert Sampite.

And then, in April, Kate Chopin took a definitive step. She had Oscar's body shipped back to St. Louis, and buried in Calvary Cemetery, near the rest of the O'Flahertys. Just four days after that, Loca Sampite withdrew her petition for a legal separation.

Loca may have harbored, once more, the hope for a peaceful and happy marriage. Like many battered women, she may have believed that if she somehow behaved in a way that did not anger her husband, he would stop beating her. The timing suggests that she also thought that Kate Chopin was a major cause of her troubles. With that woman out of the picture, Loca may have hoped, Albert would become a kind and loving husband.

Whether Kate Chopin knew all this, we cannot tell, and her later literary references to Loca Sampite (in the story "Loka") are not favorable or pleasant. Yet Chopin drew on Albert Sampite in her fiction in two major ways. The more obvious are the handsome, arrogant heroes named Alcée; the less apparent are the abusive husbands in such stories as "In Sabine" and "Désirée's Baby" — both of whom also have Albert's initial, A (Bud Aiken and Armand Aubigny).

Kate Chopin seemed to know the psychology of batterers: the outward charm, the bitterness and brutality underneath. For awhile, she and Loca Sampite no doubt regarded each other as rivals, and perhaps enemies — but both showed uncommon courage. Loca came forward publicly, naming her husband as a batterer; Kate left him, and wrote about men like him as a warning to other women. As far as we know, they did not think of themselves as sisters in any way — but they were.

Back in St. Louis, Kate Chopin was planning her career after "If It Might Be." *America* was an important and distinguished journal, with such contributors as Algernon Swinburne, Ella Wheeler Wilcox, James Russell Lowell, and the future President, Theodore Roosevelt. But polkas and poetry were not really what Kate Chopin wanted to write — and sell.

Exactly four years after her mother's death, she wrote a story about a young pianist deprived "for the second time of a loved parent," who throws "all her energies into work." It begins with a poignant epigram: "To love and be wise is scarcely granted even to a god" — but the story itself says quite the opposite. The young pianist, who lives in a city very like St. Louis, refuses to marry her rich and handsome suitor because — she tells him, to his shock — "it doesn't enter into the purpose of my life."

When the *Philadelphia Musical Journal* accepted that story, publishing it under the title "Wiser than a God" in December 1889, Kate Chopin had found her own purpose in life, as an author.

She also began developing a writing routine. She worked on several pieces at the same time, mulling them over, then writing them down, drafts and final copies, when she could. By 1889 Lélia was nearly ten years old; Jean, the eldest son, was eighteen and something of a social favorite. The house was rarely quiet, and a fixed writing regimen was hard to manage. Much later, her daughter told interested critics that Kate Chopin had never had a separate writing room and preferred to write with her children "swarming about her."

But in fact, they were much too large to swarm, and the house was big enough for Chopin to have her own writing and sitting room as well as a bedroom. Lélia liked to present her mother as putting her family first, and her writing second, and Kate Chopin herself went along with that image — but she was actually a very dedicated and ambitious author. She was never a dilettante.

Following the habits of good accounting that she had learned from the women of her family, Chopin kept meticulous records of stories she wrote, word counts, and magazines to which they were submitted. In 1888–1889 she worked on what she called, in her notebook, "Unfinished Story — Grand Isle" and also on a story called "A Poor Girl," while, in real life, she was already taking mental notes for *The Awakening* — noticing, as writers inevitably do, what her friends were up to.

Chopin's new circle included Sue V. Moore, society and feature writer for the weekly *St. Louis Spectator,* who had a six-year-old son and had been married for twelve years to Henry W. Moore, managing editor of the *Post-Dispatch.* The two were not well matched. Mrs. Moore, originally from Camden, New Jersey, was known as "a most worthy and attractive lady," but English-born Henry Moore had "a repelling air of nervous insincerity." He was a ruthless attacker of other men's reputations, and a rival newspaper — in the sensational language of the day — declared that "Something has gnawed out his self-respect, the hope of youth, his honesty, and left his face pale with the ashes of a mental fire."

In July 1888, while Kate Chopin was working on her first short stories, Henry W. Moore left his wife and son and eloped with another woman. Moore's "companion in shame" was Emma Stockman Norton, an actress married to the manager of the St. Louis Grand Opera House. The pair ran off to Kansas; Sue V. Moore went into seclusion in Colorado, a penniless but "brave little woman and an accomplished one." She, in fact, had written the newspaper pieces that gained Henry Moore his reputation as a superb drama critic.

Mrs. Moore had also been "a faithful devoted wife," who endured indignities and brutalities "with loving patience, hoping always for a change on his part." As Kate Chopin probably noticed, Sue V. Moore's situation was not unlike Loca Sampite's.

But there was another detail that evidently stuck in Chopin's mind. According to the newspaper, "It is claimed that Mr. Moore used to take particular exception to the food and the way it was prepared and would declare that Mrs. Norton's cooking was decidedly more artistic. If a salad would not please him he would get a recipe from Mrs. Norton and have the dish prepared in a style he preferred." In *The Awakening*, Kate Chopin left out the other woman, but kept the hectoring husband: one of Léonce Pontellier's bitterest whines is about bad meals at home.

After bankruptcy and an auction, Sue V. Moore did bounce back. By the early 1890s, she was editor of *St. Louis Life*, a society newspaper for which she wrote with an easy, casually witty style. She was a serious professional journalist and a lively friend who became one of Chopin's links to the growing literary community of St. Louis.

But editors in the United States in the 1890s were not interested in stories about suffering wives. They preferred New Women — and so Kate Chopin wrote what the market would buy.

In every era, some images of women arise from "real people," while others are media creations. In the 1890s, the New Woman was both. In magazines and newspapers, she was the Gibson Girl, breezily trundling about on her bicycle or playing tennis in a long skirt and white middy blouse. She was lithe and athletic, not ferociously strong, and she appealed to the male gaze.

The New Woman in real life, however, had rejected being defined by men. She defined herself, usually, as a single woman with a profession: teacher, social worker, nurse, or perhaps home economist (a newly-invented field). She lived by herself or with another woman in a lifelong "Boston marriage," and worried not a whit about whether she ever married. In the 1890s, a greater proportion of American women stayed single by choice than in any other decade before or since. And so, to many traditionalists, the New Woman was a fascinating and threatening creature.

Kate Chopin knew New Women, including the globetrotting journalist Florence Hayward and the philosopher Thekla Bernays, who could translate to or from half a dozen languages. But Chopin, early in her own career, was skittish about portraying the New Woman in a thoroughly positive light. She may have wondered how many women could truly be independent — or she may have suspected that a woman character who was too singular, too sure of herself, would not be published by the men who edited most of the magazines.

Following the classic rule, "Write about what you know," Chopin drew on contemporary controversies about women for her first stories. New Women had been talking about redefining marriage as a relationship of equals, and Chopin's married couple in "A Point at Issue!" try to do just that, living apart and freely pursuing their own intellectual interests. But jealousy strikes, and the story ends with a wink at human follies.

One minor character is Chopin's first, and only, portrayal of a women's rights activist: Margaret, "owing to a timid leaning in the direction of Woman's Suffrage," is "looked upon as slightly erratic." Margaret corresponds with "a certain society of protest" and wears "garments of mysterious shape, which, while stamping their wearer with the distinction of a quasi-emancipation, defeated the ultimate purpose of their construction by inflicting a personal discomfort that extended beyond the powers of long endurance."

Chopin was evidently alluding to bloomers, an emancipated style that had come (and gone) several decades earlier; but she had her own style, according to her son Felix's recollections: "She was not interested in the woman's suffrage movement. But she belonged to a liberal, almost pink-red group of intellectuals, people who believed in intellectual freedom and often expressed their independence by wearing eccentric clothing." (Chopin's descendants have no idea what the "eccentric clothing" was.)

The most autobiographical parts of "A Point at Issue!", though, are the side comments from disapproving observers. Still smarting from the effects of wicked wagging tongues in Cloutierville, Chopin threw in some bitterly typical quotations from public gossip: "It was uncalled for!" and "It was improper!" and "It was indecent!"

Chopin's other two New Women stories describe a self-possessed pianist who chooses music over love ("Wiser than a God"), and a fussy, confused newspaperwoman who almost botches her niece's love life ("Miss Witherwell's Mistake"). The first is celebration and the second is caricature, but all three New Women stories are romantic comedies with serious undertones, about women who are trying to define their own lives.

Chopin was already writing and thinking about the problem Edna wrestles with in *The Awakening*: can a woman be married, yet retain an independent self?

Short stories worked for brief, perceptive explorations of the self, but a novel did much more for immediate name recognition and serious sales. In July 1889, a month after writing "Wiser than a God," Kate Chopin started a novel on a subject she knew very well: a handsome Louisiana woman who suddenly finds herself widowed. Thérèse Lafirme, an "inconsolable, childless Creole widow of thirty," resembles Kate Chopin in "roundness of figure suggesting a future of excessive fullness if not judiciously guarded" (I). (In the 1890s, there were two warring beauty standards: the slim, lithe Gibson Girl and the robust, voluptuous Lillian Russell woman, named for the bountiful actress whose great size and extravagant appetite made her a legend in her own time.)

*At Fault*'s plot begins with the arrival of an outsider, the St. Louis businessman David Hosmer, at Thérèse's Cane River country plantation.

He is a sallow, earnest, humorless Yankee who resembles neither Oscar Chopin nor Albert Sampite, and he wants only one thing from Thérèse: permission to build a sawmill on her land. When she agrees, the door opens for a possible romance — but Thérèse, who deplores divorce, learns that David has a former wife, Fanny, in St. Louis. She insists that David return to his ex-wife. He obeys, the remarriage makes all three miserable, and Fanny — one of the first female alcoholics in American literature — does not stop drinking. After she drowns in a flood, Thérèse and David are finally married by Père Antoine.

Chopin set *At Fault* first in Louisiana, and then in St. Louis, cutting back and forth, sometimes with a vengeance. She presents St. Louis as cold and gray, and Louisiana as light and warm — partly for story purposes, and possibly also because she was writing most of *At Fault* during the long Midwestern winter. (Often covered with ice, St. Louis was also dark and dreary with the soot from coal-burning stoves.) Louisiana was a bright memory, and in *At Fault,* it appears as a place of happiness, hospitality, romance, and humor.

David's sister Melicent, for instance, relives some of Kate Chopin's most embarrassing Cloutierville moments, but defuses them. A St. Louis flirt with haughty urban ways, Melicent has no idea that everyone in the Cane River country is watching her, especially when she has trouble hiring servants: "the negroes were very averse to working for Northern people whose speech, manners, and attitude towards themselves were unfamiliar" (IV).

Melicent also adorns her rooms with "bizarre decorations" and "fantastic calico," and dresses even more flamboyantly than Kate Chopin did when she made a spectacle of herself in Cloutierville. Chopin wore a rose at her throat; Melicent wears giant bunches of geraniums. Like her creator, Melicent bares her ankles, and decorates her hat with a "great ostrich plume." A decade earlier, Kate Chopin might have thought she was the most fashionable creature ever to promenade Cloutierville's one street — but she makes Melicent the most ridiculous (V, VIII).

Melicent does have a flirtation with a local young man, Grégoire Santien, who suggests a bit of Albert Sampite. Compared with Melicent's

pseudosophistication, Grégoire seems primitive and uneducated, especially when he takes her on a midnight trek to the grave of "Robert
McFarlane," who is "the person that Mrs. W'at's her name wrote about
in Uncle Tom's Cabin" (VIII). Grégoire believes in ghosts; Melicent,
a smug Unitarian, scoffs at that. Clearly a romance between a St. Louis-
bred woman, with her citified ways, and a Cane River country man,
with a love for whiskey and reckless living, cannot last. Kate Chopin
knew that firsthand, and shows it in her novel when Melicent jilts Grégoire, who then comes to a bad end in a barroom.

Chopin was describing what she thought might happen to very angry young men — and as new novelists often do, she put into *At Fault*
a potpourri of the things on her mind, instead of doling them out to
different books. Her novel also has a subplot about a mixed-blood young
man, so enraged about the encroachment of a sawmill on his land that
he sets fire to it — whereupon Grégoire, another rebellious, motherless
son, kills him. As the mother of five sons, Chopin had long thought
about the best ways for a single mother to raise boys — a role her own
life had not fitted her for at all. In *At Fault,* the hotheaded young men
die, and leave everlasting disappointment and grief to their families.

With her St. Louis characters, Kate Chopin also had some scores
to settle, and she was not always kind to women. Fanny, the alcoholic
wife, borders on a caricature. Besides being a clumsy Yankee, out of
place in the Cane River country, Fanny is uneducated and crude, speaking an odd slang that makes her seem addled. Possibly Chopin, thinking
about her own past, could not afford to sympathize with a wronged
wife whose husband is drawn to a much more glamorous widow.

Fanny's friends, though, are far more colorful, with their slang and
their false hair — and Chopin used them to satirize, rather obviously,
certain real-life St. Louisans.

There were certain kinds of self-righteous reformers and high-minded
intellectuals Kate Chopin couldn't abide. Her education and her French
background had taught her to appreciate irony and sophisiticated wit —
so that clunky, single-minded earnestness bored and irritated her. It
also incited her to some rather awkward mischief in *At Fault.*

One St. Louisan who grated was Mrs. Harriet Worthington, co-founder of Forest Park University for Women, the first United States university chartered solely for women. Kate Chopin was all for women's education, but Mrs. Worthington also campaigned for temperance and trumpeted her own militant Protestantism. Chopin could not resist skewering her through Mrs. Belle Worthington in *At Fault*—a character who not only favors drinking, but is also loud and crude and a deliberate religious hypocrite: she goes to mass and confession only to keep "on the safe side" (XI).

Her husband, meanwhile, is an absent-minded and very pedantic professor whose bookshelf is weighed down with the books Kate O'Flaherty read as a schoolgirl: Bulwer (the first author in her commonplace book), Racine, Molière, Scott, Shakespeare. But Lorenzo Worthington's life's work—a chronicle of all the world's religions—is an obvious poke at Denton Snider, a St. Louis professor whose life's work was similarly grandiose: a sixteen-volume analysis of the psychological basis of all knowledge. Snider and his ponderous colleagues, with their *Journal of Speculative Philosophy* and their Hegelian jargon, were regularly lampooned by William Marion Reedy in his weekly *Mirror*—and Reedy was one of Chopin's boosters, friends, and satirical colleagues.

Working through the winter, Chopin finished *At Fault* in April 1890, writing by hand, as was her custom. She hired a Miss Keleher to type the manuscript, and then offered it to *Belford's Monthly*, a Chicago magazine that printed one novel per issue. When *Belford's* said no, Chopin decided to have *At Fault* published at her own expense. She paid Nixon-Jones Printing Company in St. Louis to produce one thousand copies, and they were ready in late September 1890.

Chopin distributed them herself to stores and news vendors, periodicals and potential reviewers, and sent them to famous editors. That kind of vanity press publishing was not frowned upon at that time, and *At Fault* did get attention. In St. Louis, there were notices in *Fashion and Fancy* ("very meritorious") and the *Spectator* ("refined and well-written"), and in New Orleans, the *Daily Picayune* noted a local angle: "The author of this interesting novel is the widow of the late Oscar

Chopin, commission merchant in New Orleans. . . . The life of a hand-some Creole widow of 30 is charmingly related in this book."

There was also an excellent notice from Chopin's friend Sue V. Moore in *St. Louis Life,* founded just the year before to be a "light and humorous" weekly, with "society comment" that would be "always bright, fresh and entertaining, without peering into the privacy of the home circle or in any way offending good taste." Moore called her friend's novel "a pleasing story, exceptionally well-told," and remarkably polished for a first book. *At Fault,* Moore wrote, showed Chopin's "in-tuitive perception of what is fitting and artistic," with characters who were "witty, tender, or commonplace, just as she means them to be."

But as an abandoned wife and single mother, making her own way and earning her own living, Sue V. Moore also knew what was impor-tant to a professional author. *At Fault,* she wrote, "proves that Mrs. Chopin possesses a talent that should prove a source of pleasure to the public and profit to herself."

There were four longer reviews of *At Fault,* and all of them picked away at Kate Chopin in one way or another. The only national review, in *The Nation,* said *At Fault* had entirely too many plots: "There is the lady who drinks and the gentleman who gets a divorce from her, the widow who loves and is beloved by him. . . . There is also the young lady of many arrangements, the negro who commits arson, the young gentleman who shoots him, the Colonel who shoots the young gentle-man, the St. Louis lady who goes to matinées and runs off with the matinée-going gentleman." *The Nation* did concede that Chopin had a knack for dialects and characterization, but its final judgment called her, tactfully, amateurish rather than unladylike: "the array of disagree-ables was born rather of literary crudity than of want of refinement."

Refinement was also an issue in the book's other three reviews, to Kate Chopin's annoyance. The *Post-Dispatch* reviewer, for instance, liked reading about St. Louis characters, and praised Chopin's plot, humor, and "ARTISTIC SKILL" (printed in capitals) in the portrayal of Fanny's death. The reviewer did object, though, to some matters: "One shudders at hearing Hosmer tell his wife to 'shut up,' and we protest against Melicent's five engagements. If she really was engaged five times it ought not to be mentioned."

The more conservative *St. Louis Republic,* edited by Chopin's childhood neighbors the Knapps, was much more critical. While the book was "a clever romance of Louisiana life," the reviewer emphasized that it was about a woman who "would rather have been married to someone else's husband." Moreover,

> Hosmer's wife, Fanny, is a fatal terror; she "guesses," she drinks to excess of whiskey, she steals from an old darkey's cabin, and uses slang that gives one shivers; but as the fair author herself, in the narrative portion of the volume, speaks of a railway station as a "depot" and a shop as a "store" — mistakes that might do in the mouth of one of the characters, who many of them use "aint" for is not, but mar the value of the book when used in the narrative portion — she may have made Fanny worse than she intended.

Although the *Republic* reviewer conceded that "some of the secondary characters are particularly well drawn," and that "the local color is excellent," the overall review made Kate Chopin bristle.

Authors — and nowadays, their publicists — disagree about whether an author should respond to hostile reviews. Some believe that the author should appear to be above the fray — and that if the author responds hotly, she will make enemies, causing her next book to be attacked or, even worse, ignored. Others argue that the only bad publicity is no publicity. If an author responds to a negative or misguided review and her response is printed, the author gets more free publicity.

Kate Chopin may have simply wanted to correct the *Republic*'s pettiness — or, being an ambitious author, she may have recognized that a correction would garner further attention for *At Fault*. In any case, she responded hotly to the Republic's review, and her rejoinder was printed:

> Will you kindly permit me through the columns of your paper to set *The Republic* book reviewer right in a matter which touches me closely concerning the use and misuse of words? I cannot recall an instance, in or out of fiction, in which an American "country store" has been alluded to

as a "shop," unless by some unregenerate Englishman. The use of the word depot or station is optional. Wm. Dean Howells employs the former to indicate a "railway station," so I am hardly ready to believe the value of "At Fault" marred by following so safe a precedent.

Chopin was indeed canny to bring in the name of William Dean Howells, a novelist who was far more important, and powerful, as a *Harper's* and *Atlantic* editor. He did indeed use the word "depot" frequently in his own divorce novel, *A Modern Instance* — and the husband in his book, Bartley Hubbard, is the shallow and crude equivalent of Chopin's Fanny. He even uses similar rude slang. Chopin was not only, as she stated, following "so safe a precedent," but she was also an admirer of Howells's work. She bought his books, wrote "good" and "excellent" in the margins next to passages she especially liked, and sent him a copy of *At Fault*. (He did not respond.)

*At Fault*'s longest, and perhaps strangest, review appeared in the Natchitoches *Enterprise*, edited by Phanor Breazeale's brother Hopkins Payne ("Hop"). The review, signed "Flora," was full of misspellings and typographical errors (silently corrected here), and much of it was just plot summary. In essence, "Flora" liked Chopin's local color writing, but not her portrayal of Fanny: "Mrs. Hosmer, who is the one 'At Fault,' and ostensibly the heroine of the story, leads the life of a drunken sot, and her manoeuvres and devices in securing her liquor form an ingenious by-play." Flora also voiced the kind of moral objections that dogged anyone trying to write about adult matters in the 1890s:

> While we have nothing but praise for the delineation of her characters and for the literary merits of the work — though at times the style is apparently swollen and high-sounding — we find that the love or lovemaking which existed and was somewhat continuous between Thérèse and Hosmer, to be out of place, or in other words improper. Such a feeling between the parties seems to mar the beauty of their lives which rests upon such a pure and high plane. In fact there is a contradiction between their lives when separated and when together. The denouement is a relief and a satisfactory solution of the situation.

Flora concluded that "The perusal of the work afforded us much pleasure . . . while we cannot accord genius to the fair authoress we are willing to admit that she is a lady who possesses talents of no common
order."

Kate Chopin was, in fact, a furious lady when she read Flora's review.
Her letter of objection was published almost immediately in the Natchi-
toches paper, under the headline "AT FAULT: A CORRECTION."
She began politely, but soon grew fierce:

> While thanking your reviewer for the many agreeable and clever things
> said of my story "At Fault," kindly permit me to correct a misconception.
> Fanny is not the heroine. It is charitable to regard her whole existence as
> a misfortune. Therese Lafirme, the heroine of the book is the one who
> was at fault — remotely, and immediately. Remotely — in her blind accep-
> tance of an undistinguishing, therefore unintelligent code of righteousness
> by which to deal out judgments. Immediately — in this, that unknowing
> of the individual needs of this man and this woman, she should yet con-
> stitute herself not only a mentor, but an instrument in reuniting them.
>
> Their first marriage was an unhappy mistake; their re-union was a crime
> against the unwritten moral law. . . .
>
> I ask to straighten this misconception — of Fanny having been "at fault,"
> because it is one, which if accepted by the reader is liable to throw the
> story out of perspective.

Flora's calling Fanny the heroine is a peculiar misinterpretation of
*At Fault* — possibly motivated by something other than literary criticism. Could Flora have been someone who knew Loca Sampite, blamed
Kate Chopin for the destruction of the Sampites' marriage, and saw
Loca as further put upon by being portrayed as an alcoholic, deserted
wife? (No one alive today knows whether Loca ever had a drinking
problem — only that Albert did.)

A century later, it is tempting to read *At Fault* as Kate Chopin's
musings about what she did, or did not do, as the other woman in a
hopeless triangle. But it is also possible that Chopin was simply writing
about what she knew: the differences between Louisiana and St. Louis,

and the different ways that people handle sexual attraction, in and out of marriage.

In any case, her letters to the *Republic* and the *Enterprise* did promote her work. If *Enterprise* readers, in particular, read her "Correction" as a reaction to local gossip, then they would have to buy her book.

Kate Chopin knew human nature.

On the day that her letter appeared in the *Enterprise,* Albert Sampite happened to be in Natchitoches. He was still legally married to Loca, after twenty-two years, but nine days after Chopin's letter appeared, the Sampites finally signed a document dividing their property, making their legal separation permanent. Loca received the house and land where they had lived (including two parcels known as the "Chopin tracts"), as well as farm animals, tools and equipment, furniture, a piano, and a thousand dollars.

Back in St. Louis, *At Fault* was not profitable: Chopin earned only $51 over the next two years. In her manuscript account book she did not record how much the printing cost her, but she almost certainly lost money. Still, *At Fault* had gotten her review attention, and that was the investment that launched her career.

She could never have had that kind of life in Louisiana.

# Chapter 8

## A Professional Writer

KATE CHOPIN had to learn how to play the role of professional writer.

She had always known how to be a widow, and she learned about marriage and motherhood from her mother, and from experience. Too, the rules for wives, mothers, and widows are always widely available — in magazines, newspapers, etiquette books, synagogues, and sermons. There are always people willing to tell a woman where to go and how to do it, if she wants to settle into a conventional destiny.

It is far more difficult for a woman to fit into a profession run by men.

In Kate Chopin's social class, few women worked outside the home. Kitty Garesché was a teacher, but nuns wore distinctive habits and had withdrawn from the world. Chopin's cousin Lovy Charleville had been a teacher, and Chopin's great-great-grandmother was the remarkable shipping entrepreneur. But otherwise the women of her family had, as far as anyone ever recorded, lived on inheritances and investments and the support of their husbands or children. When those failed, as they did for Chopin's grandmother, then the eldest daughter, Eliza, was given in marriage to a wealthy man.

Certainly the women in Kate Chopin's family did work within the home, administering mammies, nurses, cooks, laundresses, maids, and yard men. But the ladies of Chopin's social class did not work for wages, nor did their names appear in newspapers and magazines until the advent of society columns in the 1870s.

Chopin, though, had decided to step outside that familiar private realm. She would earn money from her work, and she would be written about, and promoted and criticized, just as men were. There were, of course, career women — New Women — in St. Louis, but most were single: the journalist Florence Hayward, for instance, proudly dubbed herself "An Independent Spinster." Sue V. Moore, formerly married, was a respectable woman who, it was explained, worked because her husband had deserted her. But there were no local women who aspired to be literary artists. When Kate Chopin began publishing fiction in national magazines, she was doing something no other woman in St. Louis had ever done.

She had to figure out everything: how to find the names of interested editors; how to ask for advice; how to produce a professional-looking manuscript. She wrote by hand, in pencil on cheap newsprint paper, but then copied her stories over in ink. Magazine editors would still accept handwritten copy, although some authors (notably Mark Twain) had been using the new typewriting machine for more than a decade.

Meanwhile, in her two leather-bound account books, Chopin carefully recorded stories she wrote, including word counts, where they were sent, and whether they were returned or accepted. But one account book (now called the Bonnell Book) has neatly ruled columns, while the other (now called the Wondra Book) has magazine names and abbreviations scrawled every which way. Evidently Chopin at first had no idea how difficult it might be to place some of her stories — and so, once she listed rejection after rejection, she simply ran out of space.

There was no one to tell her that the life of a writer, especially at the beginning, consists mostly of rejection.

She did, however, make her own rejection early in her career, when she traded a safe, middle-of-the-road American role model for an avant-garde French one. Her first literary model had been William Dean Howells, who was not only a powerful magazine editor, but the author of carefully crafted, serious novels about such problems as greed and divorce. Since he also liked romantic comedies, Chopin sent her one finished play, *An Embarrassing Position*, to him for comment — but he did not respond.

As a model, Howells had one great writing flaw: he was not very interested in the character and conflicts of women. Many of his creations are inexperienced American "girls," and his books have little or no sexual tension. That was not the world that interested Kate Chopin, and she began, she wrote later, "groping around; looking for something big, satisfying, convincing, and finding nothing but — myself; a something neither big nor satisfying but wholly convincing. It was at this period of my emerging from the vast solitude in which I had been making my own acquaintance, that I stumbled upon Maupassant."

In the early 1890s, Guy de Maupassant was considered a master writer and a thoroughly decadent Frenchman. In the United States, his collections of amoral short stories were not stocked by public libraries. But for Kate Chopin, he was a revelation: "I read his stories and marvelled at them. Here was life, not fiction; for where were the plots, the old fashioned mechanism and stage trapping that in a vague, unthinking way I had fancied were essential to the art of story making."

Those obvious mechanisms, as used by such authors as Howells, were comfortable and secure. But for an ambitious writer whose background and interests put her at odds with the American scene, the obvious structures were shackles and traps. Maupassant, on the other hand, "had escaped from tradition and authority." Chopin liked to "cherish the delusion that he has spoken to no one else so directly, so intimately as he does to me."

He spoke well. As a lifelong reader and speaker of French, Kate Chopin could appreciate the difficulty and classical grace of his simple, logical sentences. Further, Maupassant wrote about adult subjects that were not common, or even permitted, to American writers: not only suicide and madness, but also adultery, treated amorally and rarely punished. He was ironic and sophisticated, and his stories often ended with shocking twists.

He was the model Kate Chopin needed for writing as an adult — telling adult women's stories, and surprising the reader with a lack of moral judgment. It took awhile, though, for her to free herself from the creaking, well-made story.

In 1890–1891, besides *At Fault,* Chopin had written a heartwarming children's Christmas story called "With the Violin," and it was easy to place with the *St. Louis Spectator.* The *Post-Dispatch* published several of her translations from French articles, and she worked on a second novel, set in Paris, called *Young Dr. Gosse* or *Young Dr. Gosse and Théo.*

But her first story influenced by Maupassant was also her most-rejected story: "Mrs. Mobry's Reason," about a woman who — because of hereditary madness — does not want her son to marry. Chopin's readers would have understood (as modern readers do not) that she means the insanity that comes from third-stage syphilis ("the crime of my marriage," Mrs. Mobry calls it). The fact that men often caught incurable venereal diseases and brought them home to their wives was the subject of English moral reform, but it was not discussed or alluded to in American magazines

It does appear in Henrik Ibsen's play *Ghosts,* performed in Chicago in 1887 and published in English translation by 1890, but Continental dramatists often wrote about things immoral and amoral that were not allowed to native writers in the United States. Only the most sophisticated audiences presumably saw the productions — and they were not the mythical "Young Person" for whom magazines were edited.

With the tenacity that a professional writer needs, Chopin researched appropriate markets: not only the prestigious national magazines, such as the *Century,* the *Atlantic,* and *Harper's,* but also the avant-garde *Two Tales* and a new fashion-and-fiction magazine called *Vogue.* She sent "Mrs. Mobry's Reason" to fourteen magazines, got fourteen rejections, and learned the value of timing. She could sell a story that seemed at odds with tradition — but only if it had some urgent current appeal.

What opened the door for "Mrs. Mobry's Reason" was an English best seller, *The Heavenly Twins,* by the suffragist Sarah Grand, about a husband's syphilis and its tragic consequences to his innocent bride. As Chopin wrote in her diary, a woman friend thought the novel "calculated to do incalculable good in the world: by helping young girls to a fuller comprehension of truth in the marriage relation! Truth is certainly concealed in a well for most of us."

When, in 1893, *The Heavenly Twins* became a literary sensation, Chopin seized the opportunity. In the version of "Mrs. Mobry's Reason" accepted and published in the New Orleans *Times-Democrat,* the characters' names are suddenly very similar to those in Grand's novel. Grand wrote of Edith, while Chopin writes of Editha; Grand's infected husband was Mosley, while Chopin's is Mobry. Kate Chopin had discovered, evidently on her own, what is now called copycat publishing.

Still, she was not quite finished with Howells as a model. After "Mrs. Mobry's Reason," she wrote a romantic comedy about a haughty young miss who finds herself yearning after a farm hand ("A Shameful Affair"). But Chopin's imagination was also taking wing. In one of her last stories set in Missouri, "The Going and Coming of Liza Jane," a wife leaves her country husband because the novels she's read make her yearn for "higher life" (jewels, carriages, promenades). But the runaway wife is redeemed — and the story made publishable — when, after "sin or suffering," she returns to her husband for Christmas.

The market for conversion and happily-ever-after stories for Christmas and Easter was immense. It was also one of the best sources of income and recognition for professional writers. Chopin took advantage of it in 1892, when she syndicated the story of Liza Jane with the American Press Association under the title "The Christ Light" — thereby getting her name into newspapers all over the country.

Kate Chopin in the early 1890s was impatient to establish herself. She wrote quickly, sent her work wherever it might possibly be appreciated, and also entered every available contest. She did not win the *Short Stories* magazine competition (with "The Going and Coming of Liza Jane"); she also did not win the *New York Herald*'s drama competition (*An Embarrassing Position*). Her one historical story, "The Maid of St. Phillippe," was a loser in the *Youth's Companion* folklore contest.

It was also, Chopin admitted, rather a loser of a story, although it was her only use of her great-grandmother's St. Louis stories. "It is true I know little of the last century, and have a feeble imagination," she wrote in a wry essay some years later, but since she also found research tiresome, she came to an important piece of writerly self-knowledge: "a writer should be content to use his own faculty" to reach a sympathetic audience. A writer who does so "attains, in my opinion, somewhat to the dignity of a philosopher."

Chopin, though, was more of an entrepreneur than a philosopher. She was figuring out how to write what would sell. And then, with French practicality and women's wisdom, she found a unique way to create and promote her own career.

Kate Chopin had always had women friends in St. Louis, and in December 1890, they invited her to be a charter member of the Wednesday Club. Other charter members — all active, well-read, intellectual women — included Charlotte Stearns Eliot, a poet and biographer (now best known as the mother of T. S. Eliot, who was then a toddler named Tom). Hidee Remington Schuyler, whose husband William later set Chopin poems to music, was another member, as were the author-translator Thekla Bernays, and many activists from the Woman-Suffrage Association of Missouri.

They did not want another social club, but "an organized center of thought and action among the women of St. Louis," to promote science, education, philanthropy, literature, and art. By May 1891, the Wednesday Club had found headquarters in the Studio Building at Jefferson and Washington Avenues, and at the December meeting Kate Chopin presented an original essay on "Typical Forms of German Music." Other members gave reports on great German composers and sang selections by Bach, Mozart, and others, after which — according to club minutes — "some discussion followed in which Mrs. Green, Mrs. Chopin and others joined and the subject was closed by Mrs. Taussig with an analysis of the Symphony and the symphonic poem."

Evidently Chopin had thought that the Wednesday Club might be worthwhile for her career (her "commercial instinct"). But once the Club members set up a more complex structure of officers, essayists, and sections (Art, Current Topics, Education, History and Literature, Science, and Social Economics), Chopin resigned, in 1892. She needed a different kind of group. Although she liked the individual women, she shrank from philosophical discourse or politics, and made fun of people who thought she should be seeking wisdom from great minds. Once, she claimed in an essay, she did take someone's advice and "hurried to enroll myself among the thinkers and dispensers of knowledge, and propounders of questions. And very much out of place did I feel in these intellectual gatherings. I escaped by some pretext, and regained my corner, where no 'questions' and no fine language can reach me."

Certain kinds of over-busy clubwomen also irritated her, as she noted in a scathing diary entry about Mrs. Margaret M. B. Stone, a wealthy woman who directed the Modern Novel Club, to promote appreciation of contemporary novels about social problems. Mrs. Stone, Chopin wrote,

> looks like a woman who accepts life as a tragedy and has braced herself to meet it with a smile on her lips. . . . The condition of the working classes pierces her soul; the condition of women wrings her heart. "Work" is her watch word. She wants to work to make life purer, sweeter, better worth living. . . . Intentions pile up before her like a mountain, and the sum of her energies is Zero! It is well that such a spirit does not ever realize the futility of effort. A little grain of wisdom gained from the gospel of self-ishness — what an invaluable lesson — lost upon ears that will not hear.

Chopin truly preferred to be alone, to pursue her own thoughts, and Mrs. Stone and the Wednesday Club were distractions from her pursuit of a writing career. Once she quit the Wednesday Club, she also began writing stories critical of club women both in St. Louis ("Miss McEnders") and in Louisiana ("Loka").

Chopin also resented society people who did not share her serious professional purposes: "That class which we know as Philistines," she called them in her diary. "Their refined voices, and refined speech which says nothing — or worse, says something which offends me. Why am I so sensitive to manner." Then, after a man at an evening party praised a few performers for showing that "acting upon the stage can be done by ladies and gentlemen," Chopin wrote angrily in her diary: "It took quite an effort to withhold my wrath at such statement. God A'mighty! Aren't there enough ladies & gentlemen sapping the vitality from our every day existence! are we going to have them casting their blight upon art."

Chopin preferred her own company—unless she could summon up just the kind of people she wanted to see.

That meant people who actually were writers and artists and philosophers—not just aspirers or dilettantes. Through Sue V. Moore and Dr. Kolbenheyer, she came to know journalists, including John A. Dillon and George S. Johns of the *Post-Dispatch*. Both were said to be strong Chopin admirers (and both also had wives and children). She was also great friends with the *Post-Dispatch*'s exchange editor, Charles L. Deyo, a whiny, sometimes self-righteous fellow who amused her with his lack of self-knowledge. And she was getting to know such painters as Carrie Blackman and Cornelia Maury, both of whom worked intensely at their art.

Some St. Louis traditions were frustrating. As the society pages show, Chopin and her children, as they grew to presentable ages, frequently attended parties honoring socially prominent out-of-town guests, including ambassadors and actors. At dances and balls, her tallest son, Jean, was especially sought after as a dance partner. But all those were "occasions."

There was no term and no precedent for regularly scheduled social and literary gatherings in the evening in someone's home, where coffee and conversation, and both sexes, were the main entertainments. There was no American expectation, in general, that women might join in vigorous intellectual debate with men. For several generations, speakers for women's rights had fought newspaper editorials, churchly thunderings, and even hostile mobs for the right to express their opinions in public. Many a churchman and editor believed firmly and literally in St. Paul's dictum that women should keep silent in churches—and elsewhere. Women were expected to have babies, but not ideas, and the same was true after dinner in high society: women and men would retire to separate rooms, while the women gossiped and the men smoked. In the United States, and perhaps especially in the Midwest, little intellectual connection was expected.

That was not, however, an expectation among the upper classes in France. For centuries, kings' mistresses had been the hostesses for vigorous conversation, and Chopin in her schoolgirl diary had copied a definition of "Bas Bleu" (blue stocking). Through the nuns who taught her in the French tradition, she had learned that young women ought to know science and history to be their husbands' intellectual companions. Sacred Heart women were not discouraged from being smart, nor were they told to hide their intelligence.

Sacred Heart graduates were supposed to have opinions — and that clashed, somewhat, with the St. Louis belief that a lady should spend her days in polite visits. Years before Edna, in *The Awakening*, rebelled against calling days, Kate Chopin disliked the rituals and responsibilities of endless visiting, and her friend Sue V. Moore said so in a blind item published in *St. Louis Life* in 1893:

> A clever woman writer recommends a sort of social clearing house where women can pay off all their calls in one afternoon, and thus get rid of the greatest incubus a fashionable woman has to carry. The calling habit is the greatest drain on a woman's time that she has to contend with. It deprives her of half her pleasure in life — for when she is making her calls she wishes she might have it over, and when she is not making them the thought of a neglected duty takes all the pleasure out of what she may be doing. The social clearing house would be a building where all the women of a certain set might assemble at an appointed time and exchange visiting cards and greetings, thus getting the whole business over in a few hours, while under present regulations it occupies days and weeks.

Possibly Sue V. Moore and Kate Chopin cooked up, together, the idea of a salon in Kate Chopin's home. Moore, who worked in an office, had little time or household space to have regular guests, but Chopin had both. When she decided to reshape her social life, to make it more substantial, she drew upon the wisdom of her French ancestors.

We do not know when Kate Chopin, who was outwardly not a radical soul, began having her "day" at night, at a time when men could attend. We do not know whether she was a pioneer in overturning sex-segregated social gatherings, nor whether she was a gender bender at heart. But she does seem to have introduced the salon to St. Louis — and it was a valuable career move, a form of networking. Her salon was a booster club, and a support group.

Writers need promotion: it is never enough just to write a story or a book. A century ago, as today, readers were intrigued by personal information about famous people. "Author profiles" always help sell books, and Kate Chopin was a professional, ambitious author.

When Chopin published her first collection of short stories in 1894, she was the subject of two admiring author profiles: Sue V. Moore's in *St. Louis Life* and William Schuyler's in *The Writer*. Both Moore and Schuyler were frequent visitors to Kate Chopin's salon. Her friendships not only stimulated her own thinking, but they were also paying off in a very practical way.

No one, after all, becomes a professional writer without some help from experts. When Kate Chopin wanted to make an impact on the national book and magazine publishing world, she knew that she should choose her targets carefully.

There was, of course, William Dean Howells, who did send her a short note of praise for the story, "Boulôt and Boulotte," about two children who walk home barefoot rather than ruin their new shoes. Howells rarely mentored women (Sarah Orne Jewett was the exception), and Chopin may not have had high expectations.

Nationally, the other most important editor was Richard Watson Gilder of the *Century* magazine, whose contributors included George W. Cable, Grace King, Mark Twain, and Howells himself. Gilder's tastes could be studied. Like other editors, he had rejected Stephen Crane's *Maggie: A Girl of the Streets*, the tale of a prostitute, as too sordid. What Gilder wanted was realism softened by idealism, or travails that ended in tenderness — and Kate Chopin, with a great deal of ambition

Madame Victoire Verdon Charleville, Kate
O'Flaherty's great-grandmother
and first teacher

Early Portrait of Kate O'Flaherty

Thomas and Eliza O'Flaherty, Kate's parents

Eliza and George O'Flaherty, Kate O'Flaherty's
mother and half-brother, ca. 1850

Kate O'Flaherty as a ruffian, 1850s

Kitty Garesché, Kate O'Flaherty's
girlhood chum and lifelong friend

Oscar Chopin at the time of
his marriage, 1870

Kate O'Flaherty, 1869

Last Chopin house in New
Orleans, 1413–15 Louisiana
Avenue

Kate Chopin and her first four sons: Fred, George, Jean, Oscar

Chopin home in Cloutierville, Louisiana,
now the Kate Chopin Home/Bayou Folk Museum

Father Jean Marie Beaulieu,
Cloutierville village priest

Kate Chopin, the grande dame of a St.
Louis salon, 1893

Albert Sampite, Kate Chopin's
"Alcée"

Maria Normand DeLouche, Kate
Chopin's "Calixta"

Kate Chopin at the opera, probably in the 1890s

*Circle of Friends*
*(clockwise, facing page)*

John A. Dillon, newspaper editor and one of Chopin's first readers
George S. Johns, newspaper editor and friend
Rosa Sonneschein, editor of *American Jewess*
Dr. Frederick Kolbenheyer, physician, author, great talker

Kate Chopin's home at 3317 Morgan Street, where she held her salon, St. Louis (The house no longer exists.)

Kate Chopin's last St. Louis home, 4232 McPherson

Kate Chopin, sketch by her son Oscar, 1900

and nerve for a St. Louis widow who was scarcely published at all, set out to impress him.

In the early 1890s she spent three years, off and on, revising "Euphrasie," also called "A Maid and Her Two Lovers"; finally it was called "A No-Account Creole." *Belford's Magazine* had rejected one version ("Letter: too long — if I cut it — to 5 or 6,000 may prove acceptable," Chopin recorded). *Harper's, Home Magazine, Chaperone, Scribner's,* and *Cosmopolitan* all rejected it, two of them also calling it "too long." But on July 5, 1891, Chopin was vacationing at her usual rented cottage, at The Cedars in Sulphur Springs, Missouri, when she got her break. The *Century* returned the manuscript, but asked for a revision "with flattering letter."

Desperately wanting to appear in the magazine, Chopin wrote a rather fawning letter to Gilder: "The weakness which you found in 'A No-Account Creole' is the one which I felt." Then, laying it on thicker: "I thank you more than I can say, for your letter. My first and strongest feeling upon reading it, was a desire to clasp your hand." And "I hope I have succeeded in making the girl's character clearer. I have tried to convey the impression of sweetness and strength, keen sense of right, and physical charm besides."

But Chopin knew that characterization and even plot were only part of crafting a well-written — and salable — story. The last part of her letter shows a hint of stubbornness. She had omitted, she wrote to Gilder, passages "that seemed to me crude; but I made no attempt to condense the story. I knew that I could not without evolving something totally different in the effort. The thing drags lazily I know — I hope not awkwardly, and I believe contains nothing irrelevant. I trust a good deal to the close for rousing the interest of the reader if it may have flagged by the way."

At the end, in fact, Euphrasie's fiancé essentially hands her over to the other man, the one she really wants. Euphrasie lacks the spark of individuality that makes a female character interesting to read about. But Gilder was not interested in the New Woman or female notions of individuality. The writers he published, especially Cable and Twain, were not skilled at the characterization of women: most of their female characters are innocent virgins or aging harpies. Men's character conflicts, especially over notions of honor as in Chopin's story, were what grabbed Gilder. And so Chopin concluded her note: "I shall confess that your letter has given me strong hope that you may find the story worthy of publication."

Gilder did, directing his assistant on August 3 to write Kate Chopin that "Mr. Gilder thanks her for the alterations & accepts the story with very sincere pleasure — & that the publishers will send her a check before long." On that date, Chopin recorded her payment from the *Century*: one hundred dollars. It was by far the largest check she had received for anything in her short writing career.

It also spurred her to write quickly, in a great surge of energy during the rest of 1891. She wrote nine Louisiana stories in eight weeks and got all of them published, mostly in *Youth's Companion* and *Vogue*. "After the Winter," her last 1891 story, was bought by *Youth's Companion* as an Easter conversion tale of a bitterly lonely man, left by his wife, whose spirits are revived by the spring flowers and music.

But the story never appeared in *Youth's Companion*. Out of stubbornness or ignorance, Chopin included a line that was acceptable in France, but questionable in the United States. Not only does "After the Winter" state that the hero had an unfaithful wife (the first in a Chopin story), but the narrator describes her as a common type: "Then, there are women — there are wives with thoughts that roam and grow wanton with roaming; women who forget the claims of yesterday, the hopes of to-morrow, in the impetuous clutch of to-day." That sounds much more like Maupassant than Missouri — and "After the Winter" was not suitable for Americans. Although *Youth's Companion* paid Chopin, they never printed it, and eventually she placed it with the New Orleans *Times-Democrat* — as an Easter story.

Meanwhile, through 1892, Chopin kept writing steadily. She knew that Louisiana local color would sell, and in January alone she produced (and soon placed) four children's stories. Later that spring a few translations and children's stories did not sell, but by the end of the year she had new stories accepted by *Vogue, Youth's Companion,* and *Two Tales,* a Boston-based avant-garde magazine.

Then, in the spring of 1893, she decided to make a big push for literary attention beyond the markets where she was already known. In the 1890s, writers outside the literary centers of New York and Boston always had trouble getting national notice. The most ambitious writers—most of them men—moved to New York if they could. (Ruth McEnery Stuart of Louisiana was one of very few women to do so.)

With six children still at home, the youngest only thirteen, and with all the other ties of rootedness and family, Kate Chopin could not leave St. Louis permanently. (Stuart was a widow with one child when she made her move.) But Chopin could gather her forces and set out on a self-promoting journey, to push her career to a higher level.

She was, after all, the descendant of very self-confident women.

"I leave tonight for a two weeks absence in New York and Boston," Chopin wrote to Marion A. Baker, editor of the New Orleans *Times-Democrat,* in May 1893. Baker was a personal and professional friend: she knew his daughter, who was married to one of the Chouteaus of St. Louis, and his paper had, in April, published two Chopin stories: "Mrs. Mobry's Reason" and "A Shameful Affair." (Later it would publish "Good Night," one of very few Chopin poems ever published, plus five more stories.)

Mostly, though, Baker was a professional lead, and she wrote that in New York City she would "combine the business of seeking a publisher with the pleasure of—well, not seeking a publisher. I want to say, that any suggestion, recommendation, helpful hint, you might be kind enough to offer in the matter would be gratefully accepted and appreciated."

Carrying her novel *Young Dr. Gosse* and her "Collection of Creole Stories" (which later became *Bayou Folk*), Chopin happened to leave St. Louis on one of the worst days of the decade. On May 4, 1893, the financial panic hit New York City. Bank failures and trust closings were headlined all over the newspapers, along with a shocking story from New-Bedford, Massachusetts: an odd young woman named Lizzie Borden was accused of murdering her father and stepmother.

Nevertheless, in New York, Chopin managed to visit several publishers' offices, and even had a face-to-face meeting with *Century* editor Richard Watson Gilder — an extraordinary coup for a relatively unknown writer who simply came to Manhattan from the Midwest. Chopin must have charmed him with "A No-Account Creole," which he did not publish until the following January, two and a half years after accepting it. Possibly she used their meeting to nag him about it, in her quietly charming way. Her meeting with Gilder must have taken place at the *Century*'s magnificent office on Union Square in Manhattan, with its polished floors, stained-glass doors, and Turkish carpets. Possibly Chopin was even invited to one of the "at home" evenings that Helena and Richard Watson Gilder held on Friday nights for visiting writers.

Gilder not only agreed to have the Century Company read her story collection, but he also gave her the next lead: a much-needed note of introduction to Appleton's, which published magazines and books. She offered them both *Young Dr. Gosse* and the "Collection of Creole Stories," and followed up with a reminder note to Gilder. She made sure no one forgot meeting her.

In New York, she also knew at least one other expert: John A. Dillon, the aristocratic St. Louisan who had been editor-in-chief of the *Post-Dispatch* when Chopin returned home in 1884. Dillon, seven years her senior, was married to the daughter of one of the Chouteaus, and they had seven children. He was an oddly well-mannered figure in the rough-and-tumble world of journalism, and Kate Chopin probably knew his family all her life. In 1889, he had taken a chance on a new writer, when the *Post-Dispatch* published Chopin's short story, "A Point at Issue!"

A few months later, Chopin had asked Dillon for professional advice, after her 7,000-word story "A Poor Girl" was rejected by *Home Magazine*, with "Objection to incident not desirath [*sic*] to be handled," Chopin wrote in her account book. The magazine did find the story "well written full of interest" and "would reconsider if changed." Chopin did not record Dillon's reaction to the story or to the undesirable "incident" in it (whatever that was). Later she destroyed the story.

Dillon, raised as a Catholic, was much like Kate Chopin: well read and intellectual, with a keen sense of humor. He was also a progressive writer and father who wrote editorials supporting women's equality, but it appears there was some kind of rupture in his professional relationship with Chopin.

By mid-1891, the year Chopin committed herself to becoming a professional writer, Dillon had moved to New York to edit another Pulitzer property, the *New York World*. Chopin may have seen him, and his wife, on her 1893 trip, but she never submitted any material to his newspaper.

Something else may have been going on, at least according to Chopin family rumors. One niece heard that the widowed Kate Chopin had an admirer who had been the *Post-Dispatch*'s editor-in-chief. A granddaughter heard that Chopin had been romantically involved with a New York literary man, married to an invalid wife. Because of that romance — and the clues do point to John Dillon — it was said that Chopin stopped attending the Catholic Church.

But Kate Chopin had many reasons to stop going to mass. There were no traditional people in her family to push her to go, and she and Oscar, even on their honeymoon, had been lax about churchgoing. Her years in Cloutierville turned her against the church's position on divorce — and she very much disliked having priests poke about in her business.

Still, she and Dillon may have been more than casual friends for awhile — and if so, that was the only time that she let personal and professional relationships coincide, and collide. Possibly their attraction to one another was one reason he moved with his family to New York — and developed an antipathy to Chopin's writing that she described in her diary, a year after her New York trip. Her story collection had been published, and she had sent Dillon a copy, and she recorded his reactions:

Mr. Dillon has sent me a very frank and enthusiastic letter from New York after reading "Bayou Folk." He sent me a feeble note some weeks ago, a note of faint and damning praise, where he pretended to have read it. It must have been hard for him to set aside the prejudice which I know he has had against my work, and for that reason so much more do I appreciate his frank letter.

For whatever reason, Dillon's was the only reader response Chopin wrote down in her diary. She had a special concern for his opinion, but apparently — like so many men in her life — he proved to be rather a disappointment.

So, too, was Richard Watson Gilder, for the Century Company rejected her "Collection of Creole Short Stories" before the end of May 1893. So did Appleton's, and so did C. L. Webster, another New York publisher, though with some encouragement: "request to consider again next Winter if not placed by that time." Appleton's and the Arena Publishing Company both also rejected her novel, *Young Dr. Gosse*.

That was her first set of serious rejections, and the *Century* magazine never did become very hospitable to Chopin's writing. After "A No-Account Creole," she had a stream of rejections from them, and the only other Chopin stories the *Century* ever accepted are all tales of strong-willed Louisiana characters who give up their wild ways. All three — a thieving young girl ("Azélie"), a people-hating, middle-aged woman ("Regret"), and a lazy loafer ("Ozème's Holiday") — become nice, unselfish people who are really not very interesting.

From New York in 1893, Chopin had gone on to Boston, where, a biographer later wrote, "the atmosphere was supposed to be literary. She went, and after three days fled home to St. Louis." Both *Two Tales* (which soon folded) and *Youth's Companion* were published in Boston, but there are no records that she visited them. Possibly no one in Boston seemed professionally interested in her — although a year later, she did sign a book contract with Boston's Houghton, Mifflin.

From her 1893 attempts at self-promotion, the only editor who did not disappoint Kate Chopin was Marion A. Baker of the New Orleans *Times-Democrat*. He published virtually everything she offered him — possibly because his wife, the former Julia Wetherill, was also a poet, literary critic, and novelist (*Wings,* 1878) who appreciated women writers. But from the point of view of an ambitious writer, New Orleans was a regional center at best. It was not New York.

While she wrote to satisfy editors in New York and Boston, Kate Chopin set her stories almost exclusively in Louisiana. She visited Natchitoches Parish at least once a year, sometimes with her children, and her son Oscar sometimes stayed with relatives for months. He had not shown any interest or aptitude for formal education, and family members whispered that he could barely read. He spent most of his time in the attic, drawing. Much later, young Oscar became a professional cartoonist, and so for him — as for his mother — living in Louisiana at an impressionable age was part of a long creative apprenticeship.

Chopin still owned the large white house in Cloutierville, rented out to Dr. S. O. Colvin, his wife, and two daughters; she also owned some Cane River country land. That income, along with rent from the Seventh Street land she inherited from her father, meant that the Chopins were somewhat insulated from the financial panic of 1893. (She earned only $189 as a writer that year, despite selling eleven stories.)

Also that summer, the Columbian Exposition (World's Fair) took place in Chicago, and Kate Chopin had house guests bringing the latest news from Louisiana: her brother-in-law Lamy Chopin and his new young bride Fannie Hertzog, who had grown up on Magnolia Plantation, site of Chopin's story "Ma'ame Pélagie." Egged on by a Texas huckster, Lamy had dusted off an old sharecropper's cabin to exhibit at the fair as "The Original Uncle Tom's Cabin." But the display was not allowed on the fair grounds — whereupon Lamy's brother-in-law Phanor Breazeale denounced the cabin as a hoax, precipitating a long, sometimes comical family feud.

If Kate Chopin took sides, she left no trace. But for an author, everything is material, and the Chicago world's fair did contain inspirations for her own writing. Two decades earlier, Chopin had met Edgar Degas, at the dawn of the painting movement that would be called Impressionism: at that time, he and Berthe Morisot (and her sister Edma) did not yet have a name for the work they were doing. But by 1893, for the Chicago fair, the Impressionist painter Mary Cassatt had produced "Modern Woman," a gorgeous mural with madonnalike female figures — much like the form of Madame Ratignolle in *The Awakening*. Meanwhile, a group of African American women at the Congress of Representative Women protested their exclusion from the Women's Building, and spoke about the exploitation of female slaves.

When she came back from the fair, Kate Chopin wrote a story using the shimmering colors and sunny pastels of the Impressionists. Her Madame Delisle in "A Lady of Bayou St. John" resembles a painting, with "the brilliancy of her golden hair, the sweet languor of her blue eyes, the graceful contours of her figure, and the peach-like bloom of her flesh." The Frenchman who courts her is dressed for an Impressionists' boating party: "clad always in cool, white duck, with a flower for his buttonhole."

A few weeks later, on the day that *Vogue* published "A Lady of Bayou St. John," Kate Chopin wrote the story's darker counterpart — the version of the story that the black women might have told. This time Madame Delisle appears with her slave, Manna-Loulou, who washes her mistress's feet and tells her a tragic story from the old days. "La Belle Zoraïde" is about a light-skinned black woman, a slave, who is supposed to marry her owner's choice ("a little mulatto" she detests). Instead, Zoraïde falls in love with "le beau Mézor," whose ebony-black body she admires when he dances the Bamboula in Congo Square (now Louis Armstrong Park, in New Orleans).

Zoraïde becomes pregnant by him, and for her — a slave woman — Kate Chopin wrote the first childbirth scene that she ever published: "But there is no agony that a mother will not forget when she holds her first-born to her heart, and presses her lips upon the baby flesh that is her own, yet far more precious than her own." Zoraïde's cruel white mistress, though, tells her that the baby has died. Zoraïde goes insane with grief and spends the rest of her days clutching a bundle of rags and wailing, "Li mouri" ("She is dead").

"La Belle Zoraïde" was an extraordinary story for the daughter of slaveowners to produce, and it was not written in imitation of anyone else. Chopin was the first white American woman author to describe a dark black man as beautiful, and one of the first to show the thoughtless white world through the eyes of a woman of color — at a time when her Louisiana contemporaries, Grace King and Ruth McEnery Stuart, were writing about happy slaves and tragic octoroons. Possibly because she was both French and Midwestern in outlook, as well as Southern, Chopin had a habit of seeing life from many sides all at once.

She had a habit, too, of using Louisiana events for inspiration. On October 1, 1893, when a hurricane destroyed much of the Grand Isle she had known, she wrote the story "At Chênière Caminada" from her memories. Grand Isle in *The Awakening* is also the island pictured as it was before the great storm that killed some 2,000 people.

She was rather indiscreet, however, when she drew on real people she had known in and around Natchitoches Parish. She was the first writer to use the Cane River country as a fictional world, and she built it up gradually, by creating interlocking families and stories — among them the Laballières (with Alcée, who resembles Albert Sampite); the Santiens (hotheaded, gambling, drinking young men); the Duplans (sober planters); and the Padues (hardworking white sharecroppers).

Although Chopin made some of her characters Acadians, Natchitoches Parish was not, in reality, populated by them ("Cajuns" was an insult word in the 1890s). The Acadians, refugees from Nova Scotia in the mid-1700s, had populated southern Louisiana, in the bayou country, while the white Cane River country residents in northwest Louisiana were almost entirely "French" or "Creole" — descended from immigrants who came directly from France, not via Canada. Possibly as a stab at disguising real people, Chopin placed her Acadians in Natchitoches Parish — but real-life residents were not fooled.

After all, she used real people's names.

Sometimes they were innocuous, such as the boatman Coton Maïs ("Désirée's Baby"). Sometimes they were only slightly changed: the storekeeper Charles Bertrand, who guarded Dr. Chopin's property during the war, appears as "Chartrand" ("Love on the Bon-Dieu"). But in other instances, Chopin clearly had a point to make, or a score to settle. She could be both obvious and merciless.

In "A Rude Awakening" (1891), seventeen-year-old Lolotte almost dies because of her lazy, irresponsible father, Sylveste — a character everyone in Cloutierville would connect with the real-life drunken, irresponsible Sylvère DeLouche. A notorious "wastrel," the real-life Sylvère brought shame on both his wife, the wistfully beautiful Maria Normand, and his sister, the deeply unhappy Loca Sampite. By the early 1890s, his wife had left him, and in Cloutierville she was not even called by his name anymore. She was known as Maria Normand — never Madame Sylvère DeLouche.

In creating a character like Sylveste/Sylvère, Kate Chopin was not saying anything that people in Cloutierville would disagree with — yet many of them felt she was betraying their secrets. She had never been one of them, and they resented her even more as she became famous. Those who read national periodicals, or local newspapers where her visits were reported, could not escape hearing about Kate Chopin.

Meanwhile, she had a particular reason for thinking about passionate Cloutierville people in mid-1891, for Loca Sampite's legal separation from Albert had finally come through. Loca had charged him with desertion; their assets had been divided; and she was granted "the care and control of her children." Her husband did not keep up with child support (she had to sue him at least once), nor did he stop being threatening. Whenever she had to see him, Loca would carry a big black bullwhip for protection.

Albert had also taken up publicly with another woman, and set her up in a house across the horse pasture from his own adobe house. As a romantic gesture, he gave her the pretty hurricane lamp, with amethyst-tinted glass, that Kate Chopin had given him when she left Cloutierville. His new love was the most glamorous woman left in town: Maria Normand, his sister-in-law. Maria remained Albert's mistress for the rest of his life, and surviving pictures do not do justice to her beauty.

During the next year, Kate Chopin wrote "Loka," combining her grievances against club women with a rude use of Loca's name. Writing just five days after her resignation from the Wednesday Club, Chopin described the patronizing efforts of Christian clubwomen to convert a "half-breed Indian girl" to more responsible ways. But Loka stays indifferent and dull-witted, until her love for a baby transforms her.

The story fit a recognizable, salable niche, and *Youth's Companion* published it as a Christmas conversion story. But a century later, it is difficult to read "Loka" as inspirational. The young half-Choctaw woman is memorably unpleasant, possibly the only truly ugly female character in Chopin's fiction — with "coarse, black, unkempt hair" and "a broad swarthy face without a redeeming feature, except eyes that were not bad." Overall, she is "big-boned and clumsy," and even those who tolerate or want to civilize her cannot refrain from calling her "savage."

Chopin added another nasty twist for anyone in Cloutierville who might be reading the story. When Loka, in a savage mood, runs off to the woods, she wonders "if Choctaw Joe and Sambite played dice every night by the campfire, as they used to do; and if they still fought and slashed each other when wild with drink." ("Sambite" could be Chopin's slight revision of the original, or a typesetter's error.)

In Cloutierville, Chopin's choice of names guaranteed that the story would be read as a criticism of both Sampites: the drinking, violent man and the unattractive woman. Loca, whose children were sixteen and thirteen in 1892, might not have seen the story when it first appeared in *Youth's Companion,* but two years later it was published in Chopin's first story collection, *Bayou Folk.* Then every literate soul in Cloutierville was able to read, and cluck over, what Kate Chopin had done.

That story, with the use of her name, cemented Loca Sampite's opinion about who was at fault in her life. When she talked about who had destroyed her marriage, she did not talk about her neighbor, the other woman Maria Normand. Rather, she blamed the outsider: Kate Chopin.

Chopin, meanwhile, was moving ahead with her career, seeming not to care what people thought in Cloutierville. By 1892 she had been widowed for a decade, and her friends in St. Louis applauded her independent thinking. With "Loka," she evidently got a few things off her chest, and began leaving past romances and feuds behind. For the rest of her life, ambition would be far more important than adultery, and her writing career — which she pretended was a hobby — would be her truest passion.

As she wrote more, she learned some dismaying things. She discovered that she could publish stories hinting at sexual matters, for instance, but only if she placed her characters in quaint locales, and if she veiled, through vague words, what they actually did. She could write about male violence, but only if she coupled it with female self-sacrifice. And she could not sell stories in which women turned the tables, and won.

Three months after "Loka," in July 1892, Chopin wrote another story with recognizable Cane River country characters — including, for the first time, the earthy, impulsive, sexual planter named Alcée. Writing in Missouri, a month after a Louisiana flood destroyed most of the Sampite crops, Chopin included a natural disaster — a cyclone — but the story's pulse-pounding action is entirely human.

In "At the 'Cadian Ball," Alcée Laballière, hot and sweaty from field work, grabs his mother's graceful goddaughter, Clarisse, and pants "a volley of hot, blistering lovewords into her face. No man had ever spoken love to her like that." She rejects him, and then the cyclone destroys his crops. Like Albert Sampite, the character Alcée retreats into silence and heavy drinking, until his thoughts turn to other desires. He rides off to the 'Cadian ball, where his "handsome eyes" and "feverish glance" will make him the center of women's attentions.

He already has a past with one: Calixta, the hot-tempered "Spanish vixen." A year earlier, the two of them spent a mysterious, scandalous time together in Assumption Parish (in the bayou country of south Louisiana). Calixta and Alcée meet and flirt at the dance, and after awhile "Calixta's senses were reeling, and they well-nigh left her when she felt Alcée's lips brush her ear like the touch of a rose."

Calixta, however, is not of Alcée's social class, and a man more appropriate for her—the dull, clumsy Bobinôt—has been doggedly pursuing her. Before the night is over, dainty Clarisse has followed Alcée to the ball and thrown herself at him—whereupon he forgets the fiery Calixta. Sullenly, Calixta agrees to marry Bobinôt, and the ball is over.

To the sophisticated readers of *Two Tales,* where "At the 'Cadian Ball" appeared in October 1892, the story was a romantic and exotic piece of local color. It was more sensual than standard "American" stories, but its characters were—after all—French and Spanish in background, not Anglo-Saxon. When it appeared in *Bayou Folk,* however, Cloutierville readers had to know it was inspired, once again, by local gossip.

Alcée, of course, has his counterpart in Albert Sampite, and the woebegone Bobinôt can be read as the sodden Sylvère DeLouche. Calixta, the "Spanish vixen," does not look like the dark-haired, dark-eyed, French inhabitants of Natchitoches Parish: she is blue-eyed and blonde, with hair that "kinked worse than a mulatto's." Golden-haired Calixta is like no one else. She has a Cuban mother, and her Spanish blood accounts for her hot temper and "flashes of wit."

In Cloutierville, everyone would know who was meant by the Spanish vixen with the golden hair. Maria Normand was born in Louisiana, but when war began, her father had carried the whole family off to Cuba, where the adolescent Maria had a tempestuous romance with a Cuban lover. When she returned to the Cane River country as an adult, she was a lush beauty, with Calixta's "broad smiling mouth and tip-tilted nose" and "full figure." She liked to wear Spanish mantillas and sometimes posed with flowers draped into her naturally curly blonde hair.

Among her neighbors, "At the 'Cadian Ball" would be read as the story of a charged erotic relationship between Albert Sampite (Alcée) and Maria Normand (Calixta), with her settling for Sylvère (Bobinôt). But the dainty Clarisse—the woman the fictional Alcée does marry—has little in common with Loca, and no doubt there was endless speculation. Did *Clarisse* in some sense represent *Catherine?* Did Kate Chopin insert herself, or a hint of herself, in the story? And if so, what did she mean?

In the early 1890s, Chopin seemed to be holding a kind of dialogue with herself about women and men, sex and marriage. In 1892, in particular, she wrote several other stories suggesting that marriages made out of passion were dangerous to women. Some were easy to publish; others were impossible.

One that sold almost immediately was "A Visit to Avoyelles," a warning story about a young woman's infatuation. Gentle Mentine had been planning to marry the kind, clumsy Doudouce, when the town boy Jules captivated her "with his handsome eyes and pleasant speech." Seven years later, Mentine is thin and misshapen, bowed down with too many children, isolated in the country, as poor as "pine-woods people." Her husband is cruel, and "They seldom went to church, and never anywhere upon a visit." Doudouce, stopping to see her, abhors her swaggering husband and dreams of rescuing her. But he sees—as he leaves—the pitiful Mentine "gazing after her husband, who went in the direction of the field." He leaves her with her batterer.

Whether Kate Chopin was describing anyone in particular, we cannot know. The isolation, hopeless poverty, and endless childbearing were all characteristics of women she had seen, black and white, in rural Louisiana. "A Visit to Avoyelles" proved easy to place, because it fit certain expectations that were comfortable to readers: that rural areas were populated by poor, oppressed women, and that those women were too weakened by love or duty to rebel.

In New England, Mary E. Wilkins and Sarah Orne Jewett were also writing about poor rural women, and both were said to be describing woebegone women—but in fact, many of their best characters are happily single and self-sufficient. Kate Chopin admired the writings of Wilkins and Jewett, and sometimes succeeded in doing what they did: telling a radical, feminist story, but clothing it in traditionalist garments.

In "Désirée's Baby," for instance, Chopin created another cruel husband in the impulsive Armand, who falls in love like a pistol shot—

with a woman about whom he knows nothing. Although Désirée is a foundling, Armand declares that her ancestry does not matter. He marries her. But when she gives birth to a child who is not entirely white, Armand disowns them both. Désirée's adoptive mother pleads: "Come home to Valmondé; back to your mother who loves you. Come with your child" — but Désirée departs with her baby and walks toward the bayou, never to be seen again. And then Armand finds the chilling letter from his own late mother, who lived in France, thanking God that Armand "will never know that his mother, who adores him, belongs to the race that is cursed with the brand of slavery."

As in "A Visit to Avoyelles," Armand is a classic battering husband. He isolates Désirée in a home with a black roof coming down like a cowl, and he is cruel to everyone dependent on him. When he is madly in love with Désirée, he is kind to his slaves; when he turns against her, he beats them unmercifully. He makes everyone into his victim, including the silent slave, La Blanche, who is his mistress and the mother of quadroon boys (presumably his).

But one woman does talk back: Désirée's mother is the voice of maternal unconditional love, standing alone against the master's power. Like Eliza O'Flaherty when her daughter Kate was drowning in a morass of debts and scandal in Cloutierville, Madame Valmondé tells her daughter to "Come home." She loses, but she is a symbol of women's solidarity and a loving tribute to Eliza O'Flaherty.

Kate Chopin had more than one real-life model for Armand Aubigny. Her own father, Thomas O'Flaherty, was a powerful man who ruled over a large household — including a thoroughly dependent wife whom he had married hastily, and a young woman slave by whom he may have had children. "Aubigny" in its Louisiana pronunciation ("Oh-bean-ee") has some echoes of O'Flaherty, while Armand also shares initials with Albert Sampite.

"Désirée's Baby" is a shocking story, in the Maupassant tradition, but it is also very American. It fits Edgar Allan Poe's description of the perfect subject for poetry: the death of a beautiful young woman — a theme popular with Poe, Hawthorne, Shakespeare, and countless other male writers and readers who are fascinated by stories of young women dying violently. (Such stories still sell a century later in countless movies, while beautiful victims are a feature of nightly news reports as well as snuff films and pornography.) Audiences always find vulnerable women appealing, but Americans are ambivalent about women who — like Kate Chopin — are strong and self-confident.

"A Visit to Avoyelles" and "Désirée's Baby" both appeared nationally in *Vogue* and then in *Bayou Folk,* and they were undoubtedly read as local color stories, not as portrayals of universal patterns. In Cloutierville, they could not easily be linked with anyone in particular. But both batterer husbands do behave the way Albert Sampite did. Désirée's mother also does what Loca's mother did, when Loca ran from Albert's beatings: she welcomes her daughter home. Loca Sampite and Kate Chopin had never been friends, but both did love their mothers.

A year later, Chopin wrote her one hopeful story about a battered wife. 'Tite Reine in "In Sabine" (1893) also has a violent, demanding husband who has isolated her from everyone, and drawn out all her energy and spirit. But with help from a visitor — the charming, hotheaded Grégoire from *At Fault* — and complicity from a black handyman, 'Tite Reine escapes and goes home. Her drunken husband is tricked out of his wife and his horse, while the battered woman has an honorable and happy exit.

But Chopin could not find a magazine to publish "In Sabine." Unlike the others, it did not fit a conventional niche. It was not salable as the death of a beautiful young woman, nor as a portrayal of female self-sacrifice. It was too innovative — or too feminist — to be acceptable. And so Chopin finally slipped "In Sabine" into *Bayou Folk,* her first story collection, along with the other stories of battering, troubled marriages, and the like — as well as a few cheery, more lighthearted tales of country life.

After numerous rejections, her "Collection of Creole Stories" (*Bayou Folk*) was accepted by Houghton, Mifflin of Boston in August 1893. That was also the summer that the Sacred Heart nuns moved their convent to the country, giving up the old City House where young Katie O'Flaherty had played the piano, studied French, kept her notes on books and authors, been "a teller of marvelous stories" and a Child of Mary, and gained wisdom that would last a lifetime from the intelligent mentoring of the Sacred Heart sisters.

She was forty-three years old when she signed the contract with Houghton, Mifflin for the book that would bring her national fame and attention. Sue V. Moore, among others, crowed with delight. Meanwhile, in far-off Cloutierville, no doubt the news spread quickly, and perhaps a few people cheered. Others certainly shuddered.

# Chapter 9

## A Writer, Her Reviewers, and Her Markets

"TO BE GREAT is to be misunderstood," Ralph Waldo Emerson wrote, in his famous essay on self-reliance.

Kate Chopin, who had learned all about self-reliance from three generations of independent women, was a reader of Emerson, and so is *The Awakening*'s Edna. (Happily alone, Edna "read Emerson until she grew sleepy" — XXIV). And while Chopin might have hesitated to call herself "great" in public, she soon discovered a fact that is a great disappointment to all authors:

Their reviewers do not understand them.

Self-reliant and clever herself, Kate Chopin learned the basics of professional writing on her own initiative. She studied the experts, and she created in her salon a network of friends, supporters, and advisers. But the next career steps were beyond her control. Whatever happened would depend on the reading, writing, and thinking abilities of other people.

Reviewers, she found, were often enthusiastic, but nowhere near so knowledgeable as she expected. Readers were often worse. Chopin had to force herself to be gracious to those who misunderstood or patronized her writing, and when she travelled to her first writers' conference, she wound up as the center of a regional feud.

Chopin sometimes benefited, though, from other people's ignorance. When reviewers of *Bayou Folk* did not recognize the radical things that she was writing about women, they could not stop her from pushing against the boundaries of what was proper for American authors to say in print.

"In looking over more than a hundred press notices of 'Bayou Folk' which have already been sent to me," Chopin wrote in her diary for June 7, 1894, "I am surprised at the very small number which show anything like a worthy critical faculty." In fact, the worthwhile ones "might be counted upon the fingers of one hand. I had no idea the genuine book critic was so rare a bird. And yet I receive congratulations from my publishers upon the character of the press notices."

*Bayou Folk* was officially published by Houghton, Mifflin on March 24, 1894. It was a simple, beautiful volume bound in dark green and gold, $1.25 a copy, with a respectable first printing of 1,250 copies, and it gained reviews in all the major magazines and newspapers. Most of them described Chopin's twenty-three stories as local color tales from Louisiana — about which the reviewers were very muddled.

The *New York Times*, for instance, gave the book one of its longest notices (five paragraphs), but only two sentences were not weirdly inaccurate pronouncements about Louisiana — such as the claim that the Mississippi River, "like the Nile — lavish and deadly," is the people's "Medusa." Most other reviewers called Chopin's book "quaint" or "charming" or "agreeable" or all three, and praised her use of dialect, and her skill in mingling pathos and romance, humor and nobility of character. Two reviewers recognized Guy de Maupassant as her major influence; two others praised her subtlety and ability to convey a lot with few words.

The powerful *Atlantic* did give well-thought-out praise: "All of the stories are very simple in structure, but the simplicity is that which belongs to clearness of perception, not to meagerness of imagination. Now and then she strikes a passsionate note, and the naturalness and ease with which she does it impress one as characteristic of power awaiting opportunity."

In St. Louis, Chopin got the laudatory reviews she expected, as a local author. But at least one reviewer appeared not to have understood her: the *Post-Dispatch* reporter called "In Sabine" — the story of a battered wife — "full of humor."

Mostly, reviewers seemed to think that Chopin's *Bayou Folk* stories were about colorfully primitive rural Southerners, plus a couple of New Orleanians ("La Belle Zoraïde" and "A Lady of Bayou St. John"). But that was not Chopin's point of view. Like most local color women writers of her day, she was really writing universal stories about women, men, marriage, children, loyalty, and much more. She was saying very frank things about the power of men to limit and punish women. But when she set her stories in a distant, unusual locale, she deflected criticism — which enabled her to sail into print and even be praised by male publishers, editors, and reviewers in the Northeast. They would never have permitted such frank criticisms of patriarchy in their own back yards.

With *Bayou Folk,* Chopin's strategy worked to the extent that her book was published: that was her first goal. How women readers received it we do not know, since most published reviews were anonymous. We also have no diaries or letters from common readers. But virtually all the stories contained some kind of social criticism that was just as applicable to St. Louis — or to Boston — as it was to Louisiana.

Chopin had followed Houghton, Mifflin's request by bringing the "Santien boys" together for the first three stories — but theirs were not the real stories she was telling. In the first, the farmer Placide Santien gives up the young woman he loves ("A No-Account Creole"); in the second, the gambler Hector almost seduces a schoolteacher ("In and Out of Old Natchitoches"). But in the last, Grégoire, nursing a broken heart after his jilting in *At Fault,* actively helps a battered wife to escape ("In Sabine").

The Santien boys are all honorable and attractive, but the women characters are the ones who grow progressively stronger and more individualized. The first story's vulnerable heroine (created in 1888) expects to marry a man she does not love, while the second (February 1893) flirts with a gambler, then returns to a very impulsive man who has a famously bad temper. But the downtrodden heroine of "In Sabine" (November 1893) rides off alone, to a new life. The Kate Chopin of late 1893 was much more independent and self-confident than she had been in 1888 — and a contract with a major national publisher had much to do with it.

She arranged the rest of the stories in *Bayou Folk* for variety, and some are quick sketches: children hide and save their new shoes, or an uncooperative servant puts a household through great turmoil ("Boulôt and Boulotte" and "A Turkey Hunt"). But most of the stories that seem lighthearted have a serious edge — which reviewers, charmed by Chopin's style and colorful characters, seemed not to notice.

Many of the stories are about truly terrifying or tragic situations. In two stories, men's violence destroys women's lives; in another, a young girl is almost killed by her father's irresponsibility ("Désirée's Baby," "A Visit to Avoyelles," and "A Rude Awakening"). Former slaves also suffer: one survives only by manipulating her ex-master's family, while another is too frightened to cross the stream separating her from the rest of the world ("Old Aunt Peggy" and "Beyond the Bayou"). The title character in "Ma'ame Pélagie" has lost everything she cares about in the ruin of her home, while the one in "La Belle Zoraïde" loses her child, and then loses her mind. One of the few tender men, a father whose only wish is to spend Christmas with his son, turns out to be terminally senile, and the son is long dead ("The Return of Alcibiade").

The tone in Chopin's stories often seems light, as if — like Guy de Maupassant — she does not care deeply about her story, and refuses to tell readers what to think. Her characters banter or somehow cope or just fall silent, rather than sobbing about injustice. But even romance in *Bayou Folk* is more tense than sunny. Young men confuse falling in love with pity ("Love on the Bon-Dieu," "A Visit to Avoyelles"). Or the young men fall in love impulsively and tempestuously, as in "Désirée's Baby" and "At the 'Cadian Ball." Meanwhile, Chopin's young women characters may cling to men, but her stories show very few marriages, and only one loving husband (Baptiste in "Loka").

Not one reviewer noticed that *Bayou Folk*, as a whole, is an uncompromising critique of marriage. Of the twenty-three stories, seven show fathers without wives; two more have absent husbands who do not appear at all. Three husbands are brutal ("A Visit to Avoyelles," "Désirée's

Baby," and "In Sabine"), and the book ends with a young woman who is very happy to be a widow ("A Lady of Bayou St. John").

If Kate Chopin had written such stories and set them among white middle-class people in the Northeast — in a setting that reviewers could not consider florid or strange — she might have gotten damning reviews, as Mary E. Wilkins did for her novel *Pembroke,* about the iron will of a New England patriarch. Chopin considered *Pembroke*

> the most profound, the most powerful piece of fiction of its kind that has ever come from the American press. And I find such papers as the N. Y. Herald — the N. O. Times Democrat devoting half a column to senseless abuse of the disagreeable characters which figure in the book. No feeling for the spirit of the work, the subtle genius which created it.

Chopin's reviewers had the same problem. Not a one recognized, for instance, her unique treatment of domestic violence (then called "wife abuse") — a topic mostly ignored by men, but always written about by women. Among Chopin's contemporaries, Elizabeth Stuart Phelps had managed to publish, in the genteel *Century* magazine, a story about wife abuse in New England ("Jack the Fisherman"), while Alice Dunbar-Nelson wrote about an Italian-American abuser in New Orleans ("Tony's Wife"). But in both stories, the husband wins, and the wife goes off to starve or die. That was true to life, and it was what editors were willing to publish — and it was what Phelps and Dunbar-Nelson had seen in their lives. Both had had troubled and difficult marriages, but Kate Chopin had not. She had also grown up in a household of women where battering did not take place. Unlike Loca Sampite, she had never had to consider it acceptable, or inevitable, for a husband to abuse his wife.

"In Sabine" can be called humorous in that it has a happy ending — but the plot is anything but comical. The isolated wife 'Tite Reine, whose husband Bud regularly beats and chokes her, cannot even write home for help, because she is illiterate. A black woodsman does help 'Tite Reine — another surprising Chopin touch, for few writers in the 1890s dared to portray a black man and a white woman as allies.

Then an unexpected guest, Grégoire, turns up and plies Bud with free whiskey. When the brutal husband wakes up, he learns that his wife has fled on Grégoire's horse, while Grégoire has lit out for Texas on Bud's most prized mustang. The batterer is left fuming, helpless, and horseless.

"In Sabine" is the only published story of its era in which a battered wife escapes. And Kate Chopin had not finished punishing the batterer Bud Aiken. Three years later in "Ti Frère," an unfinished story, Chopin's title character is insulted by Bud and wants to "pound and punch and pummel him" into unconsciousness — and does. Bud loses his horse again.

But with "In Sabine," the battered woman's story with a happy ending, Kate Chopin also came to terms with what Oscar Chopin and Albert Sampite had meant in her life. One of them, in retrospect, was heroic. Oscar, at fourteen, had stood up to his violent, slave-owning father, and helped his mother to escape. Oscar is reflected in Grégoire's soft and generous feelings for women. Meanwhile, Bud Aiken, the wife beater in "In Sabine," not only shares one of Albert Sampite's initials, but also much of his behavior. Like Bud, Albert beat his wife so brutally that she could not work, and drove her out of her home — although Loca, at least, had been able to return to her mother's house. The fictional Bud humiliates his wife by forcing her to mount a horse that will throw her, and by claiming they are not really married — just as the real-life Albert, a great lover of horses, humiliated his wife by taking up with other women, as if his marriage meant nothing to him.

"In Sabine" can be read as a meditation on the men in Kate Chopin's life during her Louisiana years. A decade after she left Cloutierville, no longer blinded by grief nor dazzled by desire, she could see the many virtues of Oscar Chopin. But her story's most tender passage also describes Kate Chopin's own childhood among mother-women, at home and at the Sacred Heart Academy: "Grégoire loved women. He liked their nearness, their atmosphere; the tones of their voices and the things they said; their ways of moving and turning about; the brushing of their garments when they passed him by pleased him."

*Bayou Folk* not only criticizes men, but praises women, including honorable fiancées, devoted granddaughters, and loving mothers ("A No-Account Creole, "Love on the Bon-Dieu," "Désirée's Baby," "La Belle Zoraïde"). Both slave and free women treat children and old people with loving care ("Beyond the Bayou," "The Return of Alcibiade," "Old Aunt Peggy"). Women are the ones who give charity and second chances ("Loka," "Ma'ame Pélagie").

If the reader pays attention to the roles of women, *Bayou Folk* is not primarily a picture of the odd folkways of Louisiana. Rather, it portrays a world of women who are honorable, generous, kind, and just.

But not one reviewer saw any of that.

"I fear it was the commercial instinct which decided me. I want the book to succeed," Kate Chopin wrote in her diary six weeks after the publication of *Bayou Folk*. Being a successful author required promoting one's book, so Chopin set out gamely to do so. In April she read from her book for the Duodecimo women's club in St. Louis. In May she missed a meeting of her euchre (bridge) club, because "Mrs. Whitmore insisted upon having me go out to her house to meet Mrs. Ames and her daughter Mrs. Turner, who were anxious to know me and hear me read my stories."

Meanwhile, like most published authors, she was set upon by amateurs who thought she somehow knew the secret of publication. She dutifully read a manuscript written by her neighbor, Lizzie Chambers Hull, who "knows she can write as good stories as she reads in the magazines (such belief in her own ability is a bad omen)." The manuscript proved to be very wordy, the first thousand words all about "how a black girl came in possession of her name. It should have been told in five lines." The overall story — about a young woman with mixed blood who loves a white man, gives him up, and dies of tuberculosis — was "commonplace," and the writing had "No freshness, spontaneity or originality of perception. The whole tendency is in the conventional groove."

Those comments are in Chopin's diary, and what she actually told Mrs. Hull was almost certainly more tactful. Mrs. Hull belonged to the Wednesday Club, which by the mid-1890s was the most powerful of St. Louis's women's clubs, and she was also "a delightful little woman." Yet she needed to do what Chopin had done: "study critically some of the best of our short stories. I know of no one better than Miss Jewett to study for technique and nicety of construction. I don't mention Mary E. Wilkins for she is a great genius and genius is not to be studied. We are unfortunately being afflicted with imitations of Miss Wilkins *ad nauseum*."

The New England stories of Sarah Orne Jewett were also considered proper for everyone to read, while the tales of Guy de Maupassant, Chopin's own models, were too racy to be carried in St. Louis's libraries. And so, when she was among the conventional people whose approval she sought, Kate Chopin did not mention Maupassant. She passed as an American, and kept her Frenchness to herself.

But when Chopin did attend a conventional writers' conference, she found it unbearable, and said so — and found herself, for the first time, publicly attacked in print.

It was not supposed to happen that way.

She had gone to the Western Association of Writers convention in Warsaw, Indiana, in late June 1894, with her friend Harriet Adams Sawyer, a St. Louis association vice president and "harmless poet," and Mrs. Sawyer's musically gifted daughter, Bertha, "more rusé than her mother." Chopin was not on the Western Association program, which did include the young poet Paul Laurence Dunbar (almost certainly the only African American there).

Mostly, the four-day conference consisted of amateur poetry readings and papers on such topics as "The Schoolmaster in Literature," "Sanitization, Mentally and Physically," and "The Novel — Its Uses and Abuses." The *Indianapolis Journal* called the convention just an excuse for unpublished poets to "get together and pelt each other with verses."

Kate Chopin was also unimpressed, as she wrote in her diary: "Provincialism in the best sense of the word stamps the character of this association of writers." She called the members amateurs whose writings were "far too sentimental," conventional, and earnest, and out of touch with "human existence in its subtle, complex, true meaning, stripped of the veil with which ethical and conventional standards have draped it." They had, she wrote, "a singular ignorance of, or disregard for, the value of the highest art forms." She sounded very judicious and French in her pronouncements, but her conclusion was a concession to American upbeatness. If, she wrote, the Western Writers' "earnestness of purpose and poetic insights" made them into "students of true life and true art, who knows but they may produce a genius such as America has not yet known."

Until then, Chopin had confined her grumblings about other writers to her diary. She seemed to know that it was wiser not to make public enemies. Yet something chafed. Maybe it was her French background, or her Sacred Heart training, or simply a newcomer's faith — common to novices in any field — that if those already in the field would just learn a few simple things, everything could be improved. (A century later, Emily Toth in *Ms. Mentor's Impeccable Advice for Women in Academia* gave a name to that belief among people in their first year on a job: "I'm Surrounded By Idiots!")

Somehow Chopin wound up sending her diary entry on "The Western Association of Writers" to *The Critic*, a national journal which had favorably reviewed *Bayou Folk*. She got back an acceptance, a year's subscription to *The Critic* — and a lot of trouble. She had, after all, called the Western Association of Writers "provincial." They knew immediately what she really meant: "bumpkins."

Her piece appeared in *The Critic* on July 7, and it was reprinted in the *Indianapolis Journal* nine days later. It was published on the front page of the Brookville, Indiana *American* — not far from the conference site — and in other newspapers throughout the Midwest. Then the counterattack appeared in the *Minneapolis Journal* on July 21 and was reprinted, verbatim, in the *Cincinnati Commercial Gazette* a week later. But the response may have begun or ended elsewhere — for it seemed the whole Midwest was a-twitter with indignation against Kate Chopin.

The editorialist, unnamed, called her "Kate Chapin" and said she wrote "unkindly and bitterly of the Western Association of Writers, because it is provincial enough to stick to Indiana and meet every year at Spring Fountain Park." With insulting familiarity, the editorialist insisted that "Kate" was wrong: that James Whitcomb Riley, the Hoosier poet, was an Association member who did show great talent and accomplishment. Further, said the editorialist, the Western Association did have members outside Indiana, although "There is much Indiana talent in it, and Indianians are a little clannish; but the association is intended to have a wide, interstate scope, and it will probably have it in time."

The editorialist missed Kate Chopin's main points, and she did not respond. As an author who followed advanced European models, Chopin wanted to reach readers who were sharp and sophisticated appreciators of "the highest art forms." Haggling over the literary honor of Indiana was not what she had in mind.

But three days after the counterattack, while she was staying at The Cedars resort village, Chopin wrote a melancholy meditation: "I am losing my interest in human beings; in the significance of their lives and their actions. Some one has said it is better to study one man than ten books. I want neither books nor men; they make me suffer." But then she shifted to a more sensual mode: "The night came slowly, softly, as I lay out there under the maple tree. . . . My whole being was abandoned to the soothing and penetrating charm of the night. . . . The wind rippled the maple leaves like little warm love thrills."

Two days later, she had completely revived her spirits, and wrote a quirky story about a very large young heroine with a "fresh and sensuous beauty" that men find irresistible. She has a baby, and its father — who may or may not be her husband — is a poor, shabby, one-legged man with whom she goes off into the woods, "where they may love each other away from all prying eyes save those of the birds and the squirrels."

"Juanita," the first Chopin story in three years to be set in Missouri, was inspired by the life of a nearby postmaster's daughter. But it also violated at least half a dozen rules for short story writing. The heroine is not conventionally beautiful; the hero is neither handsome nor strong nor rich. There is no real conflict, but there is a distinct hint that the two young parents are unmarried (which would be called "living in sin" in the 1890s). And Chopin's last jaunty lines do nothing at all to make it acceptable: "For my part I never expected Juanita to be more respectable than a squirrel; and I don't see how any one else could have expected it."

Chopin evidently did not expect to publish the story, and it was ten months before she sent "Juanita" and "The Night Came Slowly" to *Moods,* a short-lived artistic magazine published in Philadelphia. Both were accepted immediately and published under the title "A Scrap and a Sketch," but the readership for *Moods* was either very small or very sophisticated. There were evidently no objections to her story of sex outside marriage.

Throughout 1894, Chopin was pushing her own career, trying to fit into some notion of a promotable author—while also, on her own, writing the kinds of stories that would eventually make her impossible to sell to conventional readers.

Three of the most striking were about wives. One is attracted to her husband's best friend; another is wildly happy to hear that her husband is dead; and a third one leaves, after her own death, hints of adultery that drive her living husband to despair ("A Respectable Woman"; "The Story of an Hour"; "Her Letters"). Only the third actually commits adultery—but the first clearly has it in mind.

Chopin had also begun translating some Guy de Maupassant stories, most of them about suicide, disillusionment, solitude, water, night, and illicit love—subjects that later appear in *The Awakening.* She may have chosen translation as a systematic way to study his writing; certainly her translations did not make much money. She was able to publish only three of them, two with Sue V. Moore's *St. Louis Life* ("It?" and

"Solitude") and the third ("Suicide") with her old friends, the Knapps, at the *St. Louis Republic.*

Her other Maupassant translations were simply impossible to publish in the United States, where magazines were supposed to preserve the innocence of "the Young Person." Maupassant (who died of syphilis in 1893) had written about parts of the body that did not exist in respectable American fiction, such as thighs and breasts and tongues. And he also imagined scenes where American readers could not go: in his story "Mad?", an insanely jealous man catches the woman he loves in a sexual rendezvous with her horse.

In the spring of 1894, Chopin did finally break into what was, besides the *Century,* the other top magazine of the 1890s. In late 1893, the *Atlantic* had solicited a story from her, but then rejected "At Chênière Caminada," the tale of a humble Grand Isle fisherman who worships a New Orleans belle. ("The motif has been used so much," *Atlantic* editor Horace E. Scudder wrote to Chopin.) He also rejected "In Sabine" and "A Gentleman of Bayou Têche," the story of a travelling artist who wants to draw an Acadian fisherman as an example of "local color."

Finally, just when *Bayou Folk* came out, the *Atlantic* accepted "Tante Cat'rinette," Chopin's tale of a devoted former slave. She received forty dollars, not her highest payment, but an *Atlantic* acceptance was an extraordinary achievement. Her contemporary Agnes Repplier, a Philadelphia writer, used to say that it took fifteen years to make it into the *Atlantic,* which she called "the taste of the brightest corner of the American literary world." Chopin did it in five years.

Still, "Tante Cat'rinette" is a rather conventional story, and right after she got the proofs, Chopin was moved to find something European and racier, according to her diary: "Received Copy of Tante Cat'rinette from Atlantic for correction. Suppose it will appear in September. Read a few delicious comedies of Aristophanes last night."

The next day she translated Maupassant's "Un cas de divorce," about a husband whose "strange sexual perversion" is an erotic obsession with orchids: "their flanks, odorant, and transparent, open for love and more tempting than all women's flesh." She never found a publisher for that.

Kate Chopin's self-promotion in 1894 included one other ritual now common to writers: the interview-profile. In the 1890s, flamboyant authors like Rudyard Kipling and Mark Twain made extended book tours — something that a St. Louis-based mother of six could not manage. But all authors were potential celebrities, and Kate Chopin had been virtually unknown when the famous Houghton, Mifflin brought out her first story collection.

Sue V. Moore was the first to take advantage of readers' curiosity. "Very few authors have made such a success with their first book as has fallen to the share of Mrs. Chopin," Moore wrote in *St. Louis Life* (June 9, 1894). Reviewers had compared Chopin with Mary E. Wilkins, Grace King, and George W. Cable, but Chopin had particular successes with dialect and descriptions of Louisiana life. She was once "one of the belles of St. Louis," but "has lived much of her life in New Orleans and on her Natchitoches plantation." (Readers in the 1890s liked to think of authors in aristocratic surroundings. To Northerners, "plantation" meant something far wealthier than "farm.")

Moore's profile also placed Kate Chopin into other conventional female categories: unambitious, physically attractive, and motherly. While her favorite authors, Moore wrote, were Guy de Maupassant and Walt Whitman, Chopin was not a driven, ambitious woman. She was "the exact opposite of the typical bluestocking," without "literary affectations," "fads," or "serious purpose in life." In person, Chopin "is a very pretty woman, of medium height, plump, with a mass of beautiful gray hair almost white, regular features, and brown eyes that sparkle with humor. Her five tall sons and pretty young daughter, who have all inherited from some ancestor a height and slenderness that the mother does not possess, make a most attactive family group, the beauty of which is greatly enhanced by the thorough *entente cordiale* that exists among them. They all take the greatest interest in their mother's work."

An autographed sketch of Kate Chopin in a fluffy hat, looking stern, accompanied Sue V. Moore's sketch. When the article was reprinted in *Current Literature* and *Book News,* Chopin was presented as one who conformed to the traditional expectations of women: she was devoted to her family and not serious about her work. Sue V. Moore evidently felt that was the way to "sell" her friend, but she also knew better. Moore knew that Chopin was a dedicated reviser and editor of her own writing, and that she was an eager and serious professional.

During the same time, Chopin's salon visitor William Schuyler wrote a profile for *The Writer,* but his took a different tack—one she preferred, according to her diary: "I don't know who could have done it better; could have better told in so short a space the story of my growth into a writer of stories."

Schuyler, the hawk-nosed, beetle-browed son of an Episcopal minister, was a man of many talents. A novelist and musician who studied the spirituals sung by Southern blacks, he was also one of the first Americans to admire Brahms and Wagner. At Central High School, where Kate Chopin's youngest son Felix ("Phil") was a 140-pound quarterback, Schuyler taught literature and writing, and sometimes on his way home he would stop at Chopin's house for a visit. Later he composed musical settings for three Chopin poems—"In Spring," "You and I," and "The Song Everlasting"—and in 1895 Chopin composed an affectionate Christmas verse to his wife, "To Hidee Schuyler."

Will Schuyler's profile reported that Kate Chopin had been a marvelous story teller as a girl, and "one of the acknowledged belles of St. Louis," and then a wife, mother, and widow, at which point she "developed much ability as a business woman." Schuyler was unusual in stressing Chopin's intelligence and managerial talents rather than her "womanly" attributes. In Louisiana, he wrote, she "not only straightened out her affairs, but put her plantations in a flourishing condition" before returning to St. Louis. She "learned how to economize her time, and all her social and household duties... were not sufficient to occupy her mind." And so she began to write for publication, studying "to better her style."

Possibly abetted by Chopin herself, Schuyler blithely lied about the hostile reactions she was getting in Louisiana. He wrote, instead, that "The people of Natchitoches always receive her enthusiastically, since they thoroughly endorse her artistic presentation of their locality and its population; for Mrs. Chopin is not, like most prophets, without honor in her own country."

He described Kate Chopin as "a most interesting and attractive woman. She has a charming face, with regular features and very expressive brown eyes, which show to great advantage beneath the beautiful hair, prematurely gray, which she arranges in a very becoming fashion. Her manner is exceedingly quiet, and one realizes only afterward how many good and witty things she has said in the course of the conversation."

Schuyler did touch on some things that made Kate Chopin unconventional—ideas that were no doubt expressed in her salon. Although she preferred French writers, especially Maupassant, she thought that American writers might even surpass the French, "were it not that the limitations imposed upon their art by their environment hamper a full and spontaneous expression." And Chopin herself had been personally hampered: "had Mrs. Chopin's environment been different, her genius might have developed twenty years sooner than it did."

That was evidently on Kate Chopin's own mind in May 1894, when she wrote her only surviving comment on the people she had lost. She did not want to contemplate graves, or those "mounds of earth out at Calvary Cemetery," but she did wonder: what if those closest to her had not died?

> If it were possible for my husband and my mother to come back to earth, I feel that I would unhesitatingly give up every thing that has come into my life since they left it and join my existence again with theirs. To do that, I would have to forget the past ten years of my growth—my real growth. But I would take back a little wisdom with me; it would be the spirit of a perfect acquiescence.

Had her mother lived, Kate Chopin would have been a dutiful daughter, a quiet custodian of her own property. Had her husband lived,

Chopin would have remained in Louisiana, and perhaps made peace with her disapproving Cloutierville neighbors — or perhaps not. In either case, she would not have become the center of St. Louis's growing literary colony, admired and pursued and envied.

In the mid-1890s, Chopin remained in the world of women she had known all her life, with lifelong women friends and an intense curiosity about other women — who sometimes, unwittingly and unwillingly, furnished story material. But men, for the first time, were not disappointments, and many were true friends. Some were personal admirers who also provided professional opportunities.

Still, there were things that non-authors would never understand.

Most authors lead rather dull lives, with hours alone at the typewriter or computer, or (as in Kate Chopin's case) with a stub pen, a block of paper, and a bottle of ink bought at the corner grocery store. She did have a favorite spot, she told inquirers: her Morris chair beside the window, where she could see a tree or two and "a patch of sky, more or less blue."

But interviewers, and the curious public, always want to know much more — about where writers get their ideas, and what tricks of the trade they're willing to reveal. Women writers are also usually asked, in some form: How do you combine being a woman and being a writer? — and they are expected to put womanhood first.

Kate Chopin was the subject of many such questions, which she did not always answer patiently. In an 1899 essay, she refused to answer the question, "Do you smoke cigarettes?" and turned aside a query about her children: "A woman's reluctance to speak of her children has not yet been chronicled. I have a good many, but they'd be simply wild if I dragged them into this." Some of her beloved children were away in Louisiana, Kentucky, and Colorado, she conceded, but "I mistrust the form of their displeasure, with poisoned candy going through the mails." And so, "In answering questions in which an editor believes his readers to be interested, the victim cannot take herself too seriously."

Kate Chopin did exactly that. She seriously and deliberately presented herself as a different creature from the dedicated writer she was. When asked about her writing, she was often evasive, and vague if not untruthful. While she did not write directly and exclusively to sell to a predictable market, as Ruth McEnery Stuart did, Chopin did want commercial success. And so she cut her image to suit a certain fashion — and made herself seem more nonchalant and breezy, and far less ambitious, than she actually was.

It began with Sue V. Moore's often-reprinted piece in *St. Louis Life*, with the claim that Chopin "has no 'fads' or 'serious purpose' in life; declares that she has never studied. She takes no notes and has never consciously observed people, places or things with a view to their use as literary material."

Chopin continued promoting that image when she responded to Waitman Barbe, a West Virginia poet who was writing a piece on "representative Southern Writers" in *Southern Magazine*. "I have no fixed literary plans," she wrote Barbe, "except that I shall go on writing stories as they come to me." Her forthcoming story in the *Century* ("Azélie") was "written in a few hours, and will be printed practically without an alteration or correction of the first draught."

Other observers agreed. According to Harrison Clark of the *St. Louis Republic*: "Mrs. Chopin writes fluently, rapidly, and with practically no revision." Similarly, William Schuyler reported that "When the theme of a story occurs to her, she writes it out immediately, often at one sitting, then, after a little, copies it out carefully, seldom making corrections. She never retouches after that." Her son Felix remembered seeing "a short story burst from her: I have seen her go weeks and weeks without an idea, then suddenly grab her pencil and old lapboard (which was her work bench), and in a couple of hours her story was complete and off to the publisher."

Chopin herself said, "I am completely at the mercy of unconscious selection," and that she relied on "the spontaneous expression of impressions gathered goodness knows where." Not that she hadn't tried to be disciplined, she claimed in an essay — but she always failed. "So

I shall say I write in the morning, when not too strongly drawn to struggle with the intricacies of a pattern, and in the afternoon, if the temptation to try a new furniture polish on an old table leg is not too powerful to be denied; sometimes at night, though as I grow older I am more and more inclined to believe that night was made for sleep." And so, "I am forced to admit that I have not the writing habit."

That was not, of course, true. By the time Chopin made that ironic claim, in November of 1899, she had published two novels, some seventy short stories, more than a dozen essays, reviews, and poems, and a play. She was undoubtedly St. Louis's finest writer—but she was also, still, caught between the expectations for women and the expectations for professional authors. She knew that a woman who seemed too pushy would have less commercial (and personal) success than one who was charming and self-deprecating. That, after all, was the successful strategy that Ruth McEnery Stuart was pursuing. Although Stuart performed onstage, much as a standup comic does today, she still preserved the façade of a Southern lady.

And so Kate Chopin presented herself as domestic, spontaneous, and casual, drawn to table legs and furniture polish, when in fact her house was organized around her writing life. She had her own writing room, shown in an 1899 drawing in the *Post-Dispatch*, and her wide day bed, specially made by carpenters, was furnished with deep cushions, suitable for napping, meditating, and dreaming. That process of mulling is common to many writers who seem to be spontaneous. For writers who live amid noise and clutter—including the social lives of half a dozen young adults—the creative stillness needed for ideas and words and images is often difficult to find. Writers have to develop strategies to clear the mind, and one of Chopin's was inadvertently revealed in a local newspaper.

"Kate Chopin loved cards, coffee, and a cigarette," everyone knew. Her favorite game was duplicate whist, which she usually played with her sons and their friends, but the *Republic* reported that "it is a sort of standing joke among her intimate friends to say that if they leave Mrs. Chopin alone for five minutes they'll find her with the cards spread out before her, on their return, deep in the fascinations of one of the many combinations of solitaire."

For writers, solitaire is a classic method for clearing the mind of distractions. Without requiring great concentration, solitaire shuts out the world, while its mindlessness and repetition somehow free the mental channels to receive ideas, images, and words. When Kate Chopin turned immediately to solitaire, what she was seeking was solitude — the unique ability true writers have, to be alone in company.

Another way to keep the world away is to claim that one's work is not a struggle — that it is easily tossed off, spontaneously and casually. Most of the surviving manuscripts from Kate Chopin's hand are clear copies, written in ink in finished form, making it appear she made few or no corrections. The stories handwritten in her 1894 diary were published just as she wrote them. Most manuscripts support her claim that she wrote easily and effortlessly — except for the 1900 story "Charlie," the tale of a tomboy transformed. Among the Chopin papers boused in the Missouri Historical Society, that story (which was not published in Chopin's lifetime) exists in at least two different drafts, one called "Jacques."

Still, until 1992 it was easy to believe that Kate Chopin was mostly a natural author, not a hardworking one.

But in 1992, Linda and Robert Marhefka bought an old warehouse in Worcester, Massachusetts, and began clearing out the lockers, some untouched for sixty years. In one they found a cache of fragile newsprint papers and a letter connecting them with Daniel Rankin, Chopin's first biographer. Rankin had evidently borrowed the papers from her descendants and never returned them.

The papers the Marhefkas found include portions and drafts of five known stories ("Alexandre's Wonderful Experience," "Charlie," "The Gentleman from New Orleans," "A Little Country Girl," and "A Vocation and a Voice"), a portion of an essay (now called "Misty," a draft for "In the Confidence of a Story Writer"), and two short story attempts that Chopin abandoned utterly (now called "Doralise" and "Melancholy").

The papers, now called the Rankin-Marhefka Fragments, show that Kate Chopin was far more disciplined and thorough than she claimed. The fragments are scrawled in pencil, with words crossed out and inserted. Her spelling is careless (if not atrocious), and she uses dashes instead of standard punctuation. Some fragments are so written over that they are illegible, and she would have had to copy them over, making revisions, before passing them on to a typist. The fragments show that she was a diligent reviser who thought deeply about minute changes in wording.

The abandoned "Vocation and a Voice" fragment, for instance, shows the protagonist (a nameless boy) trying to get into a monastery with other brothers. That scene is not in the final version, and Chopin may have felt — as some women writers do — that she could not write an all-male scene. Or she may just have lost interest in it. The published version, much faster-paced, cuts abruptly from the boy's leaving his traveling companions to his appearance as the strongest wood chopper in the monastery.

Chopin abandoned at least one other story with a male protagonist: the fragment now called "Melancholy" begins with a lonely man like those in the Guy de Maupassant stories she was translating. She may have felt — with good reason — that it would be a hard story to sell.

More promising was "Doralise," a fragment about a young watercolor artist who tries to sell her paintings on Canal Street in New Orleans. Like Mademoiselle Reisz in *The Awakening,* she wears black lace in her hair. But Chopin abandoned that fragment after a few paragraphs. As she wrote to Waitman Barbe, "It is either very easy for me to write a story, or utterly impossible; that is, the story must 'write itself' without any perceptible effort on my part, or it remains unwritten."

With some stories, though, she did make perceptible efforts, as the drafts show. She vacillated about characters' names, and worked on finding the exact word. At the beginning of "A Little Country Girl," for instance, she debated whether to show the little girl "polishing" or "scouring" her tin milk pail. In the story "Charlie" (also called "Jacques" or "Jack"), she struggled with how to describe the heroine's composing a poem. In the Rankin-Marhefka fragment, "Its composition had cost Jack much laborious breathing many drops of perspiration that had profusely besprinkled the sheet," but in what is probably the final draft, the text reads, "Its composition had cost Charlie much laborious breathing and some hard wrung drops from her perspiring brow."

The changes are small, but reflect Chopin's efforts to find the exact words and images she wanted for the reader. She was ambitious for financial success, but she also held herself to higher artistic standards than she was willing to admit — at least to her public.

Kate Chopin had had opinions all her life, and once she became a well-known writer, St. Louis periodicals asked her to write essays and reviews. For Sue V. Moore in *St. Louis Life,* Chopin reviewed three books in 1894, and disliked all of them for different reasons.

She thought the edition of the actor Edwin Booth's letters was a violation of his privacy (as someone who had passionate secrets in her past, she may have been especially attuned to that). She thought Émile Zola's *Lourdes* was overdone and full of that creaking, obvious, old-fashioned machinery that she had abandoned as a storyteller. Moreover, Zola's readers were never allowed to forget that "his design is to instruct us," she wrote. When a character appears to be just strolling to the barber shop, "we know better": we know he'll get a lecture about church abuses, or some other set piece that will stop the plot dead in its tracks.

She was a little more positive — or less disappointed — by the third male author she reviewed: Hamlin Garland, for his essay collection called *Crumbling Idols.* She agreed with his appreciation of Impressionism and innovation, but thought him unbecomingly angry for a young man, full of "hammer-strokes" and "clamor and bluster." She also twitted him for one of his pronouncements, that "in real life people do not talk love."

To which Kate Chopin, with all her French sophistication, responded: "How does he know? I feel very sorry for Mr. Garland."

But it was Zola, the French author, who continually irritated her. A few days after writing her review of his *Lourdes,* and after fuming about his overblown novels, Chopin wrote "A Sentimental Soul," with a hero quite a lot like Zola. She also killed him off.

Her character is Lacodie, a locksmith who spouts his radical opinions in Mamzelle Fleurette's shop in the French Quarter. (Mamzelle, another precursor of *The Awakening*'s Mademoiselle Reisz, wears a rusty black lace collar and has hair that is "painfully and suspiciously black.") Mamzelle Fleurette especially admires Lacodie when he gloats about gouging rich capitalists, for "she held a vague understanding that men were wickeder in many ways than women; that ungodliness was constitutional with them, like their sex, and inseparable from it." But Lacodie dies suddenly, of malaria. His widow soon remarries, and the grieving, adoring Mamzelle Fleurette quietly sets up an altar in his memory. She sees herself as his true widow, and is contented.

And so, presumably, was Kate Chopin—having buried Émile Zola, the incarnation of male bluster, in her own carefully contrived grave.

Rather than writing stories about men and men, Kate Chopin after *Bayou Folk* experimented with stories about women and women. She also tried crossing the color line in new ways.

Magazine editors in the 1890s, all of them white, liked stories of unequal relationships between blacks and whites—in which, for instance, the black character sacrifices for his or her "white folks." Chopin had written that kind of story with "For Marse Chouchoute," her first published short story set in Louisiana, in which an earnest young black boy loses his life carrying the mail in place of an irresponsible white boy. She also wrote about former slaves still devoted to their white families in such tales as "The Bênitous' Slave," "Beyond the Bayou," and "Tante Cat'rinette"—but such stories were predictable and unchallenging to write. Even before *Bayou Folk* was published, Chopin had been seeking new challenges. She tried one variation on the black-white devotion theme with "Ozème's Holiday," in which a young white man gives up his vacation to help a starving black woman. But that story still redounds to the credit of the white man, and the *Century* magazine was happy to take it.

Chopin's "Odalie Misses Mass" is a different kind of tale, about a white girl whose friend and "protégée" is a very old and helpless black woman. (Odalie is thirteen, Kate O'Flaherty's age when her great-grandmother died.) In the story, Odalie stops by to show Aunt Pinky her new dress, but finds that Pinky has been left alone. And so Odalie gives up on displaying her finery at church: sitting with her friend is more important. In the warm afternoon, the girl and the old woman sleep — and when Odalie's parents return, they find that Pinky has quietly passed away.

"Odalie Misses Mass," like "In Sabine," was not an easy story to place. Both are quirky stories in which women's needs come first. The *Atlantic,* the *Century,* and *Youth's Companion* all turned down "Odalie Misses Mass," and Chopin finally sent it to the *Shreveport Times* — which published it but paid her nothing.

"Odalie Misses Mass" is also written partly in dialect, which seems cloying or even racist to readers a century later, and they are apt to miss Kate Chopin's radical message. "Odalie Misses Mass" shows that women and girls can be friends across the races: Odalie does consider Pinky her best friend, and Pinky has no doubt about that. The white Odalie sacrifices peer approval — often the most important thing to adolescent girls — to take care of an older black person for whom she has no defined responsibility, except the ties of friendship. "Odalie Misses Mass" describes a warm female friendship that ignores barriers of race and age.

That is still a radical thought.

After *Bayou Folk,* Kate Chopin began seeking new markets for less traditional stories. The genteel tradition, as represented by William Dean Howells, was simply not hospitable to her vision of women. As the powerful editor of the *Atlantic* and then *Harper's,* Howells preferred "the more smiling aspects of life, which are the more American," rather than the tragic or melancholy themes treated by such Europeans as Guy de Maupassant. In particular, Howells insisted that American authors avoid "certain facts of life which are not usually talked of before young people, and especially young ladies." No American, Howells said, would write anything like *Madame Bovary* or *Anna Karenina,* novels about "guilty love" (he would not say adultery). And if an American writer tried to do so, Howells asked, "What editor of what American maga-zine would print such a story?"

The writers Howells chose to mentor did include one woman: Sarah Orne Jewett, a New Englander who wrote about women's relationships with each other. In those pre-Freudian days, Jewett's writings about women loving women, and her life with her intimate friend Annie Fields, were not at all controversial (the word "lesbian" was not used: Fields and Jewett had a "Boston marriage"). What would distress Howells and the other men of the genteel tradition was the hint, in print, of a sexual relationship between a woman and a man who were not mar-ried — or who were married to other people.

Adultery was, of course, the great, enduring theme of European, and especially French, literature. Kate Chopin, from the beginning of her career, had been skirting around the topic of "guilty love." "A Senti-mental Soul," with Mamzelle Fleurette's unspoken crush on the mar-ried man who visits her shop, was turned down by the *Century,* the *Atlantic,* and *Harper's,* as were many of Chopin's stories after *Bayou Folk.* When she wrote other stories of flirtations and desires outside mar-riage — among them "The Kiss" and "La Belle Zoraïde" — Chopin did not even offer them to the genteel journals.

Instead, she published them in *Vogue,* which was launched in early 1893 as a New York fashion, society, and fiction magazine. (The same *Vogue* is still being published today, a century later.) In the early 1890s, *Vogue* was almost the only periodical, besides Reedy's *Mirror* in St. Louis, to challenge the genteel tradition. "The Anglo-Saxon novelist," *Vogue* editorialized in November of 1894, "is again imploring the world to free him from the fetters imposed on him by the Young Person.... The pink and white — débutante afternoon tea — atmosphere in which convention says we must present love, means intellectual asphyxiation for us."

No doubt it helped that *Vogue* was a sophisticated women's maga-zine edited by a woman, Josephine Redding, who was more than a lit-tle eccentric. Possibly Chopin met her in her May 1893 trip to New York, for "A Visit to Avoyelles" and "Désirée's Baby" had already appeared in the January issue of *Vogue,* and "Caline" was published in May. Redding, another precursor of the assertive and unusual Mademoiselle Reisz, was known to colleagues as "a violent little woman, square and dark, who, in an era when everyone wore corsets, didn't." She did always wear a hat, however — even at home in bed.

For *Vogue,* Kate Chopin did not have to pretend to be unambitious, or to love housework above all things. In *Vogue*'s collage of "Writers Who Have Worked with Us" in December 1894, Chopin's picture appeared at the pinnacle, in an ethereal, contemplative pose, wearing a small black headdress. Vogue's caption praised both her brains and beauty: "MRS. KATE CHOPIN. — A beautiful woman, whose portrait fails to convey a tithe of the charm of her expressively lovely face, has been an honored contributor to *Vogue* almost from its first number. . . . Mrs. Chopin is daring in her choice of themes, but exquisitely refined in the treatment of them, and her literary style is a model of terse and finished diction."

In the mid- to late 1890s, *Vogue* was the place where Chopin published her most daring and surprising stories, those most in the French, Guy de Maupassant mold. In early issues, *Vogue* published, among others, "La Belle Zoraïde" and "Dr. Chevalier's Lie," as well as "A Lady of Bayou St. John," "The Kiss," and "The Story of an Hour." In later editions, *Vogue* published Chopin's stories about young women who grow tired and bored with men's excessive devotion ("Two Summers and Two Souls" and "Suzette"). She criticized youthful illusions about beauty ("The Recovery" and "The Unexpected"), and — odd for *Vogue*'s audience — wrote sympathetically about disabled men and poor women ("The Blind Man" and "A Pair of Silk Stockings"). Chopin even wrote about a hallucinogenic cigarette ("The Egyptian Cigarette").

Because she had *Vogue* as a market — and a well-paying one — Kate Chopin wrote the critical, ironic, brilliant stories about women for which she is best known today. Alone among magazines of the 1890s, *Vogue* published fearless and truthful portrayals of women's lives.

*Vogue*'s openness delighted Kate Chopin, but it may also have betrayed her. Because it was eager to publish her raciest stories, *Vogue* may have deluded her into believing that American reviewers — whose failings and shortcomings she knew very well — would somehow be ready for a novel about youthful illusions, excessive devotion, guilty love, and much more.

*Vogue,* unwittingly, may have deceived her into thinking that *The Awakening* would be welcome.

Chapter 10

# A World of Writing and Friends

A GIRL'S FIRST FRIEND is her mother. But for many nineteenth-century women writers, that first bond was broken much too soon. The mothers of Emily and Charlotte Brontë, George Eliot, and Virginia Woolf all died before their daughters were in their teens. Across the Atlantic, the same was true for Lydia Maria Child, Harriet Beecher Stowe, and Elizabeth Stuart Phelps. Even Dorothy Parker, born in 1893, was motherless before the turn of the century.

But Kate Chopin's mother lived until Kate was thirty-five, and unlike all the others except Stowe, Chopin had children of her own. Chopin's longest unbroken friendship was with her mother, and Kate's marriage changed the friendship but but did not end it. They wrote letters, visited for months at a time, and shared the most primal female experiences. When Kate gave birth, her mother was by her side. Eliza O'Flaherty's opinions also shaped the way Kate raised her children, which may be why the young Chopins adored their mother and never wanted to move away from home.

Eliza was also Kate's confidante in that time of confusion after Oscar's death — when Kate, lonely and dazed, fell into her romance with Albert Sampite. Eliza, the practical Frenchwoman, may have been the one to sound the alarm when she learned — if she did — that Kate's money was being mingled with Albert's. Certainly she was the one who induced Kate to "Come home . . . back to your mother who loves you" — the words that Madame Valmondé says to her beloved daughter in Chopin's "Désirée's Baby."

But one of the great tasks in women's lives is to negotiate between roots (home and mother) and wings (the outside world). Kate Chopin had spread her wings when she moved to New Orleans with her new husband — but once she gave birth to her first child, those wings were clipped. As a wife and mother, Chopin was following the common destiny of women, and did so until after her mother's death. Eliza and Kate never had the searing fight that embitters so many mothers and daughters — the quarrel that comes when the daughter spreads her wings in a way that violates the mother's views of what a woman should do, or strive to be.

Eliza O'Flaherty was never faced with an ambitious daughter who published her own fantasies and whims; who corresponded with powerful men in the Northeast; and who made enemies among provincial Midwesterners. All of that happened after Eliza's death. But Kate, raised by women, always appreciated and valued women's words, and was the kind of woman who does not discard friends.

Chopin kept in contact with her childhood friend Kitty Garesché throughout her life, while Kitty moved to different Sacred Heart schools in Chicago, St. Louis, and San Francisco (where she served on the house council with Mother Mary O'Meara, Kate's beloved teacher). Not long after Oscar's death, Kate visited Kitty for help and comfort — evidently believing that a nun, who had lived through none of the tensions of marriage and children and widowhood, still had knowledge and peace to impart.

From their beginnings in France, the Sacred Heart teaching sisters had been called "Mother" by their pupils: they knew that the relationship of mother and daughter can be the very best for mentoring and learning. Possibly there is something of Mother Kitty Garesché in Mademoiselle Reisz in *The Awakening*, when Mademoiselle, definitely older than Edna and not torn between the claims of motherhood and romance, gives advice about having strong wings, to "soar above the level plain of tradition and prejudice" (XXVII).

In May 1894, Chopin wrote her one story about Sacred Heart nuns, "Lilacs," and it was one that the sisters probably would not applaud.

Its central character, Adrienne, retreats once a year, bringing lilacs, to her old convent school outside Paris. There she becomes a girl again — sleeping in a white, pristine bed; folding her clothes neatly; and snuggling into the simplicity and peace of the nuns' routine. One particular nun adores her. But in Adrienne's other life in Paris, in a chaotic household, she is a demimondaine who feuds with other actresses and takes lovers. Evidently the nuns learn about her sinful side, for when she comes at lilac time the next year, she is told she cannot enter the convent. In the story's last image, a nun sweeps away the lilac blossoms. But Chopin, characteristically, does not tell her readers what to think.

The story does convey the nurturing warmth of an all-women's world, including the softness, rustlings, and graceful movements of women who are expressing their own serenity, and not striving to appeal to men.

"Lilacs" is longer than most Chopin stories: 4,820 words, she wrote in her manuscript account notebook (as compared with 3,200 for "Tante Cat'rinette," or 1,000 for "Story of an Hour"). But the content, not the length, made the story very hard to place. After working on it for three days in May 1894, Chopin sent it first to the *Century* magazine — which rejected it. By September it had also been rejected by the *Atlantic* and *Scribner's,* and later by five more magazines. Two and a half years later, it finally appeared in the New Orleans *Times-Democrat* (which paid just $10). New Orleans may have been the only place in the United States where a bittersweet portrayal of French nuns and their ways might reach a sympathetic audience.

A second story written a year later, "The Nun and the Wanton" (also called "Two Portraits"), shows a passionate woman named Alberta following two different paths. The "Nun" Alberta comes to her sensual adoration of Jesus through a holy woman who teaches her to love nature, but the other Alberta, the "Wanton," is sexually molested as a child, turns to prostitution, and carries a knife. Chopin drew no moral, and the story is much too sexual for American audiences. The wanton Alberta's body, for instance, is "made for love," and she knows "ways of stirring a man's desire and holding it." After three magazines (including *Vogue*) rejected it, Chopin stopped sending it out.

But her connection with nuns was always personal, not just story material. A few days after writing "Lilacs," Chopin made a convent visit to another Sacred Heart sister and former classmate, Liza (Elise) Miltenberger. There was loving nostalgia in the description she wrote in her diary: "Those nuns seem to retain or gain a certain beauty with their advancing years which we women in the world are strangers to. The unchanging form of their garments through years and years seems to impart a distinct character to their bodily movements." Liza looked almost unchanged, with the same happy eyes and delicious curving mouth, and no "little vexatious wrinkles." Liza's serene life kept her young and fresh, but as for her visitor:

> I wonder what Liza thought as she looked into my face. I know she was remembering my pink cheeks of more than twenty years ago and my brown hair and innocent young face. I do not know whether she could see that I had loved — lovers who were not divine — and hated and suffered and been glad. She could see, no doubt the stamp which a thousand things had left upon my face, but she could not read it.

Chopin came away thinking that Liza's life was a "phantasmagoria." Judging her life against another woman's, she preferred her own.

Kate Chopin also had many worldly friends, including odd relatives like her cousin Blanche Bordley, the wife of a tobacco millionaire, who fancied herself the reincarnation of Marie Antoinette. Blanche served delicious homegrown strawberries, but kept an obnoxious parrot that absolutely refused to talk when Chopin was present.("Perhaps I exercise an adverse influence upon them," Chopin noted sourly in her diary). Still, she gave Blanche three puffins as a Christmas gift in 1895.

Chopin had many card-playing friends, belonged to several clubs, and called herself a "euchre fiend." She also had friends who were mainly social acquaintances, such as Mrs. Otto Forster (the former Phil

Espenschied), who gave débutante parties that Chopin and her sociable sons (Jean, Fred, and Felix) attended. George was a busy medical student, while Oscar, an artist who illustrated his mother's copy of *Bayou Folk* with original drawings, was a rather solitary soul.

As Lélia grew older, into the late 1890s, there were also social obligations for the mother of a débutante-to-be. That may be why Kate Chopin began appearing in the society columns, after attending Daughters of the Confederacy events and meetings with visiting authors. Those were events that Eliza O'Flaherty would have understood, and they could have shared, with relish and sharp wit, comments on who wore what and said what to whom.

Eliza might also have been intrigued by Kate's friend Florence Hayward, the New Woman journalist who travelled frequently to London and sent back dispatches to the St. Louis *Globe-Democrat*. The word "feminist" had not yet been invented (it first appears in print in 1895), but Hayward was one. She supported votes for women; insisted on respect for professional women; and presented herself as both humorous and intrepid. In her assertive style, mingled with gawkiness and singular independence, she anticipates Mademoiselle Reisz in *The Awakening*.

Hayward and Kate Chopin liked to smoke cigarettes together, which was a great bond for women in the days when ladies supposedly did not smoke. Men withdrew to smoking rooms for their cigars; ladies had to find their own, often secret spots.

Still, Florence Hayward — Protestant, starchy and upright — could not have been more different from Chopin's other professional writer friend (besides the respectable Sue V. Moore). Rosa Sonneschein was dramatic, gorgeous, and full of ideas and opinions: like Kate Chopin in Louisiana, she was far too outspoken and fashionable for the people around her. She smoked little cigars; she dressed up as Rebecca from *Ivanhoe*; and she was miserably unhappy with the man her father had forced her to marry.

Rosa had moved to St. Louis from Hungary as the wife of a rabbi who soon began beating and abusing her. Both had affairs — Rosa with the president of their congregation, and Solomon with their cook. But once the unhappy couple decided to separate, after a quarter-century and four children, Rosa Sonneschein's revenge became one of the juiciest of St. Louis scandals.

In what seemed to be a generous gesture, she allowed her husband to be the one to get the divorce — as long as she got to choose the grounds. He agreed, whereupon she chose the reason most embarrassing to him: her "refusal to cohabit." Rabbi Sonneschein, outraged, said he would never admit in court that there might be a woman who would not sleep with him. But eventually, while everyone tittered, he had to relent, lest he lose his position as rabbi.

Pursued by scandal, Rosa moved to Chicago, where she founded *The American Jewess,* the first magazine by and for Jewish women in the United States, and her first gentile contributor was Kate Chopin. The story "Cavanelle," which appeared in the magazine's first issue, had nothing to do with Jewishness — but the Chopin name, known because of *Bayou Folk,* attracted other contributors and considerable interest. Later Dr. Kolbenheyer wrote a novella, *Jewish Blood,* for the magazine — and still later, Rosa Sonneschein would be the only American woman attending the First Zionist Congress in Basle, 1897. She was an ardent supporter of Zionism until her death at the age of 85, in 1932.

Eliza O'Flaherty would have marveled.

There was no old girl network in St. Louis, and friendships could be complicated for someone like Kate Chopin, whose feet were in both the public professional world and the private, home and family sphere. Chopin had many women friends who were part-time writers, including such would-be novelists as Anna L. Moss, Margaret M. B. Stone, and Lizzie Chambers Hull; amateur poets like Harriet Sawyer; and biographers like Charlotte Stearns Eliot. Chopin was the only one whose work kept her always in the public eye, and women who do unconventional things often have trouble making and keeping friends. While women enjoy each other's company, they also keep a certain coolness and a willingness to judge. In her one surviving diary (from 1894), Chopin does not name anyone as a particular confidante or intimate friend, and she hints that other women did not always trust her. In her private life, as an unattached widow who was dashing, handsome, and charming, Chopin sometimes made wives worry.

She liked to take notes on the women in her circle. Of Hidee Schuyler, wife of her friend Will, Chopin wrote in her diary: "I never saw her so attractive, sparkling, scintillant like a charged battery. But I do not *know* her, or even think I know her." Of the wife of Judge Franklin Ferriss: "a frank, wholesome woman, amiable & natural; no doubt a good friend and excellent mother and wife; with nothing of the *precieuse* offensiveness of manner to which I have become more sensitive than ever."

Chopin actually had much less interest in the men who visited her salon. Of Franklin Ferriss, for instance, she wrote "Ferriss came. I did not see him. I do not quite understand him. Have not got near enough."

Sometimes, too, she had apparent feuds with other women. She had a particularly standoffish, circling-around-each-other relationship with Carrie Blackman, who — with her husband George — ran a salon that met on Sunday nights and became the St. Louis Artist's Guild. Mrs. Blackman, a painter, struck Chopin as "a woman with the artistic temperament — woefully unballanced I am afraid. Her face is very beautiful and attractive — particularly her large dark eyes. I can understand how her husband gives offense to other women by losing himself in contemplation of his wife when in company. There seems however always an arrière pensé with her, which acts as a barrier between us."

At one point the barrier was serious enough for Kate Chopin to send Carrie Blackman a poem:

### *"To Carrie B."*

Your greeting filled me with distress.
I've pondered long and sore to guess
What 'twould express.

Ah, Lady fair! can you not see:
From gentlemen of high degree
I always flee!

Carrie Blackman's loveliness, her air of secrecy, and her paintings of women also seem to have inspired Kate Chopin's story "Her Letters," about a wife who has a secret lover. Dying, she makes her loyal husband swear to destroy, unread, a packet of letters. He does so, but is tormented for the rest of his life, wondering what secret a woman might have, that she would want to take with her to the grave.

Sometimes, Kate Chopin simply wanted to escape — and for that, she enjoyed the company of women.

"God! what a delight it was — the pure sensuous beauty of it, penetrating and moving as love!" she wrote in her diary about an excursion with twenty other women to the hills of Glencoe, outside St. Louis. She admired the blue sky, the silvery ribbon of the Meramec River, the rude log cabins, and the ruder local characters, including one who, she said, reminded her of a character in Hamlin Garland's writings.

The woman next to Kate Chopin "didn't seem to know what I meant and I was glad of it. I hadnt come to the Glencoe hills to talk literature! She is the little woman who calls me Mrs. Chovin and hasn't the slightest idea that I write. Its delicious."

Kate Chopin did sometimes hark back to her female ancestors for ideas, and perhaps more. She set her only historical story, "The Maid of Saint Phillippe," during the frontier days of her great-great-grandmother, the shipping entrepreneur "La Verdon." The story's tall, strong Maid refuses to marry her wealthy suitor, and instead strides off to live a free life with the Cherokees. "Athénaïse," the story named after Chopin's grandmother, is also about a woman's freedom: the title character is a young, unformed woman who marries an older man. She detests being married and runs off to New Orleans, where she has a few weeks of tantalizing freedom, including a platonic flirtation with the newspaperman Gouvernail (who appears later in *The Awakening*). When she discovers that she is pregnant, she returns, ecstatic, to her husband.

Marriage had not meant ecstasy to Chopin's grandmother, Mary Athénaïse Charleville Faris — who, at the time Chopin published the story in the *Atlantic*, was eighty-seven years old and staying with Kate's aunt Josephine. "Athénaïse," like "The Maid of Saint Phillippe," presents marriage as a snare for unwary young women, and it had certainly trapped Athénaïse Faris half a century earlier, when her husband abandoned her and their seven children. She lived only a few more months after Chopin's story was published, and whether she could read or understand it is unknown.

Chopin's most obvious use of the women in her family is, of course, "The Story of an Hour." Like Eliza O'Flaherty, the character Louise learns that her husband has been killed in a train crash. She is sad, and then happy to be free, and then, once her husband walks through the door alive, she is dead of a sudden heart attack. "The joy that kills," the doctors call it.

In all three stories, Kate Chopin is thinking back through her mothers, and criticizing the institution of marriage. But she also criticizes men, for not understanding what women really want, and for disappointing the women they say they love. Only the husband in "Athénaïse" even has an inkling of the need to change. As she grew older, Chopin understood more and more why the widows of her family chose not to remarry.

Perhaps because she was not seeking a new husband, Kate Chopin's relationships with men could be intellectual flirtations. Americans, then as now, tend to assume the possibility of a sexual escapade whenever women and men get together — but that was not the French tradition to which Chopin belonged. In a French salon, as in the Chopin salon in St. Louis, the value of women lay less in their beauty and more in what her friend Vernon (Bunnie) Knapp later said was characteristic of Kate Chopin. She possessed, he wrote, "every grace and talent essential to the maintenance of a brilliant social circle; brilliant in the sense of mentality and wit."

The men who frequented her circle were often slightly younger than she was, and often less worldly. Except for Dr. Kolbenheyer, most had never lived outside Missouri. When they wrote about her, it was in a tone of admiration — more like courtiers than lovers. When journalist William Vincent Byars, for instance, published a volume of poetry on the side, editor George Johns bragged that "Your little book has made a hit among the congregations of stubborn cranks who meet on our hill — I read some of it to Kate Chopin one night this week and she was charmed with the music of the verse and kept the book to try the contents."

George and Minne Johns, Will and Hidee Schuyler, and Kate Chopin had an informal social life, with amateur musicales and outdoor Sunday suppers, but Chopin was best known for her salon, her "Thursdays" at home at 3317 Morgan Street. Although Bunnie Knapp later called it a "modest home," he seems to have been participating (even after her death) in her self-effacement: the one surviving photo shows that it was a three-story mansion. Chopin liked to present herself as a modestly successful *bourgeoise* — but thanks mostly to real estate holdings, she sometimes bordered on being rich.

The atmosphere at Kate Chopin's salon encouraged performance, wit, and individuality. In a single visit, Will Schuyler might sing German and Italian folk songs, accompanying himself on the piano; praise and excoriate current Italian painters; and rave about the latest books. Byars, who with his wife had a dozen children in suburban Kirkwood, could not attend often, but when he did, he contributed his own peculiarities. A gaunt stringbean of a man and a dedicated linguist, Byars liked to declaim in Sanskrit, with "a curious kind of delighted whinny at the end of a speech." Or he might treat the gathering to the consolation of a good groan — "Ah me!" — in half a dozen languages.

Another complainer was Charles L. Deyo, exchange editor for the *Post-Dispatch*, who — Chopin wrote in her diary — had spoken about "the ecstatic pleasure which he finds in reading Plato," as well as (Robert) Browning and Walter Pater. "And when Plato begins to pall — as he will in a few years, he wonders what life will have to offer him and shudders already in anticipation of the nothingness." Chopin called it a "curious condition of mind," or "a total lack of inward resource.... Here is a man who can only be reached through books."

His self-centeredness also irked her: "Deyo talked anarchy to me last night," she recorded for July 4, 1894, not long after the Pullman workers' strike had thrown Chicago into chaos. She herself had just returned from the fateful Western Association of Writers meeting — but Deyo was apparently more interested in declaiming than in listening. He had "good reason for his wrath against the 'plutocrats,' the robbers of the public," Chopin wrote, but she felt his real grievance was ill health and general resentment of others: "He has had a pen in his hand for the past five years or more — what has he done with it?"

Deyo, evidently single, was what one called a "confirmed bachelor." A century later, acquaintances would certainly have speculated about his sexual orientation. But in 1894, the youthful, self-centered whininess, the emphasis on reading rather than living, and the general lack of purpose in Deyo's life all suggest a character Chopin would create only a few years later: Robert Lebrun in *The Awakening*.

George Johns, the *Post-Dispatch* editor-in-chief, was also a few years younger than Kate Chopin: he and Minne had married in 1884, the year Chopin returned from Louisiana. (Johns had courted Minne by leaving tobacco, cigarette papers, and "pash notes" in a tree for her.) A crusading newspaper editor in the take-no-prisoners Pulitzer tradition, Johns once called a rival editor "the head physician of a hospital for jackasses" and then punched him out. But by the time he met Kate Chopin, Johns had become cosmopolitan in behavior and literary tastes. He read Whitman, Swinburne, and French fiction, and would bring boorish colleagues to Kate Chopin's salon to civilize them. One convert was O. K. Bovard, a reporter fired from the *Globe-Democrat* for smoking a cigar in the bookkeeping room. Johns hired him for the *Post-Dispatch* and sent him to Chopin's "Thursdays," where he became a regular.

Minne Johns, however, did not.

In her youth, according to their son Orrick, Minne had been a talented soprano who smoked cigarettes with Kate Chopin and Florence Hayward, "our town's advanced literary ladies at that time." But later on, as the mother of five, Minne grew publicly very conservative. "I think sex is terrible, don't you?" she would say at dinner parties — or she would comment that no one, including her husband, had ever seen her naked body.

Kate Chopin would almost certainly have been embarrassed at that. In her eyes, neither sex nor nudity was terrible, and unlike Minne Johns or other friends who kept sordid truths from their children, Chopin flaunted them. When Thomas Hardy's *Jude the Obscure* was condemned, Chopin made a point of getting the book and leaving it out for young people to read — so that they would see that it was ponderous and boring and no great treat.

Some of her women visitors found her simply appalling.

Minne Johns did not care for books or ideas. Much like Madame Ratignolle in *The Awakening*, she made her home the center of her life, away from any dangerous or troublesome thoughts. But Kate Chopin was glamorous and, according to her son Felix, "pretty much the center of the party." Her young niece Julia Breazeale in Louisiana often heard that "Aunt Katie" was admired, and perhaps even pursued, by the editor-in-chief of the *Post-Dispatch*. After John Dillon left for New York, that man was George Johns.

If Kate Chopin had a romance with anyone in St. Louis, her son Felix suspected someone else: "Kolby had eyes for Mom," he used to say with a laugh. But Frederick Kolbenheyer, who had deep dark eyes and a prominent and forceful nose, had also been married for years to his Viennese childhood sweetheart, whose name was Agnes, and they had one daughter. Kolbenheyer belonged to the elite Germania Club, but at Kate Chopin's salon, he could orate for hours on "the ignorance, filth, beastiality of country life in Poland."

Chopin's diary notes about Kolbenheyer suggest a warm, deeply rooted affection, but not a romance: "My friend whose birthday I remembered with a little gift, a sip of champagne & 'wish you luck' looked positively a little sadder on the 31 of May, remembering that he was making his 51st notch. 'Ah, if it were only forty one' he sighed."

Chopin's first biographer called Kolbenheyer "a cordially accepted intimate friend, almost an ardent admirer of Kate Chopin" — someone whose agnostic beliefs helped draw Chopin permanently away from the Catholic Church. Whether the two were physically intimate is unknowable, but Dr. Kolbenheyer probably helped inspire the character of Dr. Mandelet in *The Awakening* — an open-minded man with a deep and sophisticated understanding of human frailties and possibilities.

"Kolby" may have been the smartest man Kate Chopin ever knew.

One other man in Kate Chopin's circle deserves special mention, for he did the most to boost her literary career in St. Louis.

Chopin had begun her salon as a social gesture, but also as a way to create an intellectual circle that would entertain and instruct her. It worked professionally, for Charles Deyo critiqued some of her early writings, while Sue V. Moore and Will Schuyler wrote profiles about her. Moore also kept her frequently in the society columns, and Schuyler set her poems to music. But William Marion Reedy was the one who — without a hint of romantic interest — was the greatest promoter of Kate Chopin's writings. As an editor, he was her most loyal colleague.

Twelve years younger than Kate Chopin, Reedy had grown up poor in "Kerry Patch," the Irish ghetto surrounding the Academy of the Visitation, where Kate O'Flaherty attended school in 1865–1866. Billy Reedy's mother had scrimped to get him through the Christian Brothers College, where he came to love Latin and grandiloquent words. He grew up with penetrating dark eyes and hands that were unusually white and soft for a man — both characteristics that Chopin gives to her newspaperman Gouvernail, who appears in "A Respectable Woman," "Athénaïse," and *The Awakening*. Gouvernail also has Reedy's calm tolerance for almost any human foibles.

Reedy's life was nothing like that of a young girl educated in the Sacred Heart Academy.

Much of Reedy's early life was a steamy, tormented war between the flesh and the spirit, and Chopin describes his struggle in her long story, "A Vocation and a Voice." Her nameless hero, born in "the Patch," is sexually initiated by a gypsy woman. Eventually the troubled young hero turns to religion to find peace—until he hears, again, the siren song of the gypsy woman and leaps over the wall.

After the turn of the century, Reedy himself published "A Vocation and a Voice" in his weekly newspaper, the St. Louis *Mirror* (later called *Reedy's Mirror*). But even when he began his paper in the 1890s, Reedy was a big, handsome, energetic man with wide-ranging tastes. Like Kate Chopin, he did not limit himself to safe writers, and he was one of the first American editors to publish Oscar Wilde, Fannie Hurst, and Theodore Dreiser, among others. He was also far too generous with money and had a weakness for alcohol and less-than-respectable companions. One day, during a binge, he married one of St. Louis's best-known madams—who was actually very kind to him, and helped him go through a cure, before their civil divorce.

Kate Chopin probably never met that Mrs. Reedy, but she knew the next one: Lalitte Bauduy, a distant cousin of Kitty Garesché's who had pursued Reedy secretly, unbeknownst to her high-society parents. Once they met and fell in love, Reedy applied to have his first marriage annulled—but the church court refused. The couple eloped, Reedy was excommunicated, and he denounced the archbishop as a "Tittelbat Titmouse Torquemada." Chopin no doubt agreed. But a woman with children who had to get along in the world could not use Reedy's style of invective. (And Eliza O'Flaherty, with her exquisite manners, would never have approved.)

Reedy, though, could use Chopin's writing and promote it. Early in her career, he reprinted "Désirée's Baby," and for Christmas 1895, Chopin sent him a humorous verse and a box of cigars. When a New York journal suggested that there be an American Academy of Letters, Reedy was one of very few editors to notice that no women were among the authors suggested. He had his candidates: "Mary E. Wilkins, Kate Chopin," and nearly a dozen others, among them Elizabeth Stuart Phelps and Alice Brown.

By 1897, Reedy was listing Chopin in the *Mirror* as one of St. Louis's "Minervas," the twenty most intellectual women of the city. Among the others were the novelist-reformer Margaret M. B. Stone, the essayist-translator Thekla Bernays, and his own *Mirror* reviewer Frances Porcher — who, two years later, would contribute to the chorus of disapproval against *The Awakening*.

Reedy genuinely appreciated women writers and saw them as colleagues, not as sexual prey. (His only recorded lapse was a rude comment on Fannie Hurst's first name, when they first met.) Reedy offered Kate Chopin some things a mother might give, in that his acclaim was enthusiastic and unconditional; he was warm and cuddly (though whether they cuddled is unknown); and he was a superb gossip.

On at least one occasion, both Kate Chopin and "Arbaces McFudd" (a Reedy pen name) made fun of the same subject: *A Society Woman on Two Continents*, a vanity press book by Chopin's former Sacred Heart classmate Sallie Britton — who now called herself "Sarah Maria Aloisa Spottiswood Mackin." Her book was full of name dropping and famous personages, and Reedy and Chopin were both, in their own populist ways, highly unimpressed.

Reedy roared in with Latinate verbiage, calling Sallie Mackin "a 'sassiety' woman in the fullest meaning of the slangology of the phrase." Only her modesty, he said, "induces her to refrain from spreading herself all over this terraqueous sphere." Her society balls he called "hot rags," and chortled over her having "so much name."

Chopin was more personal and more diplomatic, turning some humor against herself. When she heard that her former classmate had written memoirs, Chopin wrote, "I was seized with an insane desire to do likewise." When they were young girls, Sallie had often invited Kate to stay overnight, but Kate's mother never allowed it, "because Sallie was not a Catholic! And to-day, here she is, not only a Catholic, but actually receiving a golden rose from the Pope! While I — Well, I doubt if the Holy Father has ever heard of me, or if he would give me a golden rose if he had." Then Chopin grew sly in her satire, purporting to plan her own memoir: "I want to tell of interesting and entertaining things; whether I received much attention, and whether I was a great belle or not; that sort of thing. Do you remember if I ever met any people of distinction?"

Reedy was, in fact, the most distinguished — and the most raffish — literary figure in St. Louis. But Kate Chopin did once meet a visiting literary celebrity: Ruth McEnery Stuart, famous for short stories set in her native Louisiana. Stuart, a widow, was two years younger than Kate Chopin, but had been able to move to New York to build her career.

Stuart was on a book tour, entertained by the Wednesday Club, when Chopin met her during a big snowfall in February 1897, at the home of another society woman, Mrs. E. C. Sterling. Chopin's report in the *St. Louis Criterion* is both cloying and jarring to modern sensibilities. Stuart's "Carlotta's Intended" was, Chopin wrote, a tale of "marked excellence" with dialect that was "singularly true to nature." Further, wrote Chopin:

> Her humor is rich and plentiful, with nothing finical or feminine about it. Few of our women writers have equalled her in this respect. Even Page and Harris among the men have not surpassed her in the portrayal of that child-like exuberance which is so pronounced a feature of negro character, and which has furnished so much that is deliciously humorous and pathetic to our recent literature.

Chopin herself had, in fact, given up on dialect stories and "happy darky" stereotyped characters. Because she had an income of her own from real estate, Chopin could afford to be more experimental and more European; Stuart had to write for the market and immediate sales.

Their meeting was pleasant, and Chopin praised Stuart's "natural and sympathetic manner," with no sharp edges or "unsheathed prejudices." Perhaps, as a native Southerner, Stuart had the social graces that Chopin had never quite mastered when she lived in Louisiana. Chopin gave Stuart a copy of *Bayou Folk*, with an inscription suggesting a motherly, nurturing presence: "I heard the voice of a woman; it was like warm music; and her presence was like the sun's glow through a red pane . . . the voice of the woman lingered in my ears like a melting song, and her presence, like the warm red glow of the sun still infolded me."

The musical voice and the enfolding warmth were among the things Kate Chopin missed when she thought of her mother. They were also among the themes she would use in *The Awakening*, but only after an uneasy few years as a writer of intimate, untidy stories that kept many of her acquaintances on edge. In the five years between *Bayou Folk* and *The Awakening*, Chopin would move further and further away from what pleased others — and much closer to revealing some very unwelcome truths about women's lives.

# Chapter 11

---

# Night, Love, War

---

KATE CHOPIN was not a good candidate to be a best selling author, and her first publisher knew it.

Although publishing was still considered a gentleman's profession, most companies in the 1890s, as in the 1990s, were looking for blockbusters. *Bayou Folk* had sold out its first printing (1,250 copies) and another 500 were ordered, but those were not the roaring sales that Houghton, Mifflin wanted. The best sellers of the 1890s, with sales in the high thousands, were historical novels, such as *When Knighthood Was in Flower* by Charles Major, and *Richard Carvel* by Winston Churchill (the St. Louis novelist, not the future prime minister).

By the mid-1890s Chopin had given up on ever publishing her second novel, *Young Dr. Gosse and Théo.* She had started writing the 45,000-word book in 1890, not long after *At Fault,* and her story opened with a prologue in Paris, followed by a scene ten years later in the United States. The character of young Dr. Gosse may have been a rehearsal for Dr. Mandelet in *The Awakening* — or Dr. Gosse may have been female, inspired by the heroic Dr. Nan Prince in Sarah Orne Jewett's *A Country Doctor* (1884). Possibly the story, whatever it was, was too French to be salable to Americans: "As a piece of literature it does not satisfy me," Chopin later told a New York editor. Sometime after *Young Dr. Gosse and Théo* was rejected for the tenth time, she destroyed the manuscript.

*Bayou Folk,* though, had gotten national recognition and glowing reviews. But when Chopin asked Houghton, Mifflin about publishing her next story collection, she received some unhappy news: Horace E. Scudder of the *Atlantic,* who was also the editor-in-chief at Houghton, Mifflin, rejected her twice in the same letter. First he declined a story she had sent, probably "The Falling in Love of Fedora," with the comment that "You always make your scenes vivid to me, but sometimes they are of consequence, — a real story is involved — and sometimes there seems to be, as in this case, scarcely any story at all." (That was a problem Chopin would continually encounter. As she matured, editors would claim her stories did not have enough plot.) As for another story collection, Scudder wrote:

> I had enquiries made as to the success of *Bayou Folk*, and the result was not very encouraging. Yet the firm is always loth to seem inhospitable to one whom they have once included in the lists.... Have you never felt moved to write a downright novel? The chance of success in such a case is much greater than with collections of short stories.

That made sense to Kate Chopin, and she soon set about writing a "downright novel," the book that became *The Awakening*.

But it made less sense, she thought, to pursue book publication with representatives of the genteel tradition — such as Scudder, the *Atlantic*, and other gentlemen publishers in the Northeast. Instead, she turned to younger men.

In Chicago in the mid- to late 1890s, there was a burgeoning literary scene, with exciting, experimental publishers and periodicals, among them *The Chap-Book*, published by Stone & Kimball (Herbert S. Stone and Hannibal Ingalls Kimball, two recent Harvard undergraduates). *The Chap-Book*'s outstanding list of contributors included Aubrey Beardsley, Octave Thanet, Hamlin Garland, George Bernard Shaw, Louise Imogen Guiney, and Stephen Crane. Like *Reedy's Mirror*, the Chicagoans denounced censorship, and when the British Museum withdrew Oscar Wilde's books after his trial for homosexuality, *The Chap-Book* called it "an act of bigoted and blind fury."

Despite her own advanced thinking, Chopin's first Chicago overtures were also rejected. *The Chap-Book* ultimately turned down nine of her stories (including "The Story of an Hour" and "An Egyptian Cigarette") and two of her poems (which were rejected everywhere). But after Stone & Kimball rejected her second story collection, Chopin did get a contract with their friendly Chicago rivals, W. Irving Way and Chauncey L. Williams, who had become partners in 1895 to create a "Literary West" and stretch the boundaries of what could be published.

Chopin, meanwhile, had been chafing not only against local color (mostly the province of women writers), but also against the new social realism (mostly promoted by male writers, among them Stephen Crane and Hamlin Garland). Both were too limiting, she felt, because "Human impulses do not change and can not so long as men and women continue to stand in the relation to one another which they have occupied since our knowledge of their existence began."

Way & Williams agreed. Once they had Chopin under contract, they gave her new book a title that evoked for 1890s readers the most universal, timeless topic of all: sex. It was a transparent marketing ploy, exploiting the success of a current best seller by James Lane Allen called *Summer in Arcady* (1896).

Arcady (or Arcadia) was the term for a clean, rural setting, like Allen's in pastoral Kentucky — but by genteel standards, his book was not thoroughly clean. Allen, whose short stories Chopin admired, describes a young woman and man locked in a torrid summer romance, with a brooding refrain that anticipates Chopin's ruminations about the sea in *The Awakening*: "Nature is lashing everything . . . fiercely onward to the fulfillment of her ends . . . far out on the deeps of life Nature, like a great burying wave, was rolling shoreward."

Pushing at the censors, Allen shows his characters on the brink of consummating their passion in the fields — when they are interrupted by the attack of a great black bull. Despite his observing the ultimate taboo, reviewers attacked Allen for immorality anyway, in words that sound very like what would be said about *The Awakening*. Moaned one critic: "the wonder is that any author should be willing to put his time and talents upon such carnal evidences of our human weaknesses when the world is so full of better themes." But *Summer in Arcady*'s notoriety was good for James Lane Allen's career. A year later, his *The Choir*

*Invisible* was the best selling novel in the United States. Way & Williams's copycat title was the sincerest form of flattery: *A Night in Acadie*, by Kate Chopin.

"Acadie" or "Acadia" (or "Acadiana") means south Louisiana, but almost all of Chopin's twenty-one stories actually take place in north Louisiana, in the Cane River country. Some describe courtships, or devoted servants, or character conversions from grouchiness to goodness. Some are about young men who need to develop serious work habits (Chopin may have been thinking about her own sons' unwillingness to hold jobs). Some of her young male characters also try very hard to avoid adult emotions ("Polydore," "Mamouche," "At Chênière Caminada," "Dead Men's Shoes").

But Chopin was really more interested in women's awakenings. Although her daughter Lélia was nearly eighteen when the book was published, in November 1897, there are few stories about young women, and most are victims. In the title story, Zaïda loses all her spunk after provoking a fight; in "Azélie," the title character is caught shoplifting. "Athénaïse" winds up unexpectedly pregnant; "Caline" is forever dissatisfied. Lélia Chopin, if she wanted to, could read all the stories as warnings not to shape her life around the promises of men. (Or she could decide, as daughters sometimes do, that her mother was simply jealous of youth.)

Most of the awakenings in *A Night in Acadie* happen, as in French literature, to "women of a certain age," whose hearts are suddenly open to new sensations. Two grumpy independent women discover they love children after all ("Regret" and "A Matter of Prejudice"), while two other women become suddenly susceptible to romantic fantasies ("A Respectable Woman" and "A Sentimental Soul"). Not a great deal happens outwardly, for what interests Chopin are the changes in the heart, the inner growth that takes place after the fierce passions of youth have subsided. These stories are deeper and richer.

The strangest piece in *A Night in Acadie* is the title story, originally called "In the Vicinity of Marksville." Unlike most Chopin stories, which are crisp and well focused, "A Night in Acadie" seems written by committee — which in effect it was. It was the last time Chopin tried to write a story to suit a guardian of the genteel tradition: Richard Watson Gilder of the *Century*.

Chopin's story describes a proper and industrious young man named Telèsphore, who pursues the bold, impetuous Zaïda. After a Cane River country dance, he stumbles upon her plan to elope with a very drunk young fellow. The two men square off in a clumsy fist fight, which Telèsphore wins. In the original version, the bold Zaïda demands that Telèsphore marry her on the spot.

Gilder objected, and so Chopin wrote to him that she had made "certain alterations which you thought the story required to give it artistic or ethical value." In short, "The marriage is omitted, and the girl's character softened and tempered by her rude experience." In the published version Telèsphore takes Zaïda, now drooping and dulled, back to her home.

The story still did not please Gilder, and so it remained unpublished until *A Night in Acadie*. Chopin no doubt found it particularly irksome, months later, when the St. Louis *Republic*'s reviewer called the story's ending too vague, and suggested a better one: that the justice of the peace "marry Telèsphore and Zaïda, and then they might have gone home man and wife."

Authors always feel unappreciated by their publishers, and Kate Chopin was no different. Way & Williams did not give *A Night in Acadie* the distribution and promotion that Houghton, Mifflin — older, more established, northeastern — had given *Bayou Folk*. There were many fewer reviews. Few were more than a paragraph long.

*A Night in Acadie* was praised, blandly and unspecifically, for charm and sympathy; reviewers again blathered about bayous and quaintness. Of the national reviews, only *The Critic*, edited by Richard Watson Gilder's sister Jeanette, gave a serious critique, including two objections. First, Chopin's stories were "never very exciting or dramatic; there is even a slight feeling after reading about six of the stories, that one has read something very like the seventh before." More ominously: after praising the "delicacy of understanding of both man and woman" in the story "Athénaïse," the reviewer said the story was "marred by one or two slight and unnecessary coarsenesses."

Like most reviewers who complained about "coarseness," *The Critic* left readers to find the coarseness on their own — and Kate Chopin's salon friends no doubt engaged in lively speculation as to what was meant. Could it have been the husband's dirty feet? Or the wife's attraction to another man, the journalist Gouvernail (with his soft white hands, so like Billy Reedy's)? Or could it have been Athénaïse's response to her husband's kiss, once she knows about her pregnancy: "He felt her lips for the first time respond to the passion of his own"?

Billy Reedy, the one salon visitor with his own freedom of the press, was probably drawing on Kate Chopin's own opinions when he wrote about "Athénaïse" that "It is not the man she hates, although she makes the mistake that many wives do of thinking it is, but it is the institution, and so she runs away, as many other wives under the first impulse of rebellion would like to do."

Reedy also called *A Night in Acadie* "delightful" and "delicious," and especially praised Chopin's "pictures of the same old human nature that is old as mankind and as puzzling and new to-day as when the first murderous instinct awoke to life in the heart of Cain or the first grand passion of love entered Eden and sent a man and woman from thence to be the one compensation left for all that temptation had lost them."

Meanwhile, the *Post-Dispatch* called *A Night in Acadie* "a string of literary jewels," and the *Hesperian,* an elite literary journal, praised Chopin's "vein of quiet humor," with insight "more femininely subtle" than that of George W. Cable.

The jarring note was the *Globe-Democrat* reviewer, who rambled on about Creoles and Acadians, bayous and flowers, and concluded with the kind of mistake that comes from either carelessness or spite. Although Chopin's character Mamouche is identified as white on the story's first page, the *Globe-Democrat* called him "a mischievous little darky given to all sorts of pranks and tricks." The *Globe-Democrat* was clearly pigeonholing Kate Chopin as another mindless writer about "happy darky" characters in the quaint land of Louisiana.

Two weeks later the *Post-Dispatch* fired back with a courtly, even flirtatious review of *A Night in Acadie,* probably by Chopin's friend Charles L. Deyo. In two full columns, the reviewer praised Chopin's stories as both intellectual and artistic, and then went on to praise and flatter Chopin herself: "modern, universal and untrammeled by convention," and also—in person—something of a "rogue in porcelain," flashing her witty, provocative, and advanced opinions "right into the face of Philistia."

The reviewer's favorite example was a line from "Athénaïse": "But for all his 'advanced' opinions Gouvernail was a liberal-minded fellow; a man or woman lost nothing of his respect by being married."

"Now what may she mean by that?" asked the reviewer, and then concluded, with a smug wink, "the 'rogue' will never tell you."

What she had probably told her salon, already, was that her new novel would be her most striking critique of the institution of marriage. In March 1898, after a suggestion from Richard Watson Gilder, Chopin traveled to Chicago in a futile search for a literary agent. By then Way & Williams had accepted *A Solitary Soul,* later called *The Awakening,* and in April they also accepted her third story collection, *A Vocation and a Voice.* She had a regular publisher at last.

But she had also made enemies in St. Louis. They were behind the nasty review in the *Globe-Democrat* and the festering local animosity toward Kate Chopin.

Earlier in 1897, before *A Night in Acadie* appeared, Chopin had published two rather wicked stories under a pen name: "The Falling in Love of Fedora" and "Miss McEnders." Both appeared under the name "La Tour" in the *St. Louis Criterion,* successor to *St. Louis Life,* while Chopin—under her own name—was publishing a series of six chatty essays in the same periodical. Sue V. Moore as editor had been replaced by a retired schoolteacher named Grace Davidson, whose editor-in-chief was

Henri Dumay, a mysterious Frenchman considered — by Billy Reedy — to be a bit of a charlatan. (Reedy once called Dumay, who translated Chopin's "Story of an Hour" into French for no apparent reason, a self-appointed "intimate advisor of God").

Chopin's "Fedora" story is an odd one, about a stereotypical spinster character who disdains younger people. But one summer at a resort (always a dangerous spot in Chopin stories), Fedora is suddenly attracted to one Malthers, who has grown into being a fine young man. Under the spell of her infatuation, Fedora fetches Malthers's sister at the train station, plants a deep kiss firmly on the sister's mouth — and then drives home.

Readers a century later have debated whether it can be called a lesbian story, or a displaced crush. But Chopin, who had some trouble placing it, may have used a pen name because it resembled too closely a real-life incident. Maybe a woman who admired one of Lélia Chopin's brothers had decided to kiss Lélia instead — which would have been most annoying.

Why Chopin used a pseudonym is clearer with "Miss McEnders." She wrote the story in 1892, not long after resigning from the Wednesday Club, and the story criticizes social reformers through the character of Miss Georgie McEnders — a rich young woman who makes a point of not wearing expensive jewelry to her many committees to help factory girls, social betterment, and the like. But when faced with a social crisis closer to home — her seamstress is pregnant, with no husband — Miss McEnders fires the woman immediately. The seamstress's revenge is to ask provocative questions, including: how did Miss McEnders's father really get his money? Before the story ends, Miss McEnders learns that her father made his money illegally, in the Whisky Ring scandal.

What made the story unpublishable for years was its very obvious reference. The man who made the greatest profit from the Whisky Ring scandal in St. Louis was William McKee ("McE"), editor of the *Globe-Democrat*. He served a few months in jail, and physically resembled the fictional Miss McEnders's father — with closely cropped sideburns, thin lips, and shrewd eyes. By the time Chopin wrote her story, William McKee was dead — but his daughter Ellen, a social reformer who made a point of never wearing expensive jewelry, was very much alive.

The story languished for years, and then suddenly appeared in the March 6, 1897 *St. Louis Criterion* — which was bankrolled by none other than Ellen McKee, who also owned a controlling interest in the *Globe-Democrat*. How it came about, we cannot know, but Billy Reedy gleefully spilled the beans in his paper. Ellen McKee, he wrote,

> is devoted to charities of all kinds, including the maintenance of fashionable weeklies, and there can be no doubt that "The Criterion"'s story was a satire upon the person whose money gives it life. The publication of the tale is a splendid example of biting the hand that feeds, for it is impossible that anyone who read the story should have been ignorant of the purpose of the recital. It is said that "The Criterion"'s patroness has been terribly wounded by the fiction feature of last week, and that she has been unable thus far to bring herself to believe the "explanation": that the story was not intended to mock her philanthropic tastes and revile her father's memory.

Reedy did not unmask Kate Chopin as "La Tour," at least in print, although it must have been an open secret in St. Louis. Six months later, Ellen McKee abruptly moved *The Criterion* to New York, where Reedy wrote that it became even more noted for "priggish dullness."

Meanwhile Kate Chopin, whatever her reasons for attacking Ellen McKee in print, was probably chastened by the *Globe-Democrat*'s hostile review. It was not a good professional strategy for an author to offend potential reviewers, or to antagonize the powerful owners of publications.

After the "La Tour" stories, Chopin did stop writing about recognizable local characters, with one exception: the one St. Louis man whose reputation was so bad that he could hardly sue or complain, no matter what Kate Chopin wrote. And so her bombastic and raffish friend, Billy Reedy, the man who could not keep a secret, became the center of her story, "A Vocation and a Voice."

Meanwhile, many St. Louis audiences were eager to know more about what Kate Chopin thought. In the spring of 1898, the *Post-Dispatch* printed her opinions on two subjects: "Has High Society Struck the Pace that Kills?" and "Is Love Divine?"

The first question, inspired by several young belles' suicides around the country, got a rather testy answer from Kate Chopin, who was just then making the rounds among high society receptions, teas, and débutante parties. Of society, she said, "It is a good thing for women who have no other occupation to engage in it and endeavor to keep up with the social whirl." It could prevent women from becoming "morbid" through inactivity. And "Business men commit suicide every day, yet we do not say that suicide is epidemic in the business world." The "mere reading of a peculiar case of suicide may cause a highly nervous woman to take her own life in a similar manner, through morbid sympathy," she acknowledged. "But do not men do the same thing every day? Why all this talk about women?"

*Post-Dispatch* readers could not know, of course, that she had just written a novel in which a society woman appears to commit suicide. But with Chopin's answer to the question, "Is Love Divine?" readers got a glimpse into that very novel:

> It is as difficult to distinguish between the divine love and the natural, animal love, as it is to explain just why we love at all. In a discussion of this character between two women in my new novel I have made my heroine say: "Why do I love this man? Is it because his hair is brown, growing high on his temples; because his eyes droop a bit at the corners, or because his nose is just so much out of drawing?"

(In the published version of *The Awakening*, the words are somewhat different, showing that Chopin did revise. In chapter XXVI, Mademoiselle Reisz asks Edna why she loves Robert, and Edna replies: "Why? Because his hair is brown and grows away from his temples; because he opens and shuts his eyes, and his nose is a little out of drawing.")

Fifteen months before *The Awakening* was to appear, Chopin had more to say, and her *Post-Dispatch* answer is the only statement of her personal beliefs about love.

One really never knows the exact, definite thing which excites love for any one person, and one can never truly know whether this love is the result of circumstances or whether it is predestination. I am inclined to think that love springs from animal instinct, and therefore is, in a measure, divine. One can never resolve to love this man, this woman or child, and then carry out the resolution unless one feels irresistibly drawn by an indefinable current of magnetism. The subject allows an immense field for discussion and profound thought, and one could scarcely voice a definite opinion in a ten minutes talk. But I am sure we all feel that love — true, pure love, is an uncontrollable emotion that allows of no analyzation and no vivisection.

But before *The Awakening* could appear, and readers could see what Kate Chopin had written about animal desire and much more, the outside world, the men's world, intruded as it had three decades earlier — with war.

By the late 1890s, Kate Chopin was an established writer in St. Louis, where she had spent three-quarters of her life. Although a century later she would be called a Southern writer, she was actually a true daughter of the Midwest. Her salon gave her the intellectual stimulation and creative encouragement that she needed, while her card clubs let her enjoy friendly rivalry and gossip with women. She attended the opera regularly, kept up with the latest scientific developments (including mental telepathy), and liked to read, in French, the newest fiction from "the land where the modern holds sway."

Her children were thriving, and each of her sons had a social niche. Jean was the best dancer; Oscar, the best artist; George ("Doc"), the smartest; Fred, the most popular and most musical; and Felix ("Phil"), the best athlete. Lélia was developing into a tall, beautiful young woman with a dramatic presence and strong opinions which sometimes clashed with her mother's.

Possibly a clash of wills led them to cut short a visit to Natchitoches Parish in the summer of 1897. Kate and Lélia had planned to stay for several months with Kate's sister-in-law Eugénie at Derry, but they headed back to St. Louis after only two weeks. Possibly neither could handle the Louisiana heat anymore, without electric fans (rural Louisiana did not yet have electricity). Or maybe Lélia, who later put on public tantrums over restaurant food, was already rehearsing her finicky princess behavior. Or possibly Kate, a solitary soul by nature, found living closely with great numbers of people too tiring. ("She was, in many ways, a lone wolf," her son Felix remembered.)

Writers are people who need quiet and solitude. Even in St. Louis, Chopin had a habit of coming late to social gatherings or leaving early or missing them entirely and sending apologetic notes. But Louisiana was still her best source for salable inspiration. There is a bit of Kate Chopin in the title character's claim in "A Lady of Bayou St. John": "I have memories, memories to crowd and fill my life, if I live a hundred years!"

Still, they were just memories. By 1898, it had been fourteen years since she moved back to her mother's house. She had buried her mother and grandmother and created herself in a new form. Like Edna in her forthcoming novel, she had become "like some new-born creature, opening its eyes in a familiar world that it had never known" (XXXIX). She was no longer the harried mother and dashing widow she had been in the South.

Chopin still visited the Cane River country at least once a year, staying with in-laws in Natchitoches or on the plantation in Derry. Her arrival always meant celebrations and excitement, including whist parties, teas, musicales, and gatherings with interesting women. There was, for instance, Chopin's relative-by-marriage Camilla Lachs Breazeale, the tall, eccentrically-dressed editor of the *Natchitoches Enterprise*. Camilla was Jewish (rare in Natchitoches), and was also district chair of the Woman Suffrage Party of Louisiana, which by 1898 had gotten Louisiana women a limited voting right.

On one visit, Camilla's daughters, deputed to serve tea to Kate Chopin, could not contain their "awe and wonderment." The visiting author was so glamorous and exotic that some people did not want their impressionable children to see her, and everyone compared notes on sly things she had done. Once, when a conservative local minister called while she was playing cards, Chopin deftly concealed the cards on her lap while chatting with him about pious and innocuous topics. The minute he departed, she grabbed her cards and resumed the game.

When the Breazeale daughters finally caught a glimpse of her, Aunt Katie was smoking, with her legs crossed, and occasionally even swinging her foot jauntily in the air. At least one niece thought she was wearing a wig. And it was whispered that, in far-off St. Louis, Aunt Katie would smoke big black cigars and greet guests from her bathtub.

During her visits, Chopin had less and less to do with the adventures and intrigues of people around Cloutierville, and many of them were pleased about that. A copy of *Bayou Folk,* annotated with the names of people who thought they were in it, circulated for years, until it finally disappeared from the school library. *A Night in Acadie,* though, created less of a stir — perhaps because it has fewer wicked or sensual characters.

What did create a stir — and fear for mothers everywhere — was the sudden outbreak of war in February 1898.

On February 15, barely a week after Kate Chopin was interviewed in the St. Louis newspapers, a United State Navy battleship called the *Maine* was blown up in faraway Cuba. The Spanish overlords controlling Cuba were blamed, and American newspapers screamed for war. The Hearst newspapers led the pack, followed closely by John A. Dillon and Joseph Pulitzer's *New York World.*

In March, Chopin — obviously depressed — wrote her bitter and hopeless "Elizabeth Stock's One Story," about the death of a poor and lonely postmistress in a small Missouri town. No one wanted to publish such a somber story.

By April, Congress had declared war, and flags sprouted everywhere. Young men raced to enlist; young women rewarded them with kisses and cheers. Two "Chopin boys," far too young to know about the horrors of war, ran to sign up. Felix, despite being a star athlete, was rejected for being too small; but Fred Chopin, twenty-two years old, joined Light Battery A, and declared that he was ready for glory. His mother, who had lost her own soldier brother in wartime, in his twenty-third year, watched and agonized. Her only writing in April was a scribbled translation of Guy de Maupassant's "Father Amable," and she never finished a clear copy to send a publisher.

Possibly influenced by Kate Chopin, Billy Reedy was almost the only public voice in St. Louis to oppose the war. But after his *Mirror* editorial called the warmongering newspapers "treasonous" promoters of imperialism, he gained ten thousand new subscribers nationally, pushing *The Mirror* ahead of the *Atlantic* and the *Nation* in circulation.

Fred and the other eager recruits camped out at Jefferson Barracks — which, in Kate O'Flaherty's day, had been Camp Jackson, where the Civil War began. Now "Freddy" Chopin, according to the newspapers, was the greatest prankster there and the life of the party. When the troops left for Georgia, the *Republic* described their mothers weeping at Union Station. But at Chickamauga National Park, Fred somehow procured a piano, and between bouts of training, he became "the sweet singer of the battery."

At home, Kate Chopin and the other soldiers' mothers, many of them her cardplaying friends, dutifully organized a benefit for Battery A, a lawn party combining the United Daughters of the Confederacy and the Daughters of the American Revolution. It was "the event of the summer" at the Fair Grounds, but it hardly comforted the women who remembered the earlier war, and the outrages that were committed, and all those boys who never came back.

The adventure was not what Fred Chopin had hoped for. In mid-July, before Battery A even left for Cuba, the Spanish general surrendered — but President William McKinley, the U.S. Congress, and the Hearst newspapers demanded a wider war. Battery A finally sailed for Puerto Rico in late July, and in early September they were just about to open fire for the first time when the President's latest proclamation reached them: war was truly over. Disappointed, they returned to St. Louis, where they were honored at a great banquet.

Fred Chopin lived off that little shred of glory for the rest of his life, and even had his military service on his tombstone. But for his mother, that terrible tug at her heartstrings was more than enough. For most of 1898, even after Fred returned, her writing drifted: a few poems, a trip to White Oaks, Wisconsin.

But two days after the fight in Cuba ended in July, when she thought her warrior son was coming home, Kate Chopin had written in her diary, solely for her own enjoyment, a story called "The Storm." Possibly her son's survival made her think of another young warrior, Albert Sampite, returning barefoot and bleeding from the siege of Vicksburg so many years ago.

Whether she saw Albert Sampite when she revisited the Cane River country is unknown, but they were no longer the dashing young lovers they might once have been. When Chopin wrote "The Storm," she was forty-eight years old. Albert was fifty-four, and his grandchildren called him "Pépé Albert."

Kate Chopin created "The Storm," subtitled "A Sequel to the 'Cadian Ball," almost six years to the day after she wrote the first story — about the fiery-tempered planter Alcée and his flirtation with the "Spanish vixen" Calixta. At that story's end, both had chosen sensible marriages: Alcée to his dainty cousin Clarisse, a woman of his class, and Calixta to Bobinôt, a clumsy, good-hearted 'Cadian.

"The Storm" begins five years later. Calixta, a fussy housewife, is toiling furiously at her sewing machine, when a summer thunderstorm sweeps over her house. Alcée, riding by, comes in for shelter. A sudden thunderbolt sends her into his arms, and a wordless impulse propels them into the bedroom. Before, they had held back, but now — everything seems possible.

Chopin described their passion as mutual power and desire — laughing, generous, mysterious. "Her firm, elastic flesh that was knowing for the first time its birthright, was like a creamy lily that the sun invites to contribute its breath and perfume to the undying life of the world." No guilt disturbs them, and no deception:

> The generous abundance of her passion, without guile or trickery, was like a white flame which penetrated and found response in depths of his own sensuous nature that had never yet been reached....

When he touched her breasts, they gave themselves up in quivering ecstasy, inviting his lips. Her mouth was a fountain of delight.

And then, "when he possessed her, they seemed to swoon together at the very borderland of life's mystery."

Afterwards, the storm dies down and he rides away, while Calixta laughs aloud. She greets her husband and son with effusive kisses, while Alcée sends a loving letter to his wife, away at the Biloxi resort with their babies. Stay a month longer if you'd like, he says — and Clarisse, in turn, is pleased with that "first free breath since her marriage." And so, Chopin concludes, "The storm passed and every one was happy."

Compared with his character in "At the 'Cadian Ball," Alcée in "The Storm" is a well-behaved, charming gentleman — no longer a morose heavy drinker. The first story takes place during a warm dark night, while the second is a daring daylight tryst, in much bolder language. Although James Lane Allen in *Summer in Arcady* and Thomas Hardy in *Jude the Obscure* had written about breasts, the word was considered taboo for women writers. (As late as 1920, Willa Cather's references to a woman's breast and thigh were cut from a story in the *Smart Set* magazine.)

Also, Calixta in "The Storm" is even more recognizable as Maria Normand of Cloutierville. Not only does Calixta still have kinky blonde hair, but she also sews — and Maria was the best-known seamstress in the parish (her mother-in-law's sewing machine, the first in Cloutierville, is now in the Bayou Folk Museum). When Chopin wrote "The Storm," Maria was living across the horse lot from Albert Sampite, with her twelve-year-old daughter and thirteen-year-old son. Everyone knew that Albert — who drank a great deal but never seemed drunk — was paying her bills.

Albert might have found "The Storm" flattering, but Kate Chopin knew no American magazine would touch such a celebration of "guilty love," and she never tried to publish it. Although anthologies a century later often reprint "The Storm" as a startling story from the Victorian era, no Victorians ever read it, nor did anyone in Cloutierville.

"The Storm" was not published at all, anywhere, until 1969.

In December 1898, Kate Chopin visited Natchitoches Parish again, and told everyone that her new novel would be out soon. It had been almost a year since she finished writing *The Awakening,* but the Way & Williams firm had been dissolved, and so had their friendly rivals Stone & Kimball. Herbert S. Stone, the last partner left standing, now held the contracts for both *The Awakening* and Chopin's next story collection, *A Vocation and a Voice.* He officially accepted *The Awakening* in January 1899.

Eight days before Christmas, Chopin sold her Cloutierville home — the big white house where Lélia was born, and the only place where Kate, Oscar, and all the children had lived together. She had been renting it out since 1884, and may have needed money for Lélia's début. The buyer, for $2,500, was a German-born merchant named Pierre Rosenthal.

From Cloutierville she took a quick trip to New Orleans, where she was also very famous. The popular novelist Mollie E. Moore Davis, whose 1896 short story "A Bamboula" resembles Chopin's "La Belle Zoraïde," kept a literary salon on Fridays, attended by such visitors as Chopin and Ruth McEnery Stuart. Local literary women included "Pearl Rivers" (Eliza Nicholson, editor of the *Daily Picayune*) and "Catharine Cole" (Martha Field) of the *Times-Democrat.*

Chopin spent the Christmas before *The Awakening* at home. She planned, and then cancelled, a trip to New York. Instead, she remained home and wrote one happy story of a poor girl who gets to see the circus ("A Little Country Girl") and one chilling tale of a devoted woman who conceals a murder committed by her drunken godson ("The Godmother").

The turn of the century, even before *The Awakening* was published, had a dark underside.

Kate Chopin was turning away from Louisiana material, and setting her stories nowhere in particular. Often they were slice-of-life sketches — a character or a setting, with no moral or surprise ending. Many of them dealt with illness or vision problems, and Chopin had been seeing an eye specialist. She may have had diabetes, a risk for

women who have many children close together, and her smoking —
along with St. Louis's filthy, coal-speckled air — would have exacerbated any health problems.

Of the stories slated for her *Vocation and a Voice* collection, many
are somber. "The Blind Man," "The Unexpected," and "The Recovery"
are among those about blindness and illness. "Elizabeth Stock's One
Story" and "The Godmother" are about cold and deaths, and "The
Story of an Hour" ends with a death. Nor are the others much happier. The actress in "Lilacs" is banished from her convent retreat; the
narrator in "An Egyptian Cigarette" describes a drug experience gone
sour. "The Kiss" and "The Falling in Love of Fedora" are both about
unwanted and unappreciated kisses.

In putting together her new collection, Kate Chopin seemed bent
on ignoring commercial, entertainment considerations entirely. But she
also had very few stories in which women are kind to one another.

During the winter of 1898–1899 she turned to poetry instead, writing a dozen poems about love, nature, sensuality, and secrets. But only
one, "I Opened All the Portals Wide," ever found a publisher. She seems
to have been suffering from a deep depression, and St. Louis's winter
was one of the coldest on record. Especially after selling her home, the
last one Eliza O'Flaherty had come to visit, Kate Chopin was almost
certainly thinking back — and missing her mother. But she knew that
*The Awakening,* to be published on April 22, was her best work. She
awaited it eagerly, and apprehensively.

# Chapter 12

## The Awakening

A CENTURY AFTER the novel first appeared, teachers of *The Awakening* often ask their students to summarize the plot — and no two ever come up with the same story. Kate Chopin's 1899 novel is complex and subtle, and readers can argue endlessly about which scenes and features and characters are most important. They also wonder about the ending: is it positive? is it negative? is it over? (Novelist Jill McCorkle has suggested that Edna is still out there swimming, bent on finding a good time to come back.) Many modern readers wonder whether they are supposed to like Edna, understand her, or loathe everything about her.

Most of Kate Chopin's original critics had little trouble with any of those questions.

According to the majority of 1899 reviews, *The Awakening*'s Edna Pontellier is a selfish wife and mother who not only does not appreciate her good husband, but she also rebels in the worst possible way — by taking a lover or two. She is not sympathetic; she is wicked, foolish, or both. As for the ending, the journal *Literature* expressed the common view of 1899: "the waters of the gulf close appropriately over one who has drifted from all right moorings, and has not the grace to repent."

That was not the way Kate Chopin saw her novel. Asked to describe it, she might have said something about the imagery — the birds, the water — and about the settings: the natural wonders of Grand Isle, the urban bustle of New Orleans. But as to what happens, Kate Chopin's own plot summary might go something like this:

The central character, Edna Pontellier, is a Kentucky Presbyterian and an outsider to Louisiana and Creole culture. Twenty-eight years old, she is married to a forty-year-old New Orleans businessman who provides well for her and their two small sons. She is contented but not really happy when, during one summer at Grand Isle, a charming Creole resort, she has several awakenings.

The resort owner's young son, Robert Lebrun, attaches himself to Edna as a self-appointed friendly cavalier, but a real romance brews between them after he teaches her to swim, and she feels power and sensuality in her body. Meanwhile, Edna becomes friendly with Madame Adèle Ratignolle, a mother-woman who is gloriously contented in her traditional role — but whose affectionate ways and murmured insights draw Edna to talk about herself and learn startling things. A motherless child, an intellectual and a loner, Edna now realizes that she married Léonce Pontellier, a Louisiana Catholic, in order to annoy her family, and to close the door on infatuations and dreams that never could be. She became a mother without particularly wanting to be one, and she silenced her own voice.

During Edna's summer of awakenings, aided by female mentors, she starts regaining her voice. The peculiar, slightly sinister pianist Mademoiselle Reisz draws out Edna's deep appreciation for music and encourages her flirtation with Robert — who, suddenly and nervously, leaves for Mexico.

Back at home in the French Quarter, Edna begins to ignore her wifely obligations. She takes long solitary walks when she is supposed to be receiving callers; she has no sympathy with her husband's complaints; and she stops having relations with him ("We meet in the morning at the breakfast table," Mr. Pontellier tells Dr. Mandelet, the old Creole physician he recruits to talk with Edna, to no particular avail) (XXII). Listening to her own inner voice, Edna starts expressing opinions. She visits her friends, Madame Ratignolle (pregnant again) and Mademoiselle Reisz (grouchy as ever), and returns seriously to the sketching and painting she had abandoned earlier in life — even though Mademoiselle Reisz warns her that she may lack the artist's soul, the one that dares and defies. When Edna refuses to attend her sister's wedding in New York, her husband goes by himself. The children are with his mother, and Edna — ecstatically alone — presides over a luxurious dinner party before moving herself to a little house around the corner.

With some money from her painting, a little inheritance from her mother, and some race track winnings, Edna has enough money to support herself. She also takes up with a roué, Alcée Arobin, a lover of the night and horses and fast women. With Arobin, Edna has a passionate sexual affair and only one regret: "it was not love which had held this cup of life to her lips" (XXVIII).

Then Robert returns from Mexico and admits that he loves Edna, but knows that her husband will never let her go. Edna clasps him tightly, calls him "a foolish boy," and says that her husband does not matter: "I give myself where I choose." Robert turns pale with shock (XXXVI).

At that moment Edna is called to be with Madame Ratignolle, who is giving birth. After the scene of "torture" that reminds her of her own childbirths, Edna walks home with Dr. Mandelet, who says that "youth is given up to illusions...a decoy to secure mothers for the race" (XXXVII–XXXVIII). At her own home, Robert has gone, leaving a note: "Good-by, because I love you." Feeling hopeless, thinking of her children as chains keeping her in "soul's slavery," Edna stays awake all night, and then goes to Grand Isle (XXXIX). There she swims out into the Gulf until her strength is gone.

This summary, somewhat detached, does not tell readers what to think — nor does Kate Chopin. A century later, in fact, some parts of the plot are hazy to literal-minded readers.

Sex is a major barrier. Modern readers expect more graphic language, and are prone to misunderstand the intimacies they do see. There is, for instance, *The Awakening*'s chapter VII, in which Edna and Madame Adèle Ratignolle, both handsome women who enjoy each other's company, go down to the beach together at Grand Isle. That summer, Edna has been startled by the Creole "absence of prudery," and especially by Adèle's comforting, caressing touches. Readers a century later, confusing sexuality and sensuality, sometimes see more than what is there — and think there is a "lesbian" connection between the two.

There is indeed, if "lesbian" means love between women, or what Chopin calls, in that chapter, "the subtle bond which we call sympathy, which we might as well call love." But the word "lesbian" was not in common use in Chopin's day: women who loved women were not put in a separate category under a different label. In the 1890s Edna and Adèle are, in Chopin's terms, "intimate friends." That does not mean what it would mean, bluntly, a century later — a genital connection. It does mean a unique and sometimes wordless emotional and spiritual understanding, the kind that unlocks Edna's thoughts about herself.

There are other things in *The Awakening* that are still to be unlocked — such as the sexual orientation of Robert, Edna's summer cavalier. He is definitely different from the other fellows. They all smoke cigars, manly and phallic; Robert smokes cigarettes, as women do (he claims they're cheaper). The other men hold jobs in the city, while Robert hangs about with his mother and attaches himself to a different unattainable — usually married — woman every summer. Clean-shaven and light-haired, he resembles Edna, and the husbands regard him as a safe puppy dog. But Adèle Ratignolle, more discerning, asks Robert to leave her friend Edna alone. Edna is an outsider: "She is not one of us; she is not like us. She might make the unfortunate blunder of taking you seriously" (VIII).

When Robert objects that he is not a clown or a jack-in-the-box, Adèle gives an even stronger hint about what he really is: "If your attentions to any married women here were ever offered with any intention of being convincing, you would not be the gentleman we all know you to be, and you would be unfit to associate with the wives and daughters of the people who trust you."

Not long after that, and without consulting Edna, Robert flees to Mexico.

Before he leaves, though, Robert encounters Mr. Pontellier in the city, and Edna wonders if he seemed "gay." Her husband says Robert was cheerful, which is "natural in a young man about to seek his fortune and adventure in a strange, queer country" (XVI).

When Robert returns, he has a pouch embroidered by — he says — a girl in Vera Cruz. But homosexual male Americans frequently went to Mexico for sexual alliances with boys ("Vera Cruz" is an easy pun on cruising). Robert may very well love Edna, but when she grabs him aggressively in their last scene together, her gesture tells him that he will have to perform sexually, as a man with a woman. And so (at least according to modern queer readings), if Robert is a gay man, recognizable to other Creoles as gay, he has to run away.

If readers a century ago interpreted Robert as homosexual, no one said so in print, just four years after Oscar Wilde's sensational trial for homosexuality. Possibly the codes for recognizing a gay male character were well known to avant-garde readers in 1899, and they had no need to write down what they already knew.

Meanwhile, our language for recognizing heterosexuality has also shifted. In Kate Chopin's day, readers of *The Awakening* knew exactly what Edna was doing with Alcée Arobin, but a century later, they are less sure. They wonder, for instance, which body parts are involved — but Chopin could not have named the sexual parts of her characters and gotten her book published. She and her contemporaries used literary conventions, just as filmmakers once used symbolic images — fires flaming up, waves crashing across the sand — as shorthand for sexual acts they could not show. (In the movie version of *Gone with the Wind,* sex is understood to take place between the time Rhett carries Scarlett up the stairs and the next morning, when she awakens in bed.)

Kate Chopin's contemporaries would recognize that, in *The Awakening,* Edna has sexual relations with Alcée Arobin on three separate occasions, all indicated by suggestive language and white space. A century later, high school teachers, embarrassed by students' questions and doubtful themselves about literary conventions, often deny that Edna and Arobin actually "do it." They do, and in these chapters: (1) At the end of XXVII: "It was the first kiss of her life to which her nature had really responded. It was a flaming torch that kindled desire." In the white space after that passage, the sex takes place, followed by:

## *XXVIII*

Edna cried a little that night after Arobin left her.

(2) At the end of **XXXI**: "He did not answer, except to continue to caress her. He did not say good night until she had become supple to his gentle, seductive entreaties." (3) In **XXXV**: After a night drive with his fast, unmanageable horses, Arobin and Edna arrive at her little house "comparatively early in the evening."

> It was late when he left her. It was getting to be more than a passing whim with Arobin to see her and be with her. He had detected the latent sensuality, which unfolded under his delicate sense of her nature's requirements like a torpid, torrid, sensitive blossom.

That passage can also be read as clitoral imagery, but Chopin's contemporary readers — if they thought so — could never have said so in print.

Kate Chopin got her ideas, she said, from "the spontaneous expression of impressions gathered goodness knows where. To seek the source, the impulse of a story is like tearing a flower to pieces for wantonness." Still, bits of her life undeniably feed into the settings and characters of *The Awakening,* and at least some of her "impressions" can be traced to Impressionism. ("Impressions" is also the title of her 1894 diary.)

Chopin knew what it was like to be an outsider in Louisiana: she never lost that feeling. She had been a great walker around New Orleans; she had summered in the tropical paradise in Grand Isle. She had heard, all her life, the secrets women told each other when no men were around. And she drew on some of her own secrets, and some of other people's.

Mature readers of *The Awakening* do notice that Edna is far more candid and intelligent in her conversations with women friends than with any of the men in the book. She is more at ease with Robert than with any other man, but even their chattering is mostly little jokes and flirtations: he is the teenaged boyfriend she never had, or the rehearsal for the adult sexual relationship with Alcée Arobin (who often prefers not to talk at all).

Edna's friends Madame Ratignolle and Mademoiselle Reisz are the ones who take her art and her life seriously. They want to know about her past, her family, her dreams and her plans. They nurture and abet her and teach her about their lives, and hers; they make predictions and devise strategies (Madame Ratignolle, the mother-woman, worries about Edna's reputation). Both friends encourage Edna to spread her wings through painting. As in Kate Chopin's life, the women are the ones who listen to women, and who watch for subtle signs of change and danger.

But the men continually disappoint: all they want is for Edna to pay attention to them. Léonce Pontellier, like Sue V. Moore's husband in the late 1880s, fusses endlessly about "his" food, his career, and his wife as "the sole object of his existence" (III). Similarly, Robert "talked a good deal about himself. He was very young, and did not know any better" (II). Edna's father, the Kentucky colonel who coerced and harried his own wife to an early death, tries to dominate every conversation. (He is the domineering father Kate Chopin never had, at least after age five). As for the seductive Arobin, who wants just one thing from every woman — he still has his own ego to tend, and he complains when Edna mentions Mademoiselle Reisz "when I desired to talk of you" (XXVII). He wants to own her thoughts, and *The Awakening* can be read as a critique of inflated masculine egos.

Many bits from Kate Chopin's life feed into *The Awakening*.

The characters' names, for instance, come from different layers of her past. In her New Orleans years, she learned from Edgar Degas about his friend Berthe Morisot and her sister Edma, the painter who gave up her art when she married Adolphe Pontillon in 1869, a year before the Chopins arrived in New Orleans. (Edma Morisot Pontillon regretted that sacrifice for the rest of her life.) Degas's New Orleans neighbor Léonce Olivier, meanwhile, was the impeccable but uninteresting husband whose wife left him for another man some years later. And so Kate Chopin combined the names: Edma Pontillon, the artist silenced by marriage, and Léonce Olivier, the unsatisfactory husband, easily became Edna and Léonce Pontellier.

Degas obviously shared other gossip, too, a quarter-century before Kate Chopin used it in *The Awakening*. Besides her sister, Berthe Morisot had one other very close friend, a beautiful blonde sculptor and exceptional confidante who called herself "Marcello" — but her real name was Adèle Colonna. Hence the first name Adèle for Edna Pontellier's blonde, beautiful confidante. Adèle's last name, Ratignolle, recalls an 1870 painting that Degas knew well: "The Batignolles Studio," a very large group portrait of major contemporary artists, painted by Henri Fantin-Latour. (It may also be from Fantin-Latour that Chopin chose the pen name "La Tour" for her two pseudonymous stories, "The Falling in Love of Fedora" and "Miss McEnders.")

As for Edna's other friend Mademoiselle Reisz: she has no first name, and Chopin gives no clue as to how her name should be pronounced. But according to her friend Will Schuyler, Chopin did read the French novelist Alphonse Daudet, who in 1878 published a novel called *Le Nabab*, about a woman artist who believes herself to be monstrously different, because she defies the rules of traditional society. Daudet's artist says:

> Art is a tyrant. You have to give yourself to it entirely... there's nothing left over for your life . . . I'll never be anything but an artist, a woman set apart from others, a poor Amazon with a heart imprisoned in its iron armor, launched into combat like a man and condemned to live and die like a man.

The artist heroine's name is Félicia Ruys — an unpronounceable name too much like Reisz to be accidental.

From her Cloutierville years, Kate Chopin chose the names of Edna's lovers, giving each one part of *Albert* Sampite's first name: *Al*-cée and Ro-*bert*. Arobin also resembles Sampite as a figure of great temptation: dark, reckless, sexual, arrogant. For *The Awakening*, Chopin brought together her lifelong observation of women's dreams and desires and her knowledge of French literature, where some of those emotions could be portrayed openly.

She and the members of her salon certainly knew her famous French predecessor, Gustave Flaubert's *Madame Bovary*, the tale of an unfulfilled wife who abandons her husband and family to pursue other men. But Flaubert regards Emma Bovary as a specimen, a shallow woman with little in her head but romantic dreams. Kate Chopin saw the world differently, through the eyes of a woman. Chopin's Edna has her painting, and Edna learns and grows and changes through conversations with her friends. Her life is rich with warmth and sensual pleasures, including sexual ones; Flaubert's sexual scenes are brittle and mocking. Flaubert's coldness about his heroine was something Kate Chopin could not emulate, had she wanted to.

There were plenty of other inspirations from real life. Her brother-in-law Phanor Breazeale, for instance, told Chopin about a French Quarter woman who had desires that marriage could not fulfill—while Billy Reedy published a similar story in the *Mirror*, about a married woman from St. Louis who became enmeshed in a painful summer romance. She was "a fine figure of a woman" but "somewhat addicted to sentimentality"—which made her vulnerable to "a young Baltimorean with good looks and a taste for poetry" and "romantic professions." She hung about him in public; she claimed he was the only one who could teach her to swim. Some letters were sent, the young man's father came to take his son away, and the husband was overheard furiously saying "something about 'puppy-love letters' and an 'asylum.'" When the lady returned to St. Louis, Reedy predicted, "she will be surprised to find how much news of her season has preceded her."

When *The Awakening* appeared, less than two years later, that story may have been another reason for the "best people" of St. Louis to resent Kate Chopin. She appeared to be revealing, and trifling with, their secrets.

Reedy, though, had already revealed hers, or at least her ideas as expressed at her salon. In January 1898, the month that Chopin finished writing *The Awakening*, Reedy wrote in the *Mirror* that "Woman's truest duties are those of wife and mother, but those duties do not demand that she shall sacrifice her individuality."

Then, just after she read proofs for *The Awakening*, Chopin also wrote a rare poem in a man's voice, foreshadowing how men would misinterpret, and malign, Edna Pontellier.

### The Haunted Chamber

Of course 'twas an excellent story to tell
Of a fair, frail, passionate woman who fell.
It may have been false, it may have been true.
That was nothing to me — it was less to you.
But with bottle between us, and clouds of smoke
From your last cigar, 'twas more of a joke
Than a matter of sin or a matter of shame
That a woman had fallen, and nothing to blame,
So far as you or I could discover,
But her beauty, her blood and an ardent lover.
But when you were gone and the lights were low
And the breeze came in with the moon's pale glow,
The far, faint voice of a woman, I heard,
'Twas but a wail, and it spoke no word.
It rose from the depths of some infinite gloom
And its tremulous anguish filled the room.
Yet the woman was dead and could not deny,
But women forever will whine and cry.
So now I must listen the whole night through
To the torment with which I had nothing to do —
But women forever will whine and cry
And men forever must listen — and sigh —

In *The Awakening* itself, Chopin had written about the gulf between women and men, and symbolized it with clothing. The reader's first sight of Edna is through the eyes of her husband, and "Mrs. Pontellier," as she is called at first, is under a parasol. On the beach at Grand Isle, she and Madame Ratignolle both wear hats and veils, as ladies were supposed to do in the hot sun.

Later the narrator calls her "Edna Pontellier" and finally "Edna," while the character is "becoming herself and casting aside that fictitious self which we assume like a garment with which to appear before the world" (XIX). Edna sheds more and more veils, physically and spiritually, until at the end, she is naked, "like some new-born creature, opening its eyes in a familiar world that it had never known" (XXXIX).

*The Awakening* is the unveiling of Edna Pontellier, and the first prepublication reviewer — a woman — recognized that. She called it, in *Book News* for March 1899, "a remarkable novel," keen and subtle, "an intimate thing, which in studying the nature of one woman reveals something which brings her in touch with all women — something larger than herself." Kate Chopin "pictures, too, with extraordinary vividness, the kind of silent sympathy which is sometimes the expression of the love that goes deep." *The Awakening* shows "a brilliant kind of art."

The reviewer, Lucy Monroe of Chicago, was no stranger to the book. As Herbert S. Stone's "chief reader and literary editor," she was almost certainly the one who urged him to publish the book. She was a New Woman, an art and theater critic, a member of many writers' circles in Chicago, and the sister of Harriet Monroe, who would go on to create an internationally influential magazine, *Poetry.* Lucy Monroe almost certainly had met Kate Chopin, and they agreed on many things, including an appreciation for French realism and a dislike for Hamlin Garland's blustery writing. Lucy Monroe would eventually marry an attorney and move with him to China — but *The Awakening* is her lasting legacy to American women.

After Monroe's, there were some favorable small notices. The *St. Louis Republic,* in March, called *The Awakening* the story of an "intensely real" woman who "finally awakens to the fact that she has never lived." *The Book Buyer,* in April, called the book "analytical and fine-spun, and of peculiar interest to women."

Those were among the last good notices *The Awakening* received.

Herbert S. Stone & Company's official publication date for *The Awakening* was April 22, 1899. The book was a slim volume with a light green linen binding, decorated with graceful green and dark red vines, printed on the sides and spine in red. It sold for $1.50 a copy.

The copyright was registered on April 24, almost ten years to the day after Kate Chopin brought Oscar's body back to St. Louis for burial. Except for the poem "If It Might Be," published in January 1889, Chopin's entire literary career had taken place in those ten years. Nine days before *The Awakening* was published, Billy Reedy had written that "St. Louis is not much of a town for literature," but "Of course, the stories of Mrs. Kate Chopin continue to find ready sale all over the United States."

On the last day of April, the first real review appeared, on page 11 of the *Republic,* seven columns under large headlines: "Kate Chopin's New Book Is the Story of a Lady Most Foolish." It was the longest review *The Awakening* ever received, and it was mostly a very unsympathetic plot summary: "Given a woman at a summer resort with nothing to do, more interested in herself and her own emotions than in her husband and children, and a man who had nothing to do except make himself agreeable to the aforesaid woman . . . ." The review concluded rudely: "So the woman who did not want anything but her own way drowned herself."

The unnamed reviewer left out the joys of Edna's life, including her friendships, her art work, and her passionate susceptibility to music. There was no mention at all of Alcée Arobin, nor of Madame Ratignolle's pregnancy. In fact, Kate Chopin's depicting a blooming, voluptuously pregnant woman also violated 1890s taboos — but no one noticed that.

Everyone else was busy condemning her for other things, while her friends began, almost immediately, to write her letters of comfort and praise. Sue V. Moore, for instance, wrote Chopin that a great many copies had been sold at Barr's department store, and "Your book is great!" and "I am so proud to know 'the artist with the courageous soul that dares and defies.' "

But *The Awakening* was being pummeled by reviewer after reviewer. Reedy assigned the book to Frances Porcher, a critic and short story writer who objected to anything that strayed from "the ideal." To Porcher, Edna's character was "sensual and devilish," and "One would fain beg the gods, in pure cowardice, for sleep unending rather than to know what an ugly, cruel, loathsome monster Passion can be when, like a tiger, it slowly stretches its graceful length and yawns and finally awakens." Porcher praised Chopin's skill as a writer, but "it leaves one sick of human nature and so one feels — *cui bono?*"

Chopin had to expect a negative review from the St. Louis *Globe-Democrat*, still owned by Ellen McKee ("Miss McEnders"), and she got it. The *Globe-Democrat* praised the book's local color, but termed it "not a healthy book; if it points any particular moral or teaches any lesson, the fact is not apparent."

But as if waiting in the wings, Chopin's friend Charles L. Deyo flew out to defend *The Awakening* in the *Post-Dispatch*. His review criticizes Léonce Pontellier for treating his wife as "a bit of decorative furniture," and calls Edna, fairly, "not good enough for heaven, not wicked enough for hell." Deyo praised Chopin's "subtle understanding of motive," and said a story like Edna's calls for "compassion, not pity." No doubt abetted by discussions at Chopin's "Thursdays," Deyo also attacked the genteel insistence on bland and innocent stories and readers. "*The Awakening* is not for the young person," Deyo declared, though "not because the young person would be harmed by reading it, but because the young person wouldn't understand it." It is a book, he said, for "seasoned souls, for those who have ripened under the gracious or ungracious sun of experience." It also was not for

the old person who has no relish for unpleasant truths. For such there is much that is very improper in it, not to say positively unseemly. A fact, no matter how essential, which we have all agreed shall not be acknowledged, is as good as no fact at all. And it is disturbing — even indelicate — to mention it as something which, perhaps, does play an important part in the life behind the mask.

It is sad and mad and bad, but it is all consummate art. . . .

In short, *The Awakening* was an honest and fearless book that could be understood only by smart and sophisticated people — like those Deyo and Chopin knew best.

Evidently, though, Deyo's favorable review was controversial at the *Post-Dispatch*. On the next day another review, bylined "G. B.," was published—and this one was from an enemy. In her writings, said G. B., Kate Chopin "commits unutterable crimes against polite society, but in the essentials of her art she never blunders. Like most of her work, however, 'The Awakening' is too strong drink for moral babes, and should be labeled 'poison.'"

Nationally, reviewers were more apt to see the book as "morbid," "unhealthy," or "not wholesome," although many praised Chopin's clear, bright writing style. Some samples:

...it was not necessary for a writer of so great refinement and poetic grace to enter the overworked field of sex fiction. (*Chicago Times-Herald*)

*The Awakening* is a decidedly unpleasant study of a temperament.... the story was not really worth telling, and its disagreeable glimpses of sensuality are repellent. (*The Outlook*, New York)

In many ways, it is unhealthily introspective and morbid in feeling, as the story of that sort of woman must inevitably be...when she writes another book it is to be hoped that she will choose a theme more healthful and sweeter of smell. (*Los Angeles Times*)

But we cannot see that literature or the criticism of life is helped by the detailed history of the manifold and contemporary love affairs of a wife and mother. (*The Nation*)

The purport of the story can hardly be described in language fit for publication. (*Providence Sunday Journal*)

Even Chopin's friends at the New Orleans *Times-Democrat*, who had published some of her more risky stories, deserted *The Awakening*, calling it shocking and crude. "Certainly there is throughout the story an undercurrent of sympathy for Edna, and nowhere a single note of censure of her totally unjustifiable conduct."

Still, there were a few positive reviews. The Boston *Beacon* saw *The Awakening* as a cautionary tale, about "the immorality of a marriage of convenience." The *New York Times* said that the author "has a clever way of managing a difficult subject. . . . Such is the cleverness in the handling of the story that you feel pity for the most unfortunate of her sex."

But another up-and-coming writer, Willa Cather in the Pittsburgh *Leader,* joined the chorus of criticism. While she admired Chopin's "light, flexible, subtle" writing style, she deplored her choosing "so trite and sordid a theme." Cather used her review to attack "women of the Bovary type," who foolishly want "the passion of love to fill and gratify every need of life." Romance can never be enough, Cather declared with all the confidence of a twenty-three-year-old.

The reviews would have devastated almost any author who had written an exquisite book in which she distilled the truths she had learned in nearly half a century of living. But Kate Chopin was not felled, and not destroyed. For a while at least, she was angry and disgusted. When she sent Deyo's review to her publisher, she added in a note that "It seems so able and intelligent — by contrast with some of the drivel I have run across that I thought I should like to have you read it when you have the time."

She also had strong support from her friends, and — on one occasion only — she defended herself publicly.

Chopin chose *Book News,* Lucy Monroe's venue, as the place to publish a response that was really an ironic swipe at her critics. She wrote her satirical paragraph on May 28, only five weeks after *The Awakening*'s official publication date, but it was not published until late July. Over the summer, much of the wealthy reading public would have been away at their vacation homes, perhaps looking for soothing reading in *Book News.* But Kate Chopin's statement on *The Awakening* was brusque, and even rudely humorous:

> Having a group of people at my disposal, I thought it might be entertaining (to myself) to throw them together and see what would happen. I never dreamed of Mrs. Pontellier making such a mess of things and working out her own damnation as she did. If I had had the slightest intima-

tion of such a thing I would have excluded her from the company. But when I found out what she was up to, the play was half over and it was then too late.

Meanwhile, Chopin's friends did not think it was too late to form a loyal circle around her. When the *Globe-Democrat* published its vicious review, the attorney Lewis Ely — one of her many younger male admirers — sent a note suggesting to Chopin: "Provide yourself with ammonia salts, brandy, etc. You have had or will have hysterics, I'm sure. I didn't know there was such a fool in the world as the writer of that article."

Chopin's women friends, at least the more literary ones, also condemned the critics. Anna L. Moss, a clubwoman and sometime book reviewer, wrote to Chopin that the reviews showed "on the whole, as much discrimination as one could expect from such sources." To Moss, *The Awakening* was delicate, charming, true to life and much too good for the reviewing public: "it is not surprising that but few of the reviewers are more than funny."

Other friends chimed in. A friend signed "L." praised Chopin's "emancipation of the whole being from the trammels of conventionalism," and quoted a Mr. Paul who called Chopin "an undoubted genius."

A Louisville friend, who signed her note Lizzie L., called the book "faultless," with delicious humor, and added "In many places I can hear you speaking, describing incidents in your own cute, inimitable way." As an extra cheering-up treat, Lizzie L. enclosed gossip about a mutual friend.

But over the summer of 1899, *The Awakening* was being buffeted by mostly bad reviews from coast to coast. Chopin stayed at home even during the muggiest days of August and stubbornly kept her salon going. She needed the comfort of friends, and — as always — she attracted the admiration of younger men.

R. E. Lee Gibson was a sometime poet who worked as the head clerk at the St. Louis Insane Asylum. With his friend, the Kentucky poet Madison Cawein, Gibson was determined to curry favor with Kate

Chopin or cheer her up, or both. Even before the hostile reviews began to appear, Cawein had written to Gibson, praising the "magnolia-
scented atmosphere" and the "pathos" of the story. Gibson passed the
letter along to Chopin with his own assessment: a "splendid story."

In mid-August Cawein, visiting St. Louis, dropped in on one of
Chopin's "Thursdays," got her to autograph his copy of *The Awakening,* and wrote to a friend that Chopin was fiftyish "but still fine-look-
ing and capable of exciting the enthusiastic admiration of men much
younger than herself." Cawein, a thirty-four-year-old bachelor, could
not resist bragging about his own performance: while Will Schuyler
told "some interesting" ghost stories, Cawein's tales were "the most
thrilling. Mrs. Chopin is a great sceptic, but she seemed to be very
much interested; perhaps, if given a chance I might be able to convert
her to believing in them."

Meanwhile, Kate Chopin's faith in her own literary career was taking a beating. On November 8, she wrote a Utah correspondent that
she had had "a severe spell of illness" and was "only now looking about
and gathering up the scattered threads of a rather monotonous existence." The illness may well have been depression: she did seem to be
hiding from people.

Exactly a month earlier, most society people had returned from their
summer cottages. Lélia, who spent the summer in Minnesota, had been
back for three weeks, and her début was less than two months away.
But her mother left town that day for the Wisconsin lake country, to
stay in a cottage belonging to the Meysenburgs of St. Louis.

It was a comforting several weeks. Her friendship with the Meysenburgs, based on common interests, went back many years. Chopin had
sent the Meysenburgs a copy of *At Fault*; Lucretia Block Meysenburg
was a member of the Wednesday Club; and her husband Theodore,
president of an iron works company, had been one of the founders of
the St. Louis Public Library.

Also, while Chopin was in Wisconsin, her publisher forwarded two
very admiring letters from England. A Lady Janet Scammon Young
wrote to praise Chopin's knowledge of women and passion, and called

her paragraphs "like sunlight and like flowers." Lady Janet also enclosed a letter from a Dr. Dunrobin Thomson who praised *The Awakening*'s realism about "the accursed stupidity of men" and about most women's never being awakened to real passion. The letters were long and glowing, and Chopin showed them to friends with pride and pleasure. She probably did not know that there is no evidence that the two Londoners actually existed. They may have been fabrications to cheer her up, and their creator may well have been Chopin's smoking friend Florence Hayward, the outspoken journalist who often travelled to England. Hayward, who had a strong sense of sisterhood and loyalty toward women, was in London in the fall of 1899.

Florence Hayward and Lucretia Block Meysenburg may also have recognized the sad truth that Kate Chopin also knew by November 1899, seven months after *The Awakening* was published. The male critics and gatekeepers who controlled editing and publishing would never accept her vision of women's ambitions and passions, nor did they even notice her celebration of women's friendships. None of them noticed Edna's learning about herself, gaining trust in her own voice, in a world of women. Scarcely anyone praised Kate Chopin for writing with intelligence and maturity about a fascinating subject she had been studying all her life: how women think.

Very few reviewers even seemed to know that Kate Chopin was writing about more than sex.

That November Chopin wrote an essay suggesting that she was overwhelmed by events: "Ah! that moving procession that has left me by the road-side! ... What matters if souls and bodies are falling beneath the feet of the ever-pressing multitude! ... Oh! I could weep at being left by the wayside; left with the grass and the clouds and a few dumb animals."

She called that piece "A Reflection" and never sent it out for publication.

Whatever buzzings there may have been, Kate Chopin was not ostracized in St. Louis. Her *Post-Dispatch* friends in late November devoted almost an entire page to "A St. Louis Woman Who Has Won Fame in Literature," and the Wednesday Club rallied to honor her with one of its largest and best-attended gatherings.

The *Post-Dispatch* shrewdly positioned Kate Chopin as a Southern lady, with a drawing of her first home — made to look like a Southern mansion with galleries and columns. The article also included "Mrs. Chopin's Workroom From a Water Color Sketch By Her Son, Oscar Chopin": a well-appointed room with bookcases on either side of the fireplace, a musical clock, a nude Venus, and — in an armchair — Kate Chopin herself, leaning back and looking ethereal. The article praised Kate Chopin as a "universal" writer, "not sectional or provincial," with an appeal to "the finer taste.... Her art is not a cunning composition, but a living thing." Chopin also contributed an essay about her walking and writing habits — claiming, as always, to be un-serious and spontaneous.

A certain asperity crept in, though, when she wrote: "How hard it is for one's acquaintances and friends to realize that one's books are to be taken seriously, and that they are subject to the same laws which govern the existence of others' books!" Many an acquaintance had nagged her son with questions about where to get his mother's book. Chopin herself grew tired of telling people, politely, to try the booksellers or the libraries.

"The libraries! Oh, no, they don't keep it," a friend might claim, and "She hadn't thought of the bookseller's. It's real hard to think of everything! Sometimes I feel as if I should like to get a good, remunerative job to do the thinking for some people."

That comment about the libraries helped create a myth, generations later, that *The Awakening* had been banned and withdrawn from libraries — but it hadn't. The Mercantile Library and the St. Louis Public Library both bought multiple copies and kept them on the shelves until they wore out, as late as 1914 for the last one. Americans do like stories of banned books, but Billy Reedy — who loved to fulminate about censorship — would have gone into a volcanic rage if such a thing had happened to his friend Kate Chopin.

Sometimes with gritted teeth, Chopin strove to be polite to potential book buyers, but it was much easier to be gracious to the club women of St. Louis. Many of them were her lifelong friends, and they were loyal and enthusiastic. Nearly a decade after she had been one of its charter members, the Wednesday Club now had 250 members, all "women of brains, of wealth, or influence and undisputed power," according to the newspaper. For the Club's Reciprocity Day on November 29, nearly 400 women attended, the largest turnout in Chopin's life. It was an "Afternoon with St. Louis Authors," at which Kate Chopin was featured and honored.

The day's entertainment included poems by Chopin's admirer R. E. Lee Gibson; a performance of her poem "I Opened All the Portals Wide," with music by her friend Will Schuyler; a reading by Florence Hayward; and Chopin's own reading of her new story, "Ti Démon." Chopin wore an elegant ensemble ("black satin with white lace trimmings, jetted front and blue velvet toque," the *Post-Dispatch* reported), and her reading was a "touching little story of creole life."

A week later, Lélia's debutante season began in earnest, with a tea at the home of her wealthy aunt, Mrs. Charles Faris, whose husband — Kate's uncle — was known as "the family money man." (Clémence Benoist Faris had actually brought most of the money to the marriage: her father was the millionaire Louis A. Benoist, at whose Oakland estate Kate O'Flaherty and Oscar Chopin had begun their romance in the 1860s.) Clémence Faris also wore only white in the summer — a habit Chopin drew on for the character of Madame Lebrun in *The Awakening*. (She may also have known that Berthe Morisot, in France, wore only white in the summer.)

After Christmas, Lélia attended teas, parties, and receptions, and was a "Maid of Honor" at a ball for the Daughters of the Confederacy. Her mother, though, was not always present. Three decades earlier, Kate O'Flaherty had complained about the "general spreeing" required of a belle. For Lélia's début, she may have decided to follow her own inclinations, skip the spreeing, and stay home.

There were also some tensions between mother and daughter. Sometimes they seemed to be competing for male attention at social gatherings (or so Chopin's granddaughter heard years later). Teenagers are always embarrassed by their parents, but *The Awakening*'s notoriety must have created particularly awkward moments for Lélia. While she was the one having the début, her mother had just written a sex book that everyone was whispering about. Lélia, moreover, was not a conventional young woman. Bigger and louder than the average, she could be a trial to her charming, short, soft-spoken mother.

Kate Chopin had a bit of the Frenchwoman in her, while Lélia was thoroughly American.

In early 1900, Chopin's literary career continued, slowly. *Youth's Companion* accepted "A Little Country Girl," "Alexandre's Wonderful Experience," "The Gentleman from New Orleans," and "A December Day in Dixie," and paid for them all — although none ever appeared in print, probably because of an editorial change at the journal.

In February 1900, though, Chopin received crushing news. It was the coldest part of the winter in St. Louis, and nine months since *The Awakening* had begun receiving ignorant, berating reviews. Now her publisher, Herbert S. Stone, was cancelling the contract for her next story collection, *A Vocation and a Voice*.

The firm was cutting back on its list, but that may just have been an excuse to release an author whose books had gotten mostly bad reviews and slow sales. Chopin's royalties for *The Awakening* had added up to only $102, at a time when she was receiving as much as $50 for a single short story in *Youth's Companion*.

Stone may also have felt that he could not create an audience for an author whose new, strange stories were not bright Louisiana local color tales. Chopin's latest stories no longer had neat beginnings, middles, and ends, and they were often about loneliness, sadness, blindness, betrayal, and death. Of the twenty-two stories in the projected collection, only a few ("Suzette," "Ti Démon," and "The Godmother") were set in Louisiana, and many revolved around a variety of sins — such as reading private mail, deceiving well-meaning nuns, smoking hallucinogenic cigarettes, and rejoicing at the death of one's husband. There were also several stories about characters' having sexual relationships outside marriage. The collection, in short, could not have been marketed to "the Young Person." That would have meant more hostile reviews, and no library sales.

Yet a mystery remains, for Kate Chopin saved the warm fan letters from Sue V. Moore, Lizzie L., Anna L. Moss, and others. But she did not save Herbert S. Stone's letter cancelling *A Vocation and a Voice*. Nor is it in the Stone & Kimball correspondence collection in the Newberry Library in Chicago. Since Chopin simply noted in her manuscript account book: "R Feb. 1900," we do not know what Stone actually said. ("R" was her usual symbol for "returned.")

Stone's decision may have been commercial, or moral, or both. But Kate Chopin must have recognized that her career was slipping away from her. On her fiftieth birthday, in the same month that Stone cancelled *A Vocation and a Voice*, Chopin may have suspected that, like Edna in *The Awakening*, naked and unveiled to the world, she had swum out too far. "The shore was far behind her, and her strength was gone" (XXXIX).

# Chapter 13

## Aftermath

THROUGHOUT HER LIFE, Kate Chopin had been sustained by women friends and relatives, and only sometimes by male admirers. But her own intelligence and ambition had done the most to drive her away from the expected path — belle, wife, widow, club woman — and into a unique channel, as a writer of stories about women's dreams and conflicts and possibilities. As the new century opened, that channel seemed to be blocked, while the supports that had nurtured her throughout her life were crumbling.

Many women have a point at which they realize that they are middle-aged, and that many possibilities are forever closed to them. For someone like Kate Chopin, youth and beauty had long since become unimportant. The opportunities to express her opinions, to share her wit and insights, were what mattered most. If she had been French and a hostess rather than an author, running a salon might have been sufficient. She could nurture and cheer the talents of others, and bask in their appreciation.

But for a creative woman in St. Louis, that was not enough.

Four of her children were still living at home. Jean was a traveling salesman, Oscar an artist, and Felix a law student; Lélia, as was traditional for a débutante and a society woman, had no official occupation. The Morgan Street household also had one live-in servant, a thirty-year-old black woman named Annie Porter. In the 1900 census, Kate Chopin's occupation is listed as "capitalist."

Meanwhile, her son George was a physician living in a boarding house nearer his hospital — but her son Fred had been floundering since his short stint as one of the "spoiled darlings" in the Spanish-American

War. Fred changed jobs frequently—salesman, insurance agent, company clerk—and lived in a boarding house whose lodgers included three deputy sheriffs. He seemed to be in rebellion against the world, or perhaps against his mother, and he had become a heavy drinker. Chopin's fears about Fred may have led her to write her chilling 1899 story about a drunken young man whose godmother covers up for him—even to the extent of murder ("The Godmother").

Thinking about women seemed to make Kate Chopin happier. In April 1900, she wrote a resolutely cheerful story, "Charlie," about a tomboy, a Sacred Heart student who likes to write, but who has to learn to play the role of a sedate lady. Chopin struggled with revising the story, and with the main character's name (in some drafts, she is "Jack" or "Jacques"), and no one was interested in publishing it.

But that very month, Nina McAllister died. Nina, the odious little cousin in Kate O'Flaherty's schoolgirl diary, had never married. In her forties, she still lived with her mother, Chopin's Aunt Amanda, who was devastated by her death. Two years later, Chopin wrote to her sister-in-law that Aunt Amanda "went through so much sorrow and uneasiness in poor Nina's sickness that she has never gotten over it."

Many threads in Kate Chopin's life were being cut. A month after Nina's death, she wrote "The White Eagle," the sad story of a little girl who grows up and loses everything except her beloved cast-iron bird. *Vogue* accepted the story, and it was Chopin's last appearance in that magazine. Then, in August, for Kitty Garesché's fiftieth birthday, Kate Chopin wrote what proved to be her last poem.

### To the Friend of My Youth: To Kitty

It is not all of life
To cling together while the years glide past.
It is not all of love
To walk with clasped hands from first to last.
That mystic garland which the spring did twine
Of scented lilac and the new-blown rose,
Faster than chains will hold my soul to thine
Thro' joy, and grief, thro' life—unto its close.

That November, Chopin sold some Cane River country land to her brother-in-law Lamy Chopin, and did not attend most of the parties and receptions where her children spent their time. She was honored to be chosen for the very first edition of *Who's Who in America*, but her most important professional achievement was a long article she wrote for the December 9, 1900 St. Louis *Republic*.

The piece may have been too dull for the *Post-Dispatch*, or Chopin may have been seeking approval from the more conservative *Republic* audience, to revive her own flagging career. Possibly she was also thinking about Lélia's marital prospects, since one young man had been "rushing" her. Lélia already lacked a rich father, and having a mother who was considered hopelessly peculiar would hurt her in the eyes of conventional people.

Even in the *Republic* issue where her own article appeared, Kate Chopin was criticized. In a side article on St. Louis writers, Harrison Clark described the way Chopin claimed to write ("fluently, rapidly, and with practically no revision"), and then suddenly attacked *The Awakening*:

> This work is pretentious, and is more nearly what is known as a "problem novel" than any other St. Louis book. It has to deal with the heart and the wiles of a woman, and ends tragically. There has been much severe criticism of this book — not so much of the workmanship as of the story; but Mrs. Chopin says she does not mind that.

Apparently she minded enough that she wanted to appear ordinary, and normal, in the rest of the *Republic* spread. The front-page "Portrait of Mrs. Kate Chopin. From a Drawing Made By Her Son, Mr. Oscar C. Chopin, A St. Louis Art Student" is very different from the languishing, artfully beautiful pictures that had represented her before. The new Kate Chopin has her hair in a neat topknot and wears a brisk business suit of the kind commonly worn by suffragists, teachers, and other New Women. She sports a pince-nez (it is the only picture of her with eyeglasses), and is sorting papers with her large, capable hands. She looks dowdy but very moral — and so is her article on "Development of the Literary West," a three-column piece with very little energy or humor.

She begins by praising Father De Smet, the old Jesuit missionary who wrote about Indians and missionaries in frontier St. Louis, and she credits Bret Harte with opening up the West as a literary subject. But in her thumbnail sketches of other regionalists — Mary Hallock Foote, Ambrose Bierce, Owen Wister, and Octave Thanet — she makes only uncontroversial judgments, and even those sound apologetic. She calls Wister a "stagy fellow," for instance, but in the next sentence says "this may be a squeamish opinion, not wholly just."

Her discussion of Hamlin Garland is even more boringly fair-minded, without any of the verve or vociferousness of Billy Reedy's opinions — or her own 1894 review of Garland. Now, six years later, she says that "Hamlin Garland has been guilty of inexcusable crudities in handling men and women," but he is a good person anyway, who "believes in himself and follows his own light."

(In fact, the Garland story she praises, "The Land of the Straddle-Bug," resembles both *The Awakening* and "The Storm": a bored wife has an affair, including a rendezvous in a thunderstorm, with a younger, merrier man. Garland even ends with the same motifs as *The Awakening*: thoughts of motherhood, the smell of flowers, the humming of bees. But Chopin put none of that in print for the starchy *Republic* audience.)

Chopin does criticize the new Chicago writers and their attraction to "hideous complexities," and she claims to prefer the popular historical novelist Winston Churchill. Her final paragraph could be read as a blatant bid to be nice and middle-of-the-road, or as a drippingly ironic swipe at the Western Association of Writers she ridiculed six years earlier:

> After all, where are we to draw the line? May we not claim Mrs. Catherwood of the Northwest? James Whitcomb Riley and the whole State of Indiana that abounds in novelists and minor poets? . . . The West will surely continue to develop along the lines of a natural and wholesome growth, as yet unimpaired by intellectual complications.

Apparently Kate Chopin continued brooding and fuming through much of 1901. Or it may have been ill health, possibly diabetes or emphysema, that kept her from writing until mid-October, when R. E.

Lee Gibson sent her a copy of his newly published *Sonnets and Lyrics*, autographed to her "with admiration for her delightful stories." His book contains the only sonnet ever written in praise of Kate Chopin:

*"Bayou Folk"*
*To the Author of "Bayou Folk"*

Madam, your work is destined to receive
Still wider recognition; in these days,
Among the writers whom we justly praise,
Few pens such triumphs as your own achieve.
Witness the stories which you richly weave
Of Creole life, wherein your art portrays
Real men and women, and in charming ways,
Constrains us with them to rejoice or grieve.
This book of yours which I have read to-night
Pleases me much: my words but feebly tell
How I have followed with intense delight
The fortunes that these bayou folk befell;
The pen most truly is a thing of might
In hands like yours that wield its power so well.

Although she no longer wrote about "Creole life," Kate Chopin was delighted with the book and wrote back on October 13 that Gibson's poems showed "a fine, fine spirit and I am proud to know you. What a speaking likeness! Do come when you can and let us talk them over. Mr. Deyo and I have enjoyed reading some of the sonnets together."

Gibson's book also inspired her. For the first time in nearly a year and a half (since "The White Eagle"), she began writing short stories. Suddenly, and briefly, she was as productive and energetic as in the early 1890s, and she wrote three children's stories in three days: "Millie's First Party" (October 16); "The Wood-Choppers" (October 17); and "Toots' Nurses" (October 18). *Youth's Companion* accepted the first two, but finally published only "The Wood-Choppers," a slight, cheerful romantic comedy set in the bayou country. It was as if she had rediscovered William Dean Howells, and forgotten Guy de Maupassant.

In January 1902, Chopin wrote one more cheerful story, "Polly's Opportunity," a romantic comedy about two young people trying to save enough money to get married. In the end, the boss sends the young woman a brass teakettle with a "humorous injunction: 'Polly, put the kettle on!' " When *Youth's Companion* published that story in July, 1902, its last line — "Polly, put the kettle on!" — would be Chopin's last words to her readers.

With letters and visits, Kate Chopin kept up her Louisiana ties, cheering her brother-in-law Phanor Breazeale's election to the U.S. Congress. But on one visit with her brother-in-law Lamy and his wife Fannie, Kate and Lélia Chopin made a lifelong enemy. After a heavy meal, mother and daughter, both wearing boots, took a brisk stroll and inadvertently stepped on and killed several baby chicks who were four-year-old Julie's pets. (As of 1990, Julie Chopin Cusachs still had not forgiven them.)

In the spring of 1902, the first Chopin "child" finally decided to marry and leave home. Her eldest son Jean was thirty-one when he married twenty-eight-year-old Emelie Hughes, a college graduate, in Evansville, Indiana. They settled in St. Louis, where Oscar, Felix, and Lélia were still at home with their mother.

But there were also sorrows. That spring, Kate Chopin's sister-in-law Eugénie Chopin Henry died in Louisiana. At fifty-four, she was only two years older than Kate. That September, her old newspaper friend John Dillon fell from a horse, fractured a rib, contracted pneumonia and pleurisy, and died a few weeks later. He was fifty-nine, and had been one of the first to encourage her literary career. In 1900 he was working for the *Chicago Tribune,* and perhaps they still saw each other: he may have been the married newspaper editor who loved her. The other possibility, George Johns, served as one of Dillon's pallbearers.

In October 1902, Kate Chopin gave her brothers-in-law Lamy Chopin and Phanor Breazeale power of attorney for her Louisiana properties, and the following year, four pieces of Louisiana land were sold for her and her heirs. Her writing career was providing very little income: in 1902, $105 for three stories, plus $3.35 in royalties for *Bayou Folk*. She earned no royalties from *A Night in Acadie* or *The Awakening*.

In December 1902, Kate Chopin made a will, with special provisions for her only daughter. Her property was to be divided equally among her sons, but Lélia was to get her mother's clothes, jewelry, and the city land on Seventh Street, between Franklin and Washington, that Thomas O'Flaherty had shrewdly purchased half a century earlier. Chopin directed, pointedly, that Lélia would have that land "to her sole and separate use, free from any debts or claims against her husband." Chopin was still following the advice that the wise widows of her girlhood would have given: make sure that Lélia can be independent. Give her an income of her own.

The will was witnessed by Linn Brokaw, a twenty-three-year-old law student and friend of Chopin's sons, and by Isabel Willcox, an English and history teacher at Central High School. It was less common, in those days before women had the vote, for a woman to witness a will, and Chopin was probably making some kind of statement (at least to herself) by having a single, independent woman witness the will that would give Lélia that same freedom.

By 1903, Kate Chopin was definitely ailing, and told her children, "I hope I will die first so that I will not lose any one of you." Fred, variously working as a superintendent or a clerk, had moved back to his mother's house. Felix, an attorney, still lived at home, as did Oscar, who had become the *Post-Dispatch*'s chief editorial cartoonist. (His mother probably helped with the short poems that sometimes appeared beneath his cartoons). Lélia, years after her début, was a maid of honor in the Veiled Prophet's Court (St. Louis's equivalent of Mardi Gras), and was being courted by Frederick Hattersley, whose English-born father had made his fortune in flour.

In 1903, Kate Chopin also made a great change in her life, moving out of the Morgan Street home where she had lived for some seventeen years. She had held her "Thursdays" there, and had been the center of an admiring literary and cultural circle. But she was making her life smaller by moving into a newer, rented house at 4232 McPherson

Avenue, between Boyle and Whittier. (It is the only Chopin home still existing in St. Louis.) The two-and-a-half-story house had elegant woodwork, a winding staircase, a lovely front parlor, and a second-floor room perfect for a writing studio — if Kate Chopin had been writing.

But the house's greatest advantage was its location, virtually around the corner from the home of Jean and Emelie Chopin, who were expecting their first child. If Kate Chopin wrote about her plans for being a grandmother — and, perhaps, her hopes for a granddaughter to carry on the female line — those writings do not survive.

On the morning of July 7, something went terribly wrong. Emelie Hughes Chopin, twenty-nine years old, died in childbirth, along with her infant. They were buried two days later in the same grave, in Calvary Cemetery, and Jean Chopin was shattered. He moved back to his mother's house and was listed in the city directory the next year as a salesman. But he had had a nervous breakdown, and his mother spent much of her time caring for him. He never fully recovered from his grief.

Who comforted Kate Chopin is not known. Of her older female relatives, Aunt Amanda was still living, but also grieving over the loss of her own daughter. Clémence Benoist Faris's husband, Kate's Uncle Charles, died in May 1904, with yet another funeral at the New Cathedral and burial in Calvary Cemetery. Kate Chopin's comfort may have come from her lifelong friend Kitty Garesché, who now lived in the convent near the New Cathedral at Maryland and Taylor Avenues. It was only a short walk from Chopin's new address, and there was a quiet convent parlor for visits.

Most likely the serenity of the nuns and the quiet and sensible voices of women were — as in her childhood — Kate Chopin's refuge, consolation, and strength.

Chopin bought one of the first season's tickets to the World's Fair of 1904. Just six blocks away by railway, it was a spectacular event that is still celebrated in St. Louis. The extravagant show included artificial canals and lagoons, lovely colored lights and waterfalls, and exotic peoples and animals and customs from all over the world. Music lovers like Kate Chopin could hear the new ragtime compositions by Scott Joplin, and marvel at undreamed-of technological inventions, such as computers and automatic telephones. She could witness the Creation, the Hereafter, or the Galveston Flood, or ride the world's largest ferris wheel, or sample two special treats: iced tea and ice cream cones.

Women were well represented. The first female official World's Fair photographer was Jessie Tarbox Beals, while Helen Keller and her teacher Annie Sullivan demonstrated what people with disabilities could accomplish. Florence Hayward, the Fair's only woman commissioner, had gotten the Vatican to lend precious jewels for the show, and she went about yelling, "Hats off! Hats off!" to men who did not doff their caps for the singing of "America" at the fair's opening ceremonies.

All summer, St. Louis was humid, with stagnant air and few breezes.

August 20 was a particularly intense Saturday, with military drills, band concerts, a program by Native American school pupils, a meeting of the International Congress of the Deaf, and a display by Pennsylvania military companies in full regalia. It was also the hottest day since the fair's opening, and Kate Chopin came home very tired.

At midnight she called to her son Jean, saying she had a severe pain in her head. When he reached her bedside, she was unconscious. The next day, with her children at her bedside, she recognized her son George, but complained again about the pain in her head. The doctors thought she had had a cerebral hemorrhage, and on Sunday night, she lapsed into unconsciousness again.

The following day, on August 22, at noon, Kate Chopin died.

The obituaries praised Kate Chopin as the author of *Bayou Folk*, a charming collection of Creole tales, but most slid over *The Awakening*, calling it not her best work. Only Billy Reedy managed to pull together all her roles, calling her "a remarkably talented woman, who knew how to be a genius without sacrificing the comradeship of her children. As a mother, wife and friend she shone resplendent and her contributions to fiction, though few, showed that she possessed true literary genius." Reedy called all four of her books — *At Fault, Bayou*

*Folk, A Night in Acadie,* and *The Awakening*—"literary treasures which she has left and which have afforded many a pleasant hour."

The requiem mass was celebrated on Wednesday, August 24, 1904, at the New Cathedral, by Father Francis Gilfillan. The active pallbearers included Fred Hattersley (Lélia's fiancé), Lewis B. Ely, and Linn Brokaw, while the honorary pallbearers included her salon visitors Franklin Ferriss and George Blackman, and her dear friend from the *Post-Dispatch,* Charles L. Deyo. (Billy Reedy might have wanted to participate, but he had been excommunicated seven years earlier. Frederick Kolbenheyer, a militant atheist, probably was not invited.)

Kate Chopin was buried in Section 17, Lot 47, along the Way of the Second Dolor, in a plot originally purchased by her husband's grandmother, Suzette Rachal Benoist. Emelie Hughes Chopin and her infant had been buried there in July under a gravestone that says "June," and Kate Chopin's stone makes her a year younger than she actually was:

KATE CHOPIN

February 1851

August 1904

A lilac bush, her favorite flower, grew near the grave, casting a comforting shadow on the stone.

Later her children, who died in the same order they had been born, would be buried around her. Within a few years after her death, all of them married and established their own homes except for Jean, who died of typhoid in 1911. Oscar, the cartoonist (who died in 1933) moved to California and worked for the Hearst papers; his daughter Kate was a gifted artist. George, the physician (d. 1952), settled in Baden, a German town in north St. Louis, where he practiced for fifty years. His wife never approved of Kate Chopin (whom she'd never met) for being a lapsed Catholic, but "Doc" used to say that his mother had been ahead of her time and "too damn smart" to stay in the church.

For Fred Chopin (d. 1953), his first marriage ended in divorce because of his drinking, but then he moved to California with his second wife and became a solid citizen—a neat, precise man who worked as a candy company representative. Felix ("Phil" — d. 1955) remained in St. Louis as a lawyer in general practice, with Dr. Kolbenheyer as his family's obstetrician. The doctor, meanwhile, continued riling the establishment. A few years after Kate Chopin's death, he helped sponsor the erection of a black, larger-than-life female nude statue called "The Naked Truth" for the Compton Heights Reservoir Park. (Generations of youngsters enjoyed sitting on the statue's lap and fondling her breasts.) Kolbenheyer died in Omaha in 1921.

Lélia Chopin Hattersley (d. 1962) may have led the life her mother wanted for her. Her husband died just four years after their wedding, leaving her with a small son, and so she joined the long line of family widows, stretching back at least to her great-great-grandmother, the brilliant Madame Charleville. Lélia never remarried, and like her mother, she carved out a distinctive and unique career with the materials women had given to her.

Her mother had been a dedicated card player, a self-styled "euchre fiend," and Lélia turned her own lifelong card playing into a profession. By the 1920s, Lélia Hattersley had become an expert bridge player and teacher, who divided her time between New York and Palm Beach and eventually published six books on bridge and backgammon. She also wrote articles on New York drama for the St. Louis *Globe-Democrat* (but only after Ellen McKee, the paper's owner and her mother's nemesis, had died).

Lélia was a thoroughly dramatic character herself — a large, flamboyant woman with dark eyes mysteriously shadowed and dark-rimmed, who liked to provoke angry scenes in restaurants (frozen orange juice was her particular *bête noir*). She also enjoyed riding about in an open convertible, yelling praise and anatomical comments at young men. Her nieces and nephews, often embarrassed, compared "Aunt Lil" with Margaret Dumont, the dowager in Marx Brothers films. But Lélia Hattersley worked very hard to promote her mother's writings with critics, and sometimes did so by simply fabricating a more acceptable image: she told one critic that Kate Chopin had been Cloutierville's "Lady Bountiful," when in fact she had been more of a village scourge.

Chopin was not thoroughly forgotten in Louisiana. In New Orleans she was remembered as a vaguely scandalous figure, although most people no longer remembered quite why. But in Cloutierville, descendants of those who had known her remembered quite clearly her flirtation with Albert Sampite, her fashionable riding habits, and her refusal to fit into a simple rural environment.

Sampite himself continued keeping company with his neighbor Maria Normand and doted on her granddaughter, Ivy — but when he died in 1913, it was in the house of his estranged wife, Loca. Their daughter Marie knew that Albert had been a heavy drinker and a violent man, but she never gave up her belief that Kate Chopin, that glamorous and terrible Yankee woman, had been the reason her parents did not stay together.

After 1906, *The Awakening* was out of print for nearly half a century — although in the 1920s, students at the Louisiana Normal School (now Northwestern State University in Natchitoches) wrote and performed plays based on Kate Chopin's stories. Chopin Hall, a dormitory at "the Normal," survived until a fire destroyed it in the 1970s. Meanwhile, in 1964, Chopin's home in Cloutierville had been transformed by Mildred McCoy into the Bayou Folk Museum/Kate Chopin Home, with official landmark status. In 1980 Albert and Loca Sampite's grandson, Joseph, was elected mayor of the town of Natchitoches.

Kate Chopin's pretty amethyst hurricane lamp, the one that Albert Sampite later gave to Maria Normand, was broken by a New Orleans handyman. Her dresser, given to Emma Perrier, was kept for some two decades in a falling-down Cloutierville house, but may be transferred to the Museum, where Mrs. Scruggs's sewing machine — the one Maria Normand also used — is on display. Chopin's gaming table, with its plush green velveteen surface, is now covered over and used as a kitchen table by Albert's granddaughter, Leona Sampite.

Outside Louisiana, and despite Daniel Rankin's *Kate Chopin and Her Creole Stories* (1932), Chopin was virtually unknown in the literary world for decades after her death. Rankin, a Marist priest, was a careless researcher who interviewed very few people, and mostly men, about

Chopin's life. Lélia Hattersley considered his book a whitewash and called him "that horrible man" — something that was proved in 1992, when the new owners of a Massachusetts warehouse found Chopin manuscripts that Rankin had "borrowed" and squirreled away in a locker sixty years earlier. The new manuscripts, in crumbly newsprint (and now reprinted in *Kate Chopin's Private Papers*), confirm that Chopin was not the nonchalant writer she claimed to be, but a dedicated and ambitious reviser of her own work.

But by the 1990s, Kate Chopin's reputation had been resurrected — mostly by Per Seyersted, a Norwegian, who in 1961 read *The Awakening* during his graduate studies at Harvard. His mother had been a feminist leader in Norway, and Seyersted recognized the unique talent in the book. He spent seven years combing archives and libraries for manuscripts and unpublished papers, and Lélia's son Robert Hattersley gave him Chopin's 1894 diary, containing the shockingly sensual story "The Storm." When Seyersted's *Complete Works of Kate Chopin* and *Kate Chopin: A Critical Biography* were both published in 1969, they coincided with the rebirth of feminism in the United States. Seyersted's claim that *The Awakening* had been banned drew thousands of readers to the book.

By the 1990s, *The Awakening* was being taught in American literature and women's studies courses everywhere in the United States, and in translation in Poland, Norway, Japan, Italy, France, and elsewhere. Two film versions of *The Awakening* had been made (under the names *Grand Isle* and *The End of August*), and a new biography by Emily Toth appeared in 1990. In 1991, ninety years after it was originally scheduled to appear, Chopin's last story collection, *A Vocation and a Voice*, was finally published — as a Penguin Classic, with an introduction by Emily Toth.

The manuscripts Rankin had hidden (now called the Rankin-Marhefka Fragments), along with Chopin's diaries, letters, and other papers, were published in 1998 in *Kate Chopin's Private Papers*, edited by Emily Toth, Per Seyersted, and Cheyenne Bonnell.

All of the attention would have pleased, and certainly surprised, Kate Chopin. Like most writers, she was most interested in immediate sales and contemporary appreciation, although she liked the idea that certain writings would last. She even criticized those like Henrik Ibsen who, she said, would not endure, since he wrote about "social problems which by their very nature are mutable."

She was wrong about Ibsen, of course, and would no doubt have been wrong about the fate of her own works. A century later, *The Awakening* still speaks to women, in particular, about the war between responsibility to others and responsibility to oneself. There are always voices, often deep ones, to tell a woman that she is not doing enough for others — that she is selfish, mean, and irresponsible. Such voices have silenced women throughout the centuries.

But Kate O'Flaherty grew up with the sound of women's voices telling her that it is good for a girl to be smart, to be shrewd, to manage her own money, to be independent, to have opinions, and to tell her own stories in her own way.

Kate Chopin did exactly that in *The Awakening* and her stories — leaving us, a century later, still wondering about the "woman of mysterious fascination" who rose to fame in St. Louis, tore away many of the veils of conventionality, and flew too close to the sun.

But a century later, when we read her, we know that she opened windows, and she gave us wings.

This list includes all of Kate Chopin's known writings, both published and unpublished. Also listed here are writings recorded in her manuscript account notebooks, but now destroyed or lost. The items are arranged in order of composition, with final title, date of composition, first appearance in print, and inclusion in collections. Where titles vary, I have listed variations. CW and KCPP include information about changes from manuscript to print versions.

## Abbreviations

BF = Kate Chopin, *Bayou Folk*. Boston: Houghton, Mifflin, 1894.

CW = Per Seyersted, ed., *The Complete Works of Kate Chopin*. Baton Rouge: Louisiana State University Press, 1969.

DIR = writings appearing in "Impressions," Kate Chopin's 1894 diary, reprinted in KCPP.

DSR = Daniel S. Rankin, *Kate Chopin and Her Creole Stories*. Philadelphia: University of Pennsylvania Press, 1932.

KCM = Per Seyersted and Emily Toth, eds., *A Kate Chopin Miscellany*. Natchitoches and Oslo: Northwestern State University Press and Universitetsforlaget, 1979.

KCPP = Emily Toth, Per Seyersted, and Cheyenne Bonnell, eds., *Kate Chopin's Private Papers*. Bloomington: Indiana University Press, 1998.

NA = Kate Chopin, *A Night in Acadie*. Chicago: Way & Williams, 1897.

PS1 = Per Seyersted, "Kate Chopin: An Important St. Louis Writer Reconsidered," *Missouri Historical Society Bulletin* 19 (January 1963), 89–114.

PS2 = Per Seyersted, "Kate Chopin's Wound: Two New Letters," *American Literary Realism* 20, no. 1 (Fall 1987), 71–75.

RMF = Rankin-Marhefka Fragments, found in a Massachusetts locker in 1992, partially reprinted in KCPP.

SCB = Per Seyersted, *Kate Chopin: A Critical Biography*. Oslo and Baton Rouge: Universitetsforlaget and Louisiana State University, 1969.

TB = Thomas Bonner Jr., *The Kate Chopin Companion*. Westport, Conn.: Greenwood Press, 1988.

TKC = Emily Toth, *Kate Chopin: A Life of the Author of "The Awakening."* New York: William Morrow, 1990; Austin: University of Texas Press, 1993.

## Chronological Listing of Works

"Leaves of Affection." Autograph book (with pictures, poems, brief comments by Kate O'Flaherty). 1860–. KCPP.

"Katie O'Flaherty, St. Louis. 1867" (diary and commonplace book). 1867–1870. DSR (in part). KCM (in part). KCPP (in full).

"Emancipation. A Life Fable." Undated: late 1869 or early 1870. PS1. CW.

New Orleans diary. 1870–. Seen by Rankin; later lost.

Letter to Marie Breazeale. June 21, 1887. KCM. KCPP.

"Lilia. Polka for Piano." Undated. Published for the author by H. Rollman & Sons, St. Louis, 1888. KCM. KCPP.

"If It Might Be" (poem). Undated. *America* (Chicago) 1 (January 10, 1889), 9. CW.

("Euphrasie" (story). 1888. See "A No-Account Creole.")

Manuscript Account Books (2). 1888–. KCPP.

"Unfinished Story — Grand Isle." 1888–89. Destroyed.

"A Poor Girl" (story). May 1889. Destroyed.

"Wiser than a God" (story). June 1889. *Philadelphia Musical Journal* 4 (December 1889), 38–40. CW.

"A Point at Issue!" (story). August 1889. *St. Louis Post-Dispatch*, October 27, 1889. CW.

"Miss Witherwell's Mistake" (story). November 18, 1889. *Fashion and Fancy* (St. Louis) 5 (February 1891), 115–117. CW.

"With the Violin" (story). December 11, 1889. *Spectator* (St. Louis) 11 (December 6, 1890), 196. CW.

*At Fault* (novel). July 5, 1889–April 20, 1890. Published for the author by Nixon-Jones Printing Co., St. Louis, September 1890. CW.

"Monsieur Pierre" (story; translation from Adrien Vely). April 1890. *St. Louis Post-Dispatch*, August 8, 1892. TB. KCPP.

"Psyche's Lament" (poem). Undated; probably 1890. DSR. CW.

Letter to the *St. Louis Republic*. October 18, 1890. *St. Louis Republic*, October 25, 1890. KCM. KCPP.

"Young Dr. Gosse" (novel, also called "Young Dr. Gosse and Théo"). May 4–November 27, 1890. Destroyed.

"A Red Velvet Coat" (story). December 1–8, 1890. Destroyed or lost.

"*At Fault.* A Correction" (letter). December 11, 1890. *Natchitoches Enterprise,* December 18, 1890. TKC. KCPP.

"Mrs. Mobry's Reason" (story). January 10, 1891. *New Orleans Times-Democrat,* April 23, 1893. CW.

"The Shape of the Head" (translation of an article listed in Chopin's account book as "A Study in Heads"). Undated. *St. Louis Post-Dispatch,* January 25, 1891. KCPP.

"A No-Account Creole" (story). 1888 (called "Euphrasie"); rewritten January 24, 1891–February 24, 1891. *Century* 47 (January 1894), 382–393. BF. CW.

"Octave Feuillet" (translation?). February 1891. Destroyed or lost.

"Roger and His Majesty" (story). March 1, 1891. Destroyed.

"Revival of Wrestling" (translation). Undated. *St. Louis Post-Dispatch,* March 8, 1891. KCPP.

"For Marse Chouchoute" (story). March 14, 1891. *Youth's Companion* 64 (August 20, 1891), 450–451. BF. CW.

"The Christ Light" (story). April 4, 1891, under the title "The Going and Coming of Liza Jane." Syndicated, American Press Association. December 1892. CW calls the story "The Going Away of Liza."

"Cut Paper Figures" (also called "Manikins" and "How to Make Manikins": translation?) Undated. *St. Louis Post-Dispatch,* April 5, 1891. KCPP.

"The Maid of Saint Phillippe" (story). April 19, 1891. *Short Stories* (New York) 11 (November 1891), 257–264. CW.

"A Wizard from Gettysburg" (story). May 25, 1891. *Youth's Companion* 65 (July 7, 1892), 346–347. BF. CW.

Letter to the *Century.* May 28, 1891. KCM. KCPP.

"A Shameful Affair" (story). June 5, 7, 1891. *New Orleans Times-Democrat,* April 9, 1893. CW.

Letter to R. W. Gilder. July 12, 1891. KCM. KCPP.

"A Rude Awakening" (story). July 13, 1891. *Youth's Companion* 66 (February 2, 1893), 54–55. BF. CW.

"A Harbinger" (story). September 11, 1891. *St. Louis Magazine* 12 (apparently November 1, 1891: no copies can be found). CW.

"Dr. Chevalier's Lie" (story). September 12, 1891. *Vogue* 2 (October 5, 1893), 174, 178. CW.

"A Very Fine Fiddle" (story). September 13, 1891. *Harper's Young People* 13 (November 24, 1891), 79. BF. CW.

"Boulôt and Boulotte" (story). September 20, 1891. *Harper's Young People* 13 (December 8, 1891), 112. BF. CW.

"Love on the Bon-Dieu" (story). October 3, 1891, as "Love and Easter." *Two Tales* (Boston) 2 (July 23, 1892), 148–156. BF. CW.

"An Embarrassing Position. Comedy in One Act." October 15–22, 1891. *Mirror* (St. Louis) 5 (December 19, 1895), 9–11. CW.

"Beyond the Bayou" (story). November 7, 1891. *Youth's Companion* 66 (June 15, 1893), 302–303. BF. CW.

"Typical Forms of German Music." Paper read at the Wednesday Club, St. Louis, December 9, 1891. Possibly the same as "Typical German Composers," essay offered in 1899 to the *Atlantic*. Destroyed or lost.

"After the Winter" (story). December 31, 1891. *New Orleans Times-Democrat,* April 5, 1896. NA. CW.

"The Bênitous' Slave" (story). January 7, 1892. *Harper's Young People* 13 (February 16, 1892), 280. BF. CW.

"A Turkey Hunt" (story). January 8, 1892. *Harper's Young People* 13 (February 16, 1892), 287. BF. CW.

"Old Aunt Peggy" (story). January 8, 1892. BF. CW.

"The Lilies" (story). January 27–28, 1892. *Wide Awake* 36 (April 1893), 415–418. NA. CW.

"Mittens" (story). February 25, 1892. Destroyed.

"Ripe Figs" (story). February 26, 1892. *Vogue* 2 (August 19, 1893), 90. NA. CW.

"Croque-Mitaine" (story). February 27, 1892. PS1. CW.

"A Trip to Portuguese Guinea" (translation?). February 27, 1892. Destroyed or lost.

"A Visit to the Planet Mars" (translation?). March 1892. Destroyed or lost.

"Transfusion of Goat's Blood" (translation?). March 1892. Destroyed or lost.

"Miss McEnders" (story). March 7, 1892. *Criterion* (St. Louis) 13 (March 6, 1897), 16–18, signed La Tour. CW.

"Loka" (story). April 9–10, 1892. *Youth's Companion* 65 (December 22, 1892), 670–671. BF. CW.

"Bambo Pellier" (story). May (?) 1892. Destroyed or lost.

"At the 'Cadian Ball" (story). July 15–17, 1892. *Two Tales* (Boston) 3 (October 22, 1892), 145–152. BF. CW.

"A Visit to Avoyelles" (story). August 1, 1892. *Vogue* 1 (January 14, 1893), 74–75. BF. CW.

"Ma'ame Pélagie" (story). August 27–28, 1892. *New Orleans Times-Democrat,* December 24, 1893. BF. CW.

"A Fancy" (poem). Probably 1892. DSR. KCM. KCPP.

"Désirée's Baby" (story). November 24, 1892. *Vogue* 1 (January 14, 1893), 70–71, 74. BF. CW.

"Caline" (story). December 2, 1892. Vogue 1 (May 20, 1893), 324–325. NA. CW.

"The Return of Alcibiade" (story). December 5–6, 1892. *St. Louis Life* 7 (December 17, 1892), 6–8. BF. CW.

"In and Out of Old Natchitoches" (story). February 1–3, 1892. *Two Tales* 5 (April 8, 1893), 178–179. NA. CW.

"Mamouche" (story). February 24–25, 1893. *Youth's Companion* 67 (April 19, 1894), 178–179. NA. CW.

Letter to Marion A. Baker. May 4, 1893. KCM. KCPP.

Letter to R. W. Gilder. May 10, 1893. KCM. KCPP.

"Madame Célestin's Divorce" (story). May 24–25, 1893. BF. CW.

"The Song Everlasting" (poem). Before June 1893. Published in the program for the St. Louis Wednesday Club's "Reciprocity Day: An Afternoon with St. Louis Authors," November 29, 1899. CW.

"You and I" (poem). Before June 1893. Published in the program for the St. Louis Wednesday Club's "Reciprocity Day: An Afternoon with St. Louis Authors," November 29, 1899. CW.

"It Matters All" (poem). Before June 1893. DSR. CW.

"If the Woods Could Talk" (poem). Before June 1893. KCM. KCPP.

"A Sentimental Serenade" (poem). Before June 1893. KCM. KCPP.

"A Message" (poem). Before June 1893. KCM. KCPP.

"An Idle Fellow" (story). June 9, 1893. CW.

"A Matter of Prejudice" (story). June 17–18, 1893. *Youth's Companion* 68 (September 25, 1895), 450. NA. CW.

"Azélie" (story). July 22–23, 1893. *Century* 49 (December 1894), 282–287. NA. CW.

"A Lady of Bayou St. John" (story). August 24–25, 1893. *Vogue* 2 (September 21, 1893), 154, 156–158. BF. CW.

"La Belle Zoraïde" (story). September 21, 1893. *Vogue* 3 (January 4, 1894), 2, 4, 8–10. BF. CW.

"At Chênière Caminada" (story). October 21–23, 1893. *New Orleans Times-Democrat,* December 23, 1894. NA. CW.

"A Gentleman of Bayou Têche" (story). November 5–7, 1893. BF. CW.

"In Sabine" (story). November 20–22, 1893. BF. CW.

"A Respectable Woman" (story). January 20, 1894. *Vogue* 3 (February 15, 1894), 68–69, 72. NA. CW.

"Tante Cat'rinette" (story). February 23, 1894. *Atlantic Monthly* 74 (September 1894), 368–373. NA. CW.

"A Dresden Lady in Dixie" (story). March 6, 1894. *Catholic Home Journal* (March 3, 1895). NA. CW.

*Bayou Folk* (collected stories). Published March 1894, by Houghton, Mifflin & Co., Boston.

"The Dream of an Hour" (story). April 19, 1894. *Vogue* 4 (December 6, 1894), 360. CW calls the story "The Story of an Hour," and modern editors use that title.

"Impressions. 1894" (diary). May 4, 1894–October 26, 1896. Published in part in SCB. KCM. KCPP.

"Lilacs" (story). May 14–16, 1894. *New Orleans Times-Democrat,* December 20, 1896. CW.

"Good Night" (poem). Undated. *New Orleans Times-Democrat,* July 22, 1894. CW.

"The Western Association of Writers" (essay). June 30, 1894. *Critic* 22 (July 7, 1894), 15. CW. DIR.

"A Divorce Case" (story; translation of "Un cas de divorce," by Guy de Maupassant). July 11, 1894. TB. DIR.

"A Scrap and a Sketch": "The Night Came Slowly" (story). July 24, 1894; "Juanita" (story). July 26, 1894. *Moods* (Philadelphia) 2 (July 1895), n. p. CW prints the two separately as "The Night Came Slowly" and "Juanita." DIR.

"Dorothea" (untitled story, possibly a real-life observation — not listed separately in manuscript account notebook, and not sent out separately for publication). July 25, 1894, in 1894 diary. KCM. KCPP. DIR.

"Cavanelle" (story) July 31–August 6, 1894. *American Jewess* 1 (April 1895), 22–25. NA. CW. DIR.

"Mad?" (story; translation of "Fou?" by Guy de Maupassant). September 4, 1894. TB. DIR.

Letter to Stone & Kimball. September 10, 1894. KCM. KCPP.

"Regret" (story). September 17, 1894. *Century* 50 (May 1895), 147–149. NA. CW. DIR.

"The Kiss" (story). September 19, 1894. *Vogue* 5 (January 17, 1895), 37. CW. DIR.

"Ozème's Holiday" (story). September 23–24, 1894. *Century* 52 (August 1896), 629–631. NA. CW. DIR.

"'Crumbling Idols' by Hamlin Garland" (essay). Undated. *St. Louis Life* 10 (October 6, 1894), 13. CW.

Letter to Waitman Barbe. October 2, 1894. KCM. KCPP.

"The Real Edwin Booth" (essay). Undated. *St. Louis Life* 10 (October 13, 1894), 11. CW.

"Emile Zola's 'Lourdes'" (essay). Undated. *St. Louis Life* 10 (November 17, 1894), 5. CW.

"A Sentimental Soul" (story). November 18–22, 1894. *New Orleans Times-Democrat,* December 22, 1895. NA. CW.

"Her Letters" (story). November 29, 1894. *Vogue* 5 (April 11, 18, 1895), 228–230, 248. CW.

Letters to A. A. Hill. December 26, 1894; January 1, 11, 16, 1895. KCM. KCPP.

"Odalie Misses Mass" (story). January 28, 1895. *Shreveport Times,* July 1, 1895. NA. CW.

"It?" (story; translation of "Lui?" by Guy de Maupassant). February 4, 1895. *St. Louis Life* 11 (February 23, 1895), 12–13. TB.

"Polydore" (story). February 17, 1895. *Youth's Companion* 70 (April 23, 1896), 214–215. NA. CW.

"Dead Men's Shoes" (story). February 21–22, 1895. *Independent* (New York) 49 (February 11, 1897), 194–195. NA. CW.

"Solitude" (story; translation of "Solitude" by Guy de Maupassant). March 5, 1895. *St. Louis Life* 13 (December 28, 1895), 30. TB.

"Night" (story; translation of "La Nuit" by Guy de Maupassant). March 8, 1895. TB.

Letter to J. M. Stoddart. March 31, 1895. KCM. KCPP.

"Athénaïse" (story). April 10–28, 1895. *Atlantic Monthly* 78 (August, September 1896), 232–241, 404–413. NA. CW.

"A Lady of Shifting Intentions" (story). May 4, 1895. Destroyed or lost; extant fragment in KCM, KCPP.

"Two Summers and Two Souls" (story). July 14, 1895. *Vogue* 6 (August 7, 1895), 84. CW.

"The Unexpected" (story). July 18, 1895. *Vogue* 6 (September 18, 1895), 180–181. CW.

"Two Portraits" (story). August 4, 1895. DSR. CW.

"If Some Day" (poem). August 16, 1895. CW. DIR.

"Under My Lattice" (poem). August 18, 1895. KCM. KCPP. DIR.

"To Carrie B." (poem). Autumn 1895. CW. DIR.

"The Falling in Love of Fedora." November 19, 1895, as "Fedora." *Criterion* (St. Louis) 13 (February 20, 1897), 9, signed La Tour. Published in CW as "Fedora."

Letter to Cornelia F. Maury. December 3, 1895. KCM. KCPP.

"For Mrs. Ferriss" (poem). December 1895. KCM. KCPP. DIR.

"To Blanche" (poem). December 1895. KCM. KCPP. DIR.

"Vagabonds" (story). December (?) 1895. DSR. CW.

"Suicide" (story; translation of "Suicide" by Guy de Maupassant). December 18, 1895. *St. Louis Republic,* June 5, 1898. TB.

"To Hidee Schuyler — " (poem). Christmas 1895. CW. DIR.

"To 'Billy' with a Box of Cigars" (poem). Christmas 1895. CW. DIR.

Letter to Stone & Kimball. January 2, 1896. KCM. KCPP.

"Madame Martel's Christmas Eve" (story). January 16–18, 1896. CW.

"The Recovery" (story). February 1896. *Vogue* 7 (May 21, 1896), 354–355. CW.

"A Night in Acadie" (story). March 1896. NA. CW.

"A Pair of Silk Stockings" (story). April 1896. *Vogue* 10 (September 16, 1897), 191–192. CW.

"Nég Créol" (story). April 1896. *Atlantic Monthly* 80 (July 1897), 135–138. NA. CW.

"Aunt Lympy's Interference" (story). June 1896. *Youth's Companion* 71 (August 12, 1897), 373–374. CW.

"The Blind Man" (story). July 1896. *Vogue* 9 (May 13, 1897), 303. CW.

"In the Confidence of a Story-Writer" (essay). October 1896. *Atlantic Monthly* 83 (January 1899), 137–139, published without an author's name. CW. (An earlier version, written September 1896 and entitled "Confidences," is also published in CW.)

"Ti Frère" (story). September 1896. KCM. KCPP.

"For Sale" (story; translation of "A Vendre" by Guy de Maupassant). October 26, 1896. TB. DIR.

"A Vocation and a Voice" (story). November 1896. *Mirror* (St. Louis) 12 (March 27, 1902), 18–24. CW.

"A Mental Suggestion" (story). December 1896. CW.

"To Mrs. R" (poem). Christmas 1896. CW. DIR.

"Let the Night Go" (poem). January 1, 1897. CW.

Letter to the *Century*. January 5, 1897. KCM. KCPP.

Inscription for Ruth McEnery Stuart. February 3, 1897. KCM. KCPP.

"Suzette" (story). February 1897. *Vogue* 10 (October 21, 1897), 262–263. CW.

"As You Like It" (a series of six essays). Undated, individual essay titles supplied by Per Seyersted. *Criterion* (St. Louis) 13:

    I. "I have a young friend..." (February 13, 1897), 11. CW.

    II. "It has lately been..." (February 20, 1897), 17. CW.

    III. "Several years ago..." (February 26, 1897), 11. CW.

    IV. "A while ago..." (March 13, 1897), 15–16. CW.

    V. "A good many of us..." (March 20, 1897), 10. CW.

    VI. "We are told..." (March 27, 1897), 10. CW.

"The Locket" (story). March 1897. CW.

"An Easter Day Conversion" (story). April 1897, as "A Morning Walk." *Criterion* (St. Louis) 15 [*sic*] (April 17, 1897), 13–14. CW calls the story "A Morning Walk."

"An Egyptian Cigarette" (story). April 1897. *Vogue* 15 (April 19, 1900), 252–254. CW.

*A Night in Acadie* (collected stories). Published November 1897, by Way & Williams, Chicago.

The Awakening (novel). June (?), 1897–January 21, 1898, listed in Chopin's notebook as "A Solitary Soul." Published April 22, 1899, by Herbert S. Stone & Company, Chicago & New York. CW.

"A Family Affair" (story). December (?), 1897. Syndicated, American Press Association, January, 1898. *Saturday Evening Post* 172 (September 9, 1899), 168–169. CW.

" 'Is Love Divine?' The Question Answered by Three Ladies Well Known in St. Louis Society" (interview). *St. Louis Post-Dispatch*, January 16, 1898, 17. TKC. KCPP.

"Has High Society Struck the Pace That Kills?" (interview). *St. Louis Post-Dispatch*, February 6, 1898, 12. TKC. KCPP.

Letter to Lydia Arms Avery Coonley Ward. March 21, 1898. PS2. KCPP.

"Elizabeth Stock's One Story" (story). March 1898. PS1. CW.

"A Horse Story" (story). March 1898. KCM. KCPP.

"Father Amable" (story; translation of "Le père Amable" by Guy de Maupassant). April 21, 1898. TB.

"There's Music Enough" (poem). May 1, 1898. DSR. CW.

"An Ecstasy of Madness" (poem). July 10, 1898. DSR. CW.

"The Roses" (poem). July 11, 1898. KCM. KCPP.

"The Storm" (story). July 19, 1898. CW.

"Lines to Linn" (poem). July 31, 1898. KCM. KCPP.

"White Oaks" (poem). August 24, 1898. KCM. KCPP.

"Lines Suggested by Omar" (poem). August 1898. KCM. KCPP.

"The Lull of Summer Time" (poem). Undated, but probably August 1898. KCM. KCPP.

"To Henry One Evening Last Summer" (poem). October 21, 1898. KCM. KCPP.

"By the Meadow Gate" (poem). October 24, 1898. KCM. KCPP.

"Old Natchitoches" (poem). December 1898. KCM. KCPP.

"An Hour" (poem). Undated, but before January 1899. DSR. KCM. KCPP.

"In Spring" (poem). Undated, but before January 1899. *Century* 58 (July 1899), 361. KCM. KCPP.

"I Wanted God" (poem). Undated, but before February 1899. CW.

"My Lady Rose Pouts" (poem). Undated, but before February 1899. KCM. KCPP.

"Come to Me" (poem). Undated, but before February 1899. KCM. KCPP.

"O! Blessed Tavern" (poem). Undated, but before February 1899. KCM. KCPP.

"As Careless as the Summer Breeze" (poem). Undated, but before February 1899. KCM. KCPP.

"One Day" (poem). Undated, but before February 1899. KCM. KCPP.

"Ah! Magic Bird!" (poem). Undated, but before February 1899. KCM. KCPP.

"With a Violet-Wood Paper Knife" (poem). Undated, but before February 1899. KCM. KCPP.

"Because —" (poem). Undated, but probably 1899. CW.

"The Godmother" (story). January–February 6, 1899. *Mirror* (St. Louis) 11 (December 12, 1901), 9–13. CW.

"The Haunted Chamber" (poem). February 1899. CW.

Letter to the *Youth's Companion*. February 11, 1899. KCM. KCPP.

"A Little Country Girl" (story). February 11, 1899. CW. RMF.

"Life" (poem). May 10, 1899. DSR. CW.

Letter to Herbert S. Stone. May 21, 1899. KCM. KCPP.

Statement on *The Awakening*. May 28, 1899. *Book News* 17 (July 1899), 612. KCM. KCPP.

Letter to Herbert S. Stone. June 7, 1899. KCM. KCPP.

"A Little Day" (poem). Undated, but probably 1899. KCM. KCPP.

Inscription for Madison Cawein. August 17, 1899. KCM. KCPP.

Letter to Richard B. Shepard. August 24, 1899. KCM. KCPP.

Letter to Richard B. Shepard. November 8, 1899. PS2. KCPP.

"A Reflection" (story). November 1899. DSR. CW.

"On certain brisk, bright days" (untitled essay, title supplied by Per Seyersted). Undated, but undoubtedly November 1899. *St. Louis Post-Dispatch*, November 26, 1899. CW.

"Ti Démon" (story). November 1899. CW.

Letter to the *Century*. December 1, 1899. KCM. KCPP.

"A December Day in Dixie" (story). January 1900. DSR (in part), CW (in full).

"Alexandre's Wonderful Experience" (story). January 23, 1900. KCM. KCPP. RMF.

"The Gentleman from New Orleans" (story). February 6, 1900. CW. RMF.

Letter to the *Youth's Companion*, February 15, 1900. DSR. KCM. KCPP.

"Charlie" (story). April 1900. CW. Also known as "Jacques" in RMF.

"The White Eagle" (story). May 9, 1900. *Vogue* 16 (July 12, 1900), 20, 22. CW.

"Alone" (poem). July 6, 1900. KCM. KCPP.

"To the Friend of My Youth: To Kitty" (poem). DSR (who dates it August 24, 1900). CW. KCPP.

"Development of the Literary West: A Review" (essay). Undated. *St. Louis Republic*, December 9, 1900, 1. TKC. KCPP.

Letter to R. E. Lee Gibson. October 13, 1901. KCM. KCPP.

"Millie's First Party" (story). Also called "Millie's First Ball." October 16, 1901. Destroyed or lost.

"The Wood-Choppers" (story). October 17, 1901. *Youth's Companion* 76 (May 29, 1902), 270–271. CW.

"Toots' Nurses" (story). October 18, 1901. Destroyed or lost.

"Polly" (story). January 14, 1902 as "Polly's Opportunity." *Youth's Companion* 76 (July 3, 1902), 334–335. CW.

Letter to Marie Breazeale. February 4, 1902. KCM. KCPP.

Kate Chopin's Last Will and Testament. December 1902. KCPP.

# Undatable Materials

Reminiscences about Kitty Garesché. Undated; 1900? DSR. KCM. KCPP.

Letter to Mrs. Tiffany. Undated. KCM. KCPP.

Letter to Professor Otto Heller (Washington University). December 26, year unknown. KCPP.

Letter to Mrs. Douglas. July 10, year unknown. KCM. KCPP.

"The Impossible Miss Meadows" (story). CW. Possibly a sketch for "The Falling in Love of Fedora."

"The Boy." RMF. KCPP.

"Melancholy." RMF. KCPP.

"Doralise." RMF. KCPP.

"Misty." RMF. KCPP.

## Abbreviations Used in the Notes

CW = Per Seyersted, ed. *The Complete Works of Kate Chopin*. Baton Rouge: Louisiana State University Press, 1969.

DSR = Daniel S. Rankin, *Kate Chopin and Her Creole Stories*. Philadelphia: University of Pennsylvania Press, 1932.

HKT = Heather Kirk Thomas, "'A Vocation and a Voice': A Documentary Life of Kate Chopin." Dissertation, University of Missouri, 1988.

KCM = Per Seyersted and Emily Toth, eds. *A Kate Chopin Miscellany*. Natchitoches: Northwestern State University Press, and Oslo: Universitetsforlaget, 1979.

KCPP = Emily Toth, Per Seyersted, and Cheyenne Bonnell, eds. *Kate Chopin's Private Papers*. Bloomington: Indiana University Press, 1998, in press (page numbers not yet available).

MHS = Missouri Historical Society in St. Louis, repository for most of Kate Chopin's papers.

TKC = Emily Toth, *Kate Chopin: A Life of the Author of "The Awakening"*. New York: William Morrow, 1990; London: Random Century, 1991; Austin: University of Texas Press, 1993.

## Introduction

xix. Reviews of *The Awakening*: TKC, 336–355.

xix. Posthumous history of *The Awakening*: TKC, Epilogue.

xx. Polish reactions to *The Awakening*: Bernard Koloski, conversation, 1986.

xx. Critical reactions: See Suzanne Green and David Caudle, eds., *Kate Chopin: An Annotated Bibliography of Critical Works, 1976–1997* (Westport, Conn.: Greenwood, in press).

xxi. My previous writings: see Bibliography, in this volume.

xxi. Theorists about biography include Sara Alpern, Joyce Antler, Elisabeth Israels Perry, and Ingrid Winther Scobie, eds., *The Challenge of Feminist Biography: Writing the Lives of Modern American Women* (Urbana: University of Illinois Press,

1992); Carol Ascher, Louise DeSalvo, Sara Ruddick, eds., *Between Women: Biographers, Novelists, Critics, Teachers and Artists Write about Their Work on Women* (Boston: Beacon Press, 1984); Carolyn Heilbrun, *Writing a Woman's Life* (New York: Norton, 1988); and Linda Wagner-Martin, *Telling Women's Lives* (New Brunswick, N.J.: Rutgers University Press, 1994). Also of interest is a dissertation comparing the three biographies of Kate Chopin by Rankin, Seyersted, and Toth: Maria Fernandez Snitzer, "Telling the Lives of Kate Chopin, Edith Wharton, and Willa Cather: The Effects of Social Change and Ideology upon Literary Biography." Dissertation, St. Louis University, 1992.

XXI. Alleged banning of *The Awakening*: TKC, Appendix III.

XXII. Battering: See Susan Koppelman, ed., *Women in the Trees: U.S. Women's Short Stories about Battering and Resistance, 1839–1994.* Boston: Beacon Press, 1996, esp. Introduction, xvii–xxxi.

## Chapter 1: Girls and Women

3ff. Kate O'Flaherty's childhood: TKC, chaps. 1–4. TKC chapters also give census and other data about slaves, as well as genealogical information and school attendance records.

3. Levee outing: DSR, 29–31. Rankin is the source for most of our information about Kate O'Flaherty's childhood.

4ff. Eliza O'Flaherty's family: TKC, chaps. 1–2. Thomas's youth: DSR, 16–22. Edmund O'Flaherty: letters and conversations with Madeleine Matthews, 1997.

7. It is unlikely that there are documents proving that Thomas O'Flaherty was — or was not — the father of the slave children in his household. According to genealogist Elizabeth Shown Mills, an exhaustive search of church records, court records, city directories, and other filings might — or might not — yield helpful information. She suggests that the slave children could have been fathered by a neighbor. Mills, personal communication, 1997. Census takers sometimes categorized people as "black" or "mulatto" on the basis of appearance only.

7. For a modern discussion of the *droit de seigneur,* the master's presumed right to sex with his slaves, see Susan Koppelman, "Headnote" to Charlotte Perkins Gilman's "Turned" in Koppelman, ed., *The Other Woman: Stories of Two Women and a Man* (New York: Feminist Press, 1984), 133–134.

10. About "Story of an Hour" as Eliza O'Flaherty's story: See Emily Toth, "Kate Chopin Thinks Back Through Her Mothers: Three Stories by Kate Chopin," in *Kate Chopin Remembered: Beyond the Bayou,* eds. Lynda S. Boren and Sara deSaussure Davis (Baton Rouge: Louisiana State University Press, 1992), 15–25.

11. About white children and mammies: Susan Tucker, *Telling Memories Among Southern Women: Domestic Workers and Their Employers in the Segregated South* (New York: Schocken Books, 1988), 1–18.

15. Major Sacred Heart sources include papers at the National Archives of the Society of the Sacred Heart, Villa Duchesne, St. Louis; Louise Callan, *Society of the Sacred Heart in North America* (New York: Longmans Green, 1937); M. O'Leary, *Education with a Tradition: An Account of the Educational Work of the Society of the Sacred Heart* (New York: Longmans Green, 1936); and V. V. Harrison, *Changing Habits: A Memoir of the Society of the Sacred Heart* (New York: Doubleday, 1988).

16. What friends share: See "Introduction" to Susan Koppelman, ed., *Women's Friendships: A Collection of Short Stories* (Norman: University of Oklahoma Press, 1991), xix–xxv, and "Afterword," 280–301. Kitty Garesché's reminiscences and family information appear in early chapters of DSR and TKC, passim.

20. "Leaves of Affection": The book is at MHS; contents are transcribed in KCPP.

## Chapter 2: The Spoils of War

22ff. Civil War: TKC, chap. 4.

24. Confirmation: It is not clear what catechism Kate O'Flaherty and Kitty Garesché studied for their first communion. The Baltimore Catechism was not yet standard. I am grateful to Barbara Ewell and then to John May for this information, which May received from Father Donald Martin, a New Orleans Province Jesuit, in April 1998.

30. Rape in war: See Susan Brownmiller, *Against Our Will: Men, Women and Rape* (New York: Simon & Schuster, 1975), esp. the early chapters.

31. Eliza's letter to her uncle: The full text of the letter appears in KCM, 103–104. The original is at MHS.

## Chapter 3: The Voice of a Young Woman

34ff. Postwar years: TKC, chap. 5.

34. About "loss of voice" and adolescent girls: see Mary Field Belenky, Blythe McVicker Clinchy, Nancy Rule Goldberger, and Jill Mattuck Tarule, eds., *Women's Ways of Knowing* (New York: Basic Books, 1986); Joan Jacobs Brumberg, *The Body Project: An Intimate History of American Girls* (New York: Random House, 1997); Carol Gilligan, *In a Different Voice: Psychological Theory and Women's Development* (Cambridge: Harvard University Press, 1982); Carol Gilligan and Lyn Mikel Brown, *Meeting at the Crossroads: Women's Psychology and Girls' Development* (Cambridge: Harvard University Press, 1994); Peggy Orenstein, *SchoolGirls: Young Women, Self-*

*Esteem, and the Confidence Gap* (New York: Anchor, 1995); Mary Pipher, *Reviving Ophelia: Saving the Selves of Adolescent Girls* (New York: Ballantine, 1994). I am not claiming that all young women, past and present, have suffered a "loss of voice"; in particular, it is not a pattern in the lives of African American girls. But Kate O'Flaherty does seem to fit the pattern described for middle-class white girls today.

39. Commonplace book: The commonplace book, housed at MHS, is transcribed in KCPP.

## Chapter 4: Belle and Bride

45ff. Belle and bride: TKC, chaps. 6–7.

47. Diary: The diary quoted here and elsewhere is part of the commonplace book, KCPP.

52. Oscar Chopin's letters: "little rods" is a better translation than "our pipes," in TKC, 93. I am grateful to Katharine Jensen for the new translation.

54ff. Honeymoon diary: The diary is in the same notebook as the commonplace book, and it is also transcribed in KCPP. Kate O'Flaherty Chopin's spelling was imperfect, and I have kept her spellings.

## Chapter 5: Walking in New Orleans, Swimming at Grand Isle

62ff. New Orleans years: TKC, chap. 8.

62. Woman and person: see Heilbrun, *Writing a Woman's Life* and other sources noted for p. xxi, above. Also of interest is Gail Sheehy, *Pathfinders* (New York: Bantam, 1982).

62. Androgynous mind, woman thinking back through mothers: Virginia Woolf, *A Room of One's Own* (New York: Harcourt, Brace & World, 1929), esp. 79, 101, 102.

63. "Americans" and Creoles: See Arnold R. Hirsch and Joseph Logsdon, eds., *Creole New Orleans: Race and Americanization* (Baton Rouge: Louisiana State University, 1992).

65. "The Irish voice": That is a quotation from Kate Chopin's story, "A Matter of Prejudice."

71. Louisiana Avenue house: That house now belongs to a women's historical association.

73. Degas, Morisot: Christopher Benfey, *Degas in New Orleans: Encounters in the Creole World of Kate Chopin and George Washington Cable* (New York: Knopf, 1997); Anne Higonnet, *Berthe Morisot* (New York: Harper & Row, 1990); Denis Rouart, comp., *The Correspondence of Berthe Morisot*, trans. Betty W. Hubbard (London: Lund Humphries, 1957), all passim.

74. Edma Pontillon/Edna Pontellier: My Louisiana State University student Michelle Bergeron noticed the similar names in 1996. Apparently no one else has done research linking Berthe Morisot and Kate Chopin.

77. Ogden Guards: HKT, 163.

## Chapter 6: Cloutierville: The Talk of the Town

82ff. TKC chaps. 9–11. Virtually all the Cloutierville historical and cultural information in this chapter comes from Lucille Tinker Carnahan, in numerous interviews between 1984 and 1997.

84. Lil Chouteau: Kate Chopin mentions her in the honeymoon diary, reproduced in KCPP.

88. Not having more children: Most small towns had midwives who were also part-time abortionists and experts on herbal remedies, such as pennyroyal. Whether it is legal or illegal, about a third of U. S. pregnancies have always ended in abortion. Oscar may also have begun using condoms, possibly at Kate's insistence — and he may have gotten them at Hot Springs. Conversations with Lucille Tinker Carnahan (1997) and with Rickie Solinger (1993).

## Chapter 7: St. Louis and At Fault

101ff. TKC, chaps. 11–12.

102. Eliza O'Flaherty's cancer: HKT, 298.

103. New home as mansion: I have this description from Frederick Medler, St. Louis architectural historian, personal conversation, 1997. The Lafayette Park type of house is also described and pictured in "Lafayette Square: Inside and Out," in *Where: St. Louis* (June 1997), 8.

103. The photo of Kate Chopin's Morgan Street home is from the collection of Dr. William Swekosky (1894–1963), a dentist and historian in St. Louis. The photo was obviously taken years after Chopin's death (note the car). Dr. Swekosky's collection was donated to Notre Dame College, which closed in 1977, whereupon the collection was transferred to the Cardinal Ritter Library, School Sisters of Notre Dame, in St. Louis. I am grateful to Frederick Medler for directing me to Sister M. Dionysia Brockland, director of the collection.

103. Visit to Kitty: Interview with Sister Marie Louise Martinez, R.C.S.J., 1994.

108. Psychology of batterers: See Susan Koppelman's introduction to *Women in the Trees*, esp. xx–xxi.

109. Record keeping: Chopin's manuscript account books are transcribed in KCPP.

109ff. Sue V. Moore's troubles: St. Louis *Republic*: "Eloped," (July 8, 1888), Part I, 9; "Captured" (July 10), 1; "A Bold Pair" (July 11), 1; "The Wages of Sin" (July 15), 4; "Moore Still in Jail" (July 15), 16; "Unhappy Moore" (July 16), 1; "Moore's Nerve" (July 17), 1; "The Birds Flown" (July 18), 1; "A Dismantled Home" (July 19), 8.

110. Images of women: Susan Koppelman Cornillon, ed., *Images of Women in Fiction: Feminist Perspectives* (Bowling Green: Bowling Green State University Popular Press, 1972).

111. Boston marriages: Lillian Faderman, *Surpassing the Love of Men: Romantic Friendship and Love Between Women from the Renaissance to the Present* (New York: William Morrow, 1981), 190–230; Susan Koppelman, ed., *Two Friends and Other Nineteenth-Century Lesbian Stories by American Women Writers* (New York: Meridian, 1994), 124–127.

111. Stories of New Women: Susan Koppelman, ed., *Old Maids: Short Stories by Nineteenth-Century U.S. Women Writers* (Boston: Pandora, 1984).

## Chapter 8: A Professional Writer

121ff. TKC chaps. 13–14. About the publishing industry: Susan Coultrap-Mc-Quin, *Doing Literary Business: American Women Writers in the Nineteenth Century* (Chapel Hill: University of North Carolina Press, 1990); Ellery Sedgwick, *The Atlantic Monthly, 1857–1909: Yankee Humanism at High Tide and Ebb* (Amherst: University of Massachusetts Press, 1994).

122. Writing by hand: Some of Kate Chopin's pencil-written manuscripts, on cheap newsprint paper, are at MHS, but only photocopies are available for researchers' use. In KCPP the manuscripts are called the Rankin-Marhefka Fragments.

122. Manuscript account books: These two books are named the Bonnell and Wondra Books in KCPP, and those names will presumably be used by future researchers. All information about Chopin's rejections and acceptances comes from those notebooks.

123. Chopin and Maupassant: She writes about his inspiring her in several versions of an essay called "In the Confidence of a Story Writer." Two versions appear in CW; a fragment, "Misty," is reprinted in KCPP.

125. Market for Easter and Christmas stories: Some of the "occasional" stories from Chopin's era appear in Susan Koppelman, ed., *"May Your Days Be Merry & Bright": Christmas Stories by Women* (New York: New American Library, 1988).

125. Historical loser, escaping to her corner: "In the Confidence of a Story Writer," CW, 704.

127. Mrs. Stone: June 2, 1894 diary. KCPP.

127. Chopin's diaries: The 1894 diary and the commonplace book are Chopin's only surviving diaries. Both are transcribed in KCPP.

129. Calling rituals: TKC, 256 and 477 n.

135. Possible relationship with Dillon: The niece was Julia Breazeale Waters; the granddaughter was Marjorie Chopin McCormick. Both are cited in TKC, esp. chap. 14.

140. A very old photograph shows Maria with golden curls, with her sisters, but it is too light to be reproduced. The one picture that is reproducible, a painting on a piece of wood, is cracked and damaged.

143. Because of Calixta's kinky hair, some readers have thought that Chopin intended her to be of mixed race, but the story states clearly that "Any one who is white may go to a 'Cadian ball." If the others did not consider Calixta white, she could not attend.

144. The best discussions of battered women in literature appear in the introductory material in Susan Koppelman's *Women in the Trees*, xvii-xxxi.

146. The portrayal of rape victims as beautiful is analyzed brilliantly in Jane Caputi's *The Age of Sex Crime* (Bowling Green: Popular Press, 1990).

## Chapter 9: A Writer, Her Reviewers, and Her Markets

149ff. TKC, chaps. 13, 15–16, 18. The diary quoted in this chapter is the 1894 one, transcribed in KCPP.

150. Local color and universal: The use of local color as a mask for social criticism is discussed in Susan Koppelman's headnote to Mary Austin's "Papago Wedding" in *The Other Woman*, 191–192.

150. *Bayou Folk*: The stories in *Bayou Folk* are "A No-Account Creole," "In and Out of Old Natchitoches," "In Sabine," "A Very Fine Fiddle," "Beyond the Bayou," "Old Aunt Peggy," "The Return of Alcibiade," "A Rude Awakening," "The Bênitous' Slave," "Désirée's Baby," "A Turkey Hunt," "Madame Célestin's Divorce," "Love on the Bon-Dieu," "Loka," "Boulôt and Boulotte," "For Marse Chouchoute," "A Visit to Avoyelles," "A Wizard from Gettysburg," "Ma'ame Pélagie," "At the 'Cadian Ball," "La Belle Zoraïde," "A Gentleman of Bayou Têche," and "A Lady of Bayou St. John."

152. *Pembroke*: Chopin's discussion is from June 7 entry, 1894 diary. KCPP.

152. Wife battering stories: Susan Koppelman's studies of U.S. women's battering stories, reported in the introduction to her *Women in the Trees*, are the most complete surveys ever made. Koppelman, who has spent some 25 years reading American women's short stories, has found no other battered wife stories from the 1890s in which a wife escapes. Personal conversation, 1997.

154. "Commercial instinct": Diary, May 4 and 12, 1894. KCPP. Western Association of Writers: Chopin's 1894 diary, June 2, June 30, July 5. KCPP.

156. "Idiots": Emily Toth, *Ms. Mentor's Impeccable Advice for Women in Academia* (Philadelphia: University of Pennsylvania Press, 1997), 60.

159. Diary entries: Aristophanes—July 6, 1994; Schuyler—May 28, 1894; Calvary Cemetery—May 22, 1894. KCPP.

160ff. Moore and Schuyler profiles are both reprinted in KCM.

163ff. Writing habits: "On Certain Brisk, Bright Days," CW, 721; TKC, chaps. 13, 16.

166. Rankin-Marhefka Fragments: KCPP.

168. Chopin's reviews are reprinted in CW.

## Chapter 10: *A World of Writing and Friends*

174ff. TKC, 15–17, 20.

175ff. Much of this discussion comes from the introduction to Susan Koppelman, ed., *Between Mothers & Daughters: Stories Across a Generation* (New York: Feminist Press, 1985), xv–xxxix. See also Adrienne Rich's *Of Woman Born: Motherhood as Experience and Institution* (New York: Norton, 1976).

175. About Kitty: Sister Marie Louise Martinez, R.C.S.J., 1994 interview.

177. Nun: diary, May 22, 1894. Information about Elise Miltenberger: Sister Marie Louise Martinez, R.C.S.J., 1994 interview. See also KCPP.

177ff. Influence on birds: diary, May 12, 1894. "Euchre fiend": diary, May 28, 1894. KCPP. *Bayou Folk* drawings: The copy with Oscar Chopin's drawings is in the Olin Library, at Washington University.

178. Rosa Sonneschein: TKC and Walter Ehrlich, *Zion in the Valley: The Jewish Community of St. Louis.* Vol. I: 1807–1907. (Columbia: University of Missouri, 1997), 191, 219–20, 287n, 299n, 406n.

179ff. Diary entries for May 4, May 28, June 2.

181. Chopin's use of women's stories: See Emily Toth, "Kate Chopin Thinks Back Through Her Mothers: Three Stories," note to p. 10 above.

182. Knapp: Vernon Knapp, "Is There an Interesting Woman in St. Louis?" St. Louis *Republic* (September 11, 1910), part 1, p. 1, reprinted in KCM.

183. Architectural drawings: Frederick Medler, 1997 conversation.

183. Chopin on Deyo: diary, June 7, July 5, 1894. KCPP.

185. On *Jude the Obscure*: "As You Like It" essay, CW, 713.

185. Kolbenheyer: Chopin's 1894 diary, May 4, June 2. KCPP.

188. Chopin on Sallie Britton: "As You Like It" essay, CW, 715.

189. Chopin on Stuart: "As You Like It" essay, CW, 711–713. Stuart's copy of *Bayou Folk* is in the Howard-Tilton Library at Tulane University. The entire inscription is in KCM and KCPP.

## Chapter 11: *Night, Love, War*

191ff. TKC, chaps 18–21.

191. "not satisfy me": March 31, 1895 letter to J. M. Stoddart. KCM, KCPP.

193. "Human impulses": Review of Hamlin Garland's *Crumbling Idols*, CW, 693.

194. Stories in *A Night in Acadie*: "A Night in Acadie," "Athénaïse," "After the Winter," "Polydore," "Regret," "A Matter of Prejudice," "Caline," "A Dresden Lady in Dixie," "Nég Créol," "The Lilies," "Azélie," "Mamouche," "A Sentimental Soul," "Dead Men's Shoes," "At Chênière Caminada," "Odalie Misses Mass," "Cavanelle," "Tante Cat'rinette," "A Respectable Woman," "Ripe Figs," and "Ozème's Holiday."

195. Gilder letter: January 5, 1897 letter. KCM. KCPP. *Republic* review: TKC, 301.

195ff. Reviews: TKC, 298–305. See also Anthony Paul Garitta, "The Critical Reputation of Kate Chopin." Dissertation, University of North Carolna at Greensboro, 1978, 104–113.

196, 198. Reedy: on "Athénaïse," TKC, 300–301; on Dumay, TKC, 291. Dumay's translation of "Story of an Hour" is in MHS.

198. "Fedora" as lesbian: "The Falling in Love of Fedora" is anthologized in Susan Koppelman's 1994 collection, *Two Friends and Other Nineteenth-Century Lesbian Stories by American Women Writers*.

200. *Post-Dispatch* opinions: "High Society" appeared on February 6, 1898, p. 12; "Is Love Divine?" appeared on January 16, 1898, p. 17.

201. "Land where modern holds sway": This was a common Reedy term for France.

202. "Lone wolf": Felix Chopin interview with Charles van Ravenswaay, 1949, reprinted in KCM.

202. Visits to Natchitoches: Interviews with Julia (July) Breazeale Waters, Carmen Breazeale, Julie Chopin Cusachs, 1975–1988.

203ff. Fred Chopin in army: newspaper accounts in TKC, 312–316.

206. Breasts as taboo: TKC, 320–321.

206. Maria Normand and Albert Sampite: Interviews with Ivy DeLouche, Mary DeLouche, Lucille Tinker Carnahan, 1983–1988.

207. Mollie E. Moore Davis: TKC, 325–326. See also Patricia Brady, "Mollie Moore Davis: A Literary Life," in Dorothy H. Brown and Barbara C. Ewell, eds., *Louisiana Women Writers* (Baton Rouge: Louisiana State University Press, 1992), 99–118.

207. Eye specialist: TKC, 286–287.

208. *Vocation and a Voice* stories: The stories planned for the collection were "A Vocation and a Voice," "Elizabeth Stock's One Story," "Two Portraits (The Nun and the Wanton)," "An Idle Fellow," "A Mental Suggestion," "An Egyptian Cigarette," "The White Eagle," "The Story of an Hour," "Two Summers and Two Souls," "The Night Came Slowly," "Juanita," "The Unexpected," "Her Letters," "The Kiss," "Suzette," "The Falling in Love of Fedora," "The Recovery," "The Blind Man,"

"An Easter Day Conversion (A Morning Walk)," "Lilacs," "Ti Démon," and "The Godmother."

## Chapter 12: The Awakening

209ff. TKC, chaps. 21–23. Jill McCorkle, TKC, 405.

212. Robert's sexual orientation: I am indebted to Suzanne Green for discussions and an unpublished paper about this. An entertaining and thought-provoking article is Harriet Kramer Linkin's "'Call the Roller of Big Cigars': Smoking Out the Patriarchy in *The Awakening*," *Legacy* 11 (1994), 130–142. Also of related interest are two articles: Elizabeth LeBlanc, "The Metaphorical Lesbian: Edna Pontellier in *The Awakening*," *Tulsa Studies in Women's Literature* 15, no. 2 (1996), 289–307; and Kathryn Lee Seidel, "Art as an Unnatural Act: Mademoiselle Reisz in *The Awakening*," *Mississippi Quarterly* 46 (Spring 1993), 199–214.

212. "Gay" and "queer": These words may be coded homosexual references, or they may be accidents.

213. Edna and Arobin's doing it: I am indebted to my Louisiana State University students Cynthia Clark, Summer Doucet, and Mona Goudeau for discussing whether the sex scenes are recognizable to modern readers, and for posing a question: if fictional characters have sex but readers don't recognize that fact, do the characters really have sex? That intriguing philosophical question is beyond the scope of this book.

214. Edna and conversation: See E. Laurie George, "Women's Language in *The Awakening*," in Bernard Koloski, ed., *Approaches to Teaching Kate Chopin's "The Awakening"* (New York: Modern Language Association, 1988), 53–59.

214. "Spontaneous expression": "On certain brisk, bright days," CW, 722.

215. Degas, Morisot and related connections: Higonnet, *Berthe Morisot,* about Adèle Colonna (33–34); Batignolle studio (65–66); Daudet's novel (79). Schuyler's 1894 profile is discussed in chap. 9 of this book; he mentions Daudet.

217. Reedy: TKC, 309, 334.

219. Lucy Monroe: TKC, 328–329 and Alma Bennett, "Any Enthusiasm is Welcome: Lucy Monroe's 'Chicago Letter' as Social Commentary," unpublished paper, delivered at Popular Culture Association meeting in 1998. Bennett did not find any references to Kate Chopin in Monroe's columns (personal communication, 1998).

220. Reedy: TKC, 335. Reviews of *The Awakening*: TKC, 336–355.

223. Chopin's letter to Herbert S. Stone: TKC, 344, KCM, KCPP.

223. Self-defense: TKC, 344, 345; KCM, KCPP.

224. Chopin's friends' letters — TKC 19, 21; 338; 349–351. The letters are all at MHS. KCM.

224. Gibson and Cawein: TKC, 328, 356–357.

225. Utah correspondent: TKC, 361. KCPP. Re Chopin's possible depression, see also Heather Kirk Thomas, "'What Are the Prospects for the Book?': Rewriting a Woman's Life," in Lynda S. Boren and Sara deSaussure Davis, eds., *Kate Chopin Reconsidered: Beyond the Bayou* (Baton Rouge: Louisiana State University Press, 1992), 36–57.

225. Londoners' letters: TKC, 358–360. Per Seyersted's research turned up no proof that they existed: *Kate Chopin: A Critical Biography* (Baton Rouge: Louisiana State University Press, and Oslo: Universitetsforlaget, 1969), 179, 225.

227. *Post-Dispatch*: "St. Louis Woman Who Has Won Fame in Literature" (November 26, 1899), pt. 4, p. 1. Chopin's article: "On Certain Brisk, Bright Days," CW, 721–723.

227. Myth of banning: "The Alleged Banning of *The Awakening*," Appendix III in TKC, 422–425.

228. Wednesday Club: Newspaper report on "Reciprocity Day" is excerpted in HKT, 502–503.

228. "Family money man": Interview with Maryhelen Wilson, 1984. TKC, 371. Morisot in white: Higonnet, 89.

228–229. Social life and Lélia: TKC, 371–372. Tensions: Interview with Marjorie Chopin McCormick, 1984.

229. *Vocation and a Voice*: stories listed above, 208 n. Also see Emily Toth, "*A Vocation and a Voice*: Why Was It Killed?" in Bernard Koloski, ed., *Kate Chopin: A Study of the Short Fiction* (New York: Twayne/Simon & Schuster, 1996), 135–140.

## Chapter 13: Aftermath

231ff. TKC, chap. 24.

232. Aunt Amanda: TKC, 377. Chopin's note is in KCM and KCPP.

233. *Republic* article: TKC, 378–385, reprinted in KCPP. TKC includes Harrison Clark piece. Suit worn by New Women: I am indebted to Pamela Dean for this observation.

235. Gibson sonnet: Gibson book, autographed to Chopin, is in the Bayou Folk Museum/Kate Chopin home in Cloutierville. TKC, 385–386, 404–405.

236. Julie Chopin Cusachs: Interview, 1990.

236. Selling land: HKT, 539–541.

237. Will, ailing: TKC, 389; HKT, 346–347, 532–533; KCPP.

237. Chopin home: The McPherson house is a private home, with landmark status. The original winding staircase still exists. TKC, 501 n 390.

238. Kitty nearby: Martinez, 1994.

238. World's Fair: TKC, 391–393.

239. Death, obituaries: TKC, 393–396.

240. Date on Chopin's tombstone: Most sources record her birthdate as 1851, but that is wrong. Her baptismal certificate and the 1850 U.S. Census both show that she was born in 1850. See TKC, 24–25. There seems to be no way to correct the error, however, and it is enshrined in the Library of Congress database and virtually everywhere else.

240. Children after her death: TKC, Epilogue, 397–400. "Euchre fiend": Diary entry May 28, 1894, KCPP. "Lady Bountiful": Lélia to Leonidas Whipple, DSR, 102.

242. Louisiana memories: TKC, 401–402.

243. Revival of KC's repute: TKC, 404–406.

244. Human problems as mutable: Chopin essay on Hamlin Garland's "Crumbling Idols," CW, 693. "Woman of mysterious fascination": DSR, 106.

# SELECT BIBLIOGRAPHY OF WORKS
## RELATED TO KATE CHOPIN

This book draws on years of Kate Chopin research, including my three previous books, my dissertation, and research for my Penguin Classic edition of Chopin's *A Vocation and a Voice*. This bibliography lists only the major sources, and those that have been most useful for this particular book. Readers interested in extensive source lists should check the forthcoming bibliography by Suzanne Green and David Caudle (below), the other bibliographies listed below, and the bibliography in my *Kate Chopin: A Life of the Author of "The Awakening"*.

Readers seeking earlier discussions of Chopin's works may find useful *The Kate Chopin Newsletter* (which I edited from 1975 to 1979, the last two years under the title *Regionalism and the Female Imagination*). It is indexed in PMLA, and copies of individual articles are available at a nominal charge from the Penn State Room, Fred Lewis Pattee Library, Pennsylvania State University, University Park, PA 16802.

*A Kate Chopin Miscellany* (KCM) is difficult to obtain, but the articles listed from it below can all be obtained from the Missouri Historical Society in St. Louis. Most are also quoted extensively in TKC.

## Abbreviations

KCM = Per Seyersted and Emily Toth, eds., *A Kate Chopin Miscellany*. Natchitoches: Northwestern State University Press; and Oslo: Universitetsforlaget, 1979.

KCPP = Emily Toth, Per Seyersted, and Cheyenne Bonnell, eds., *Kate Chopin's Private Papers*. Bloomington: Indiana University Press, 1998.

KCR = Lynda S. Boren and Sara deSaussure Davis, eds., *Kate Chopin Reconsidered: Beyond the Bayou*. Baton Rouge: Louisiana State University Press, 1992.

TKC = Emily Toth, *Kate Chopin: A Life of the Author of "The Awakening"*. New York: Morrow, 1990; London: Random Century, 1991; Austin: University of Texas, 1993.

## Books and Book-Length Studies

Bardot, Jean. "L'influence française dans la vie et l'oeuvre de Kate Chopin." Thèse de doctorat, Université de Paris IV, 1985–1986.

Beer, Janet. *Kate Chopin, Edith Wharton, and Charlotte Perkins Gilman: Studies in Short Fiction.* New York: St. Martin's, 1998.

Benfey, Christopher. *Degas in New Orleans: Encounters in the Creole World of Kate Chopin and George Washington Cable.* New York: Knopf, 1997.

Bonner, Thomas Jr. *The Kate Chopin Companion, with Chopin's Translations from French Fiction.* Westport, Conn.: Greenwood Press, 1988.

Boren, Lynda S., and Sara deSaussure Davis, eds. *Kate Chopin Reconsidered: Beyond the Bayou.* Baton Rouge: Louisiana State University Press, 1992. [Abbreviated as KCR]

Chopin, Kate. *A Vocation and a Voice* (edition of Kate Chopin's last story collection). Edited by Emily Toth. New York: Penguin Classics, 1991.

Culley, Margaret, ed. *The Awakening: An Authoritative Text, Contexts, Criticism.* New York: Norton, 1976, 1994.

Ewell, Barbara C. *Kate Chopin.* New York: Ungar, 1986.

Fick, Thomas, and Eva Gold, eds. "Special Section: Kate Chopin." *Louisiana Literature* 11, no. 1 (spring 1994).

Garitta, Anthony Paul. "The Critical Reputation of Kate Chopin." Dissertation, University of North Carolina at Greensboro, 1978.

Koloski, Bernard. *Kate Chopin: A Study of the Short Fiction.* New York: Twayne/Simon & Schuster, 1996.

Koloski, Bernard, ed. *Approaches to Teaching Kate Chopin's "The Awakening".* New York: Modern Language Association of America, 1988.

Papke, Mary E. *Verging on the Abyss: The Social Fiction of Kate Chopin and Edith Wharton.* Westport, Conn.: Greenwood Press, 1990.

*Perspectives on Kate Chopin.* Proceedings of the Kate Chopin International Conference, Northwestern State University, Natchitoches, La. Natchitoches: Northwestern State University Press, 1990.

Petry, Alice Hall, ed. *Critical Essays on Kate Chopin.* New York: G. K. Hall/Simon & Schuster, 1996.

Rankin, Daniel S. *Kate Chopin and Her Creole Stories.* Philadelphia: University of Pennsylvania Press, 1932.

Seyersted, Per. *Kate Chopin: A Critical Biography*. Baton Rouge: Louisiana State University Press; and Oslo: Universitetsforlaget, 1969.

Seyersted, Per, and Emily Toth, eds. *A Kate Chopin Miscellany*. Natchitoches: Northwestern State University Press; and Oslo: Universitetsforlaget, 1979. [Abbreviated as KCM]

Skaggs, Peggy. *Kate Chopin*. Boston: G. K. Hall, 1985.

Taylor, Helen. *Gender, Race, and Region in the Writings of Grace King, Ruth McEnery Stuart, and Kate Chopin*. Baton Rouge: Louisiana State University Press, 1989.

Thomas, Heather Kirk. "'A Vocation and a Voice': A Documentary Life of Kate Chopin." Dissertation, University of Missouri, 1988.

Toth, Emily. "That Outward Existence Which Conforms: Kate Chopin and Literary Convention." Dissertation, Johns Hopkins University, 1975.

————. *Kate Chopin: A Life of the Author of "The Awakening"*. New York: William Morrow, 1990; London: Random Century, 1991; Austin: University of Texas Press, 1993. [Abbreviated as TKC]

Toth, Emily, Per Seyersted, and Cheyenne Bonnell, eds. *Kate Chopin's Private Papers*. Bloomington: Indiana University Press, 1998. [Abbreviated as KCPP]

## Bibliographies

Green, Suzanne, and David Caudle, eds. *Kate Chopin: An Annotated Bibliography of Critical Works, 1976–1997*. Westport, Conn.: Greenwood Press, in press.

Inge, Tonette Bond. "Kate Chopin." In Maurice Duke et al., eds., *American Women Writers: Bibliographical Essays*, 47–69. Westport, Conn.: Greenwood Press, 1983.

KCM, pp. 201–261.

Springer, Marlene. *Edith Wharton and Kate Chopin: A Reference Guide*. Boston: G. K. Hall, 1976.

Thomas, Heather Kirk. "Kate Chopin: A Primary Bibliography, Alphabetically Arranged." *American Literary Realism* 28, no. 2 (1996), 71–88.

TKC, pp. 426–506.

## Some Useful Articles

Bardot, Jean. "French Creole Portraits: The Chopin Family from Natchitoches Parish." KCR, 26–35.

Chopin, Felix. "Statement on Kate Chopin." January 19, 1949 interview with Felix Chopin (Kate's son), notes taken by Charles van Ravenswaay of the Missouri Historical Society. KCM.

(Knapp, Vernon.) "Is There an Interesting Woman in St. Louis?" *St. Louis Republic*, September 11, 1910, part 5, 1. KCM.

Mills, Elizabeth Shown. "Colorful Characters from Kate's Past." *Kate Chopin Newsletter* 2, no. 1 (Spring 1976), 7–12.

Moore, Sue V. "Mrs. Kate Chopin." *St. Louis Life* 10 (June 9, 1894), 11–12. KCM.

"The Practical Side of Oscar Chopin's Death." *Kate Chopin Newsletter* 1, no. 3 (winter 1975–1976), 29.

Schuyler, William. "Kate Chopin." *The Writer* 7 (August 1894), 115–117. KCM.

Thomas, Heather Kirk. "'What Are the Prospects for the Book?': Rewriting a Woman's Life." KCR, 36–57.

Toth, Emily. "A Vocation and a Voice: Why Was It Killed?" In *Kate Chopin: A Study of the Short Fiction*. Ed. Bernard Koloski, 135–140. New York: Twayne/Simon & Schuster, 1997.

———. "Kate Chopin." In *The Oxford Companion to Women's Writing in the United States*, edited by Cathy N. Davidson and Linda Wagner-Martin, 187–189. New York: Oxford University Press, 1995.

———. "Introduction: A New Generation Reads Kate Chopin." *Louisiana Literature* 11, no. 1 (spring 1994), 8–17.

———. "What Teachers Should Know about Kate Chopin." *Louisiana English Journal* 1, no. 1 (new series) (October 1993), 47–52.

———. "Kate Chopin Thinks Back Through Her Mothers: Three Stories by Kate Chopin." KCR, 15–25.

———. "Kate Chopin's *The Awakening* as Feminist Criticism." Reprint, for special Thirtieth Anniversary Issue of *Southern Studies* 2, nos. 3/4 (new series) (fall/winter 1991), 231–241.

———. "Kate Chopin on Divine Love and Suicide: Two Rediscovered Articles." *American Literature* 63, no. 1 (March 1991), 115–121.

———. "The Shadow of the First Biographer: The Case of Kate Chopin." *Southern Review* 26, no. 2 (April 1990), 285–292.

———. "A New Biographical Approach." In *Approaches to Teaching Kate Chopin's "The Awakening"*, edited by Bernard Koloski, 60–66. New York: Modern Language Association, 1988.

Wilson, Maryhelen. "Kate Chopin's Family: Fallacies and Facts, Including Kate's True Birthdate." *Kate Chopin Newsletter* 2 (winter 1976–1977), 25–31.

Wilson, Maryhelen. "Woman's Lib in Old St. Louis: 'La Verdon.'" *St. Louis Genealogical Society* 14, no. 4 (n.d.), 139–140.

## Unpublished Papers

Most of Kate Chopin's papers are in the Missouri Historical Society (MHS) in St. Louis. With KCPP, all are now published, except for some of the Rankin-Marhefka Fragments (versions of stories already published) which are virtually illegible.

Also of interest to scholars at MHS are recently deposited research notes by Per Seyersted, showing what he learned in interviews and how he conducted his research in the days before computers, faxes, and photocopies. KCPP has materials from that collection, and from MHS's acquisitions files, useful for studying the conduct of Father Daniel Rankin, Kate Chopin's first biographer.

Emily Toth's research materials will eventually be donated to the Louisiana State University archives.